The Transition of Legacy Systems to a Distributed Architecture

The Transition of Legacy Systems to a Distributed Architecture

Narsim Ganti, Ph.D.

and

William Brayman

A Wiley–QED Publication

John Wiley & Sons, Inc.

New York • Chichester • Brisbane • Toronto • Singapore

Publisher: K. Schowalter
Editor: Rich O'Hanley
Managing Editor: Robert S. Aronds
Editorial Production & Design: Publishers' Design and Production Services

Designations used by companies to distinguish their products are often claimed as trademarks. In all instances where John Wiley & Sons, Inc., is aware of a claim, the product names appear in initial capital or all capital letters. Readers, however, should contact the appropriate companies for more complete information regarding trademarks and registration.

This text is printed on acid-free paper.

This publication is designed to provide accurate and authoritative information in regard to the subject matter covered. It is sold with the understanding that the publisher is not engaged in rendering legal, accounting, or other professional service. If legal advice or other expert assistance is required, the services of a competent professional person should be sought.

Library of Congress Cataloging-in-Publication Data:

Ganti, Narsim.
    The transition of legacy systems to a distributed architecture /
Narsim Ganti and William Brayman.
        p.   cm.
    Includes Index.
    ISBN 0-471-06080-1
    1. Electronic data processing—Distributed processing.
I. Brayman, William.   II. Title.
QA76.9.D5G36   1995
004′ .36—dc20   94-23583
                                                                CIP

Printed in the United States of America

10 9 8 7 6 5 4 3 2 1

*For Elizabeth Lucille Brayman, who was an inspiration,
and for Eric, Daniel, and Jennifer—
may their hopes and dreams flourish.*

- W.B.

To Annayya, Amma, and Nannagaru

- N.G.

Contents

Preface

Businesses have found themselves competing worldwide in a very dynamic marketplace. In order to survive, a business must continuously improve its business process while operating in a highly distributed environment. Unfortunately, as businesses have found out, most information systems built on older technology, legacy systems as they are often called, are not very adaptable. Moreover, many businesses have discovered that their business processes are intertwined with their legacy information systems. Consequently, business improvements are frustratingly slow to occur.

Business process redesign, as practiced today, places reduced emphasis on a hierarchical authority structure. Teams and individuals are vested with the authority to operate and redefine business process in a flattened horizontal organization. The effect of the horizontal corporation for information technology is to place a strong demand on data integration and the ability to communicate and share information instantaneously. However, legacy information systems are often notoriously poor at sharing information across the company.

Information systems are more organic than other constructed systems like bridges, dams, or vehicles. They are a bit like buildings. They change by evolving, part by part, with smatterings of new technology applied to different parts at different times. It is easy for such a system to become a tangled hodgepodge. We can look back at the systems that we developed 10 years ago, knowing that we did the best with what we had to work with, but also knowing that the systems have, at best, become part of a tangled system.

Commercial computing and information technology has evolved radically over the last few years. There is abundant new technology ranging from artificial intelligence to word-processors, cheap technology, down from million dollar mainframes to thousand dollar PCs, and inter-connected technology expanding from the office to the globe. This abundance has emerged quite recently. Ask yourself how long have the computers in your environment been networked? Probably not that long, 5 or 10 years perhaps. Yet, surprisingly, there are currently an estimated 50 million Ethernet-connected computers in the world.[1] How long do you think it will be before you are sending greeting cards to your relatives over the Internet?

Mainframe computers have become culprits in an ironic way. They were very good for certain requirements. Unfortunately, though, they were also deployed for nearly all large-scale requirements. Their value stems from several key characteristics. They can process data very fast. Because they are a central resource, they can coordinate many concurrent users contending for common resources. They provide a single address space that simplifies certain programming challenges. Finally, centralized systems simplify failure and security approaches. These are key requirements for data processing. The situation has changed in that there are new requirements and new solutions. There are many new requirements for information technology such as personal productivity tools and geographically dispersed work groups that do not fit the centralized processor model. For many information technology tasks there are better solutions than mainframes. Technology and its operational support has evolved enough to supply adequate solutions for distributed processing.

However, simply migrating off the mainframe will not automatically produce adaptable systems that enable business process improvement. Mainframes are still the most effective at certain tasks. Conversely, PCs or other small systems can become just as tangled and maladaptive as mainframe systems. Distributed computing provides irresistible opportunities for the business trying to compete in a changing global marketplace. However, technical issues such as concurrency, disjoint address spaces, security, and failure are extremely large issues.

The approach to deploying distributed information technology will take a sharp turn from the approaches used in the centralized, mainframe environment. This book is about new approaches more suitable for the distributed environment.

---

[1]Metcalfe, Bob. The origin of Ethernet and its link to the information superhighway. InfoWorld. October 31, 1994.

The book has, perhaps, three main themes. One theme is that business improvements are enabled only by information technology that is integrated, yet diverse. Helter-skelter evolution won't do. A second theme is that information systems will always be extended and therefore, growth and change must be built in. A third theme is that information technology is inherently about abstractions. We can't keep up with technical evolution if we deploy information technology only in terms of hardware, software, and data records. Instead, information technology must implement ordinary metaphors such as business processes, objects, and services.

The transition to a distributed environment is more than migrating data and applications to a new computing environment. The transition requires applying new approaches to solve existing problems.

Horizontal integration implies a data reengineering task. Date reengineering is complex in a legacy situation. The tasks requires definition of new processes to perform empirical legacy-data analysis and standardization. Data from multiple sources have to be integrated. The reengineered data will be the life blood for the newly acquired or newly developed forward engineered applications.

Legacy systems transition does not mean rehosting a mainframe application on different desktop Client/Server operating system. However, the new logical computing architecture model of choice is client/server. Legacy systems transition does not mean "surrounding" legacy applications with new data-access methods such as 3270 screen scrapping, PC emulators, and Graphical User Interface front ends. These techniques may be good Band Aids and can provide some benefits in understanding the corporate data resource.

Legacy systems transition means a more broadly scoped process. It requires understanding the existing data better in terms of information that the company needs to integrate their processes. Transition requires acquisition of reusable service modules that are flexible building blocks. Transition requires formulating policies that balance cooperation with autonomy. Transition implies performing data reengineering, forward engineering new applications in accordance with newly redefined business processes in an architected environment. Legacy applications will be phased out gracefully. Whether mainframes are a permanent part of the environment is *not* at issue. Any technology will run its course if we do not specify an architecture that has a longer shelf life than the products used to implement it. This book considers architecture, business processes and incremental practical implementation strategies in a holistic fashion to guide the reader through the transition process.

This book is organized to first focus on conceptual foundations required to make the shift. Then, the book provides a process and road map for untangling the Gordian knot of legacy systems to better align information technology with changing business strategies. The book considers these topics from several points of view: the *enterprise perspective* concerning strategic social, managerial, and financial issues; the *information perspective* concerned with generating, communicating, and protecting information; the *engineering perspective* concerned with the design and implementation of mechanisms to achieve transparent distribution of functionality; and the *computational perspective* concerned with assembling and structuring information service components.

BOOK CONTENTS

This book is organized into 12 chapters. Chapters 1 through 3 develop the context and strategic issues surrounding legacy information systems and the distributed information technology environment. This material will appeal to a broad audience concerned with the complexities and opportunities for modernizing, even revolutionizing, business information systems.

- Chapter 1, *Introduction*, describes the context.
- Chapter 2, *Architecture and the Distributed Environment,* introduces major design principles that focus on the fundamentals of integrating business objectives with technology opportunities.
- Chapter 3, *Distributed Systems Are a New Paradigm,* discusses emerging visions of business information technology and the relationship to business process redesign.

Chapters 4 through 7 develop the conceptual foundations for information technology in a distributed environment. Architects, students, technology suppliers, and strategic planners will be most at home in these sections. However, developers, analysts, and planners who are looking for design patterns will find many important concepts. Information technology suppliers will find that the material helps them better understand the needs of business.

- Chapter 4, *Information in Transition,* looks at data in terms of data abstraction and the process of communicating facts and knowledge. The chapter discusses information in terms of its form, function, and fit for purpose.
- Chapter 5, *Service-based Architecture,* introduces recent advances in the approaches to architecting and designing information sys-

tems for an open and distributed environment. Critical technologies for incremental transition to a distributed environment are discussed.

- Chapter 6, *Cooperative Environment,* reviews sources of diversity and ways to achieve cooperation and integration among diverse elements of the system. The chapter describes an approach for regenerating data and knowledge embedded in legacy systems to be broadly shared by the whole business process.
- Chapter 7, *Application Systems,* discusses application design issues in the context of legacy system transition and strategic approaches for reengineering applications.

Chapter 8, *Alignment of Business Systems with Information Systems,* examines the transition process from an enterprise- and people-issues perspective. The chapter discusses the concept of linking business objectives with the deployment of information technology. This material will appeal to a broad audience of persons interested in applying information technology to business needs.

Chapters 9 through 12 describe the deployment process to make the transition from legacy systems to a distributed environment. Planners, developers, and managers will benefit from material in these chapters.

- Chapter 9, *The Transition Process,* integrates the discussion up to this point by describing an overall process for making the transition from legacy information systems to information systems in a distributed environment.
- Chapter 10, *Transition Design Considerations,* applies the concept of business process redesign to the business of information systems itself.
- Chapter 11, *Transition Overview,* revisits the transition process to discuss business management concerns such as recovering early benefits, fine-tuning the approach, and product acquisition.
- Chapter 12, *Road Map of Transition Process of Legacy Systems,* provides a road map for planning and deploying the transition.

INTENDED AUDIENCE

This book will be useful for people in industry and universities who may be strategists for business-oriented development strategy, who may be designing information technology solutions, or who may be managing information systems. The book could serve as reference material to supplement undergraduate computer science courses concerned with systems engineering or information architecture. The book could serve as supplementary material for courses on business process engineering that are taking a technical approach.

Readers should have some background knowledge in information technology and experience with business information systems. Although some of the material is fairly intense in some places, there is substantial introductory material for the less experienced reader.

ACKNOWLEDGMENTS

This book is a collaborative effort between Bill Brayman and myself (Narsim Ganti). The idea to write the book was conceived when I met Bill Inmon. I thank him for providing some guidance in formalizing the idea and pointing me toward a publisher. As the book took form, Bill wrote the first six chapters and I wrote the second six. I thank Bill Wright, Harvey Kriloff, and Ed Edwards for many discussions over a period of time that helped me clarify approaches and ideas described in the book. Finally, I give particular thanks to Padma "Pam" Ganti for her well-disposed nature and keeping me motivated while writing this book.

I (Bill Brayman) benefited from the spirit of invention and discovery that developed while working with John Thompson, Bill McClay, Roger Speigle, and the other members of a team developing a state-of-the-art information mediation tool and enterprise architecture during the first part of the 1990s. I would like to mention Mark Jones, who inspired me to think more profoundly and broadly about computing architecture. Ashutosh Tiwary was a critical catalyst for this book because of his insights and our many probing and fruitful discussions about the fundamentals of distributed computing. Finally, I give special thanks to my wife, Mary Brayman, for her gracious and consistent encouragement while writing this book.

1

Introduction

This book is about how information technology can enable business process innovation. It is also about making the transition to an information technology environment that is distributed from one based on centralized information systems. Although this book concentrates on information technology, the primary driver of change is improvements to business processes. It is true that information technology exerts a *push* on business process change, but the major change factor and *pull* on information technology is business process redesign. Leading business experts consider business process redesign and continuous quality improvement to be key strategies to enable businesses to become and remain competitive in the world marketplace.

1.1 THE CONTEXT

As part of business process redesign, business leaders are reducing their emphasis on a hierarchical authority structure. In its place they are encouraging a flattened, horizontal structure where teams and individuals are vested with the authority to operate and improve the business process. Many chief executives are not only permitting a change to the business culture, they are also inviting wholesale changes from the line workers and management. Moreover, some top executives are encouraging workers to push back hard on any management efforts to continue "the way we always do things around here." The effect of the horizontal corporation on information technology is to place a strong demand on data integration and the ability to communicate and share information and knowledge. Workers are shifting to smarter roles in the business. Heads-down clerical activities are more often performed by information systems. The ordinary worker is more involved in the analysis and decision-making process. Workers are becoming highly specialized information specialists or knowledge workers who proactively address customer satisfaction. More often, specialized workers form teams that cut across multiple disciplines.

The reshaping of the business model is a response to an increasingly dynamic and competitive marketplace. Business objectives have begun to shift towards increased customer satisfaction. Mazda, the Japanese automobile manufacturer, uses the phrase, "An intense commitment to your total satisfaction." Many manufacturers have commited to bringing out new products in cycle times measured in weeks and months rather than years. Consequently, business processes must be much more adaptable and flexible to meet shifting demand and expectations.

The 1990s has become a time to regroup and recognize the patterns emerging from business and technology sophistication. In business, the "Henry Ford assembly line" archetype is being challenged. As with many great ideas, it is not the original impetus that is being challenged, but rather the implementation. Ford's impetus was to design a process to make things better and faster. The implementation has been to rigidify the process rather than redesign it as the situation changed. More recently, it has become clear that the way to improvement is to constantly improve the process itself, not freeze it. Improvement means change. Too often, existing legacy information systems impede change. Therefore, the transition to a distributed environment is an opportunity to create systems that are intended to be continually improved.

1.2   CONFLICTING FORCES

Information Overload.   Dynamic business processes place enormous burdens on existing information systems. Businesses are becoming much more complex and, as a result, they process enormous amounts of information. There is complexity at both ends of the spectrum. Tools for individuals are becoming complex such as design and planning tools. At the same time there is great complexity trying to integrate business processes across the enterprise. Business and information professionals alike suffer from information overload. There is too much detail and not enough organization of the information. There is an enormous need to coordinate the highly divided labor specializations. In a medium or large company it is becoming a challenge just discovering what all the ongoing projects, programs, and departmental functions are

Sins of the Past.   The rapidly changing world is making it apparent that many existing legacy information systems have become obstacles to change. Recent industrial literature has pointed out that current legacy information systems are mired in problems. For example, Brodie and Stonebraker[1] have this to say about legacy information systems:

> Most large organizations are deeply mired in their information sins of the past. Typically, their information systems are large (e.g., 10^7 lines of code), geriatric (e.g., more than 10 years old), written in COBOL, and use a legacy database service (e.g., IBM's IMS or no database management system at all). These information systems are mission critical (i.e., essential to the organization's business) and must be operational at all times. These characteristics define what we call legacy information systems.

Legacy information systems are those business information systems that have been in use for a long time to run the day-to-day operations of an enterprise. Typically, these systems are hosted on mainframes and are supported by large, centralized, in-house information systems groups that operate a large data center and perform software maintenance and development. Legacy information systems present an inconsistent decision environment, where computing systems have become a patchwork quilt. There are high levels of waste, lost opportunity, and failing projects. Data quality can be surprisingly poor. Redman[2] cites studies that report data error rates up to 75 percent.

The history of efforts to change and modernize legacy systems is filled with failure. In many cases, failures occur despite well-funded, well-planned, and well-managed efforts to upgrade or replace legacy systems. There are a number of reasons for this failure. Frequently, the economic return is often not enough to warrant the expense. A substantial mainframe application overhaul can easily cost tens of millions of dollars and take three to four years. Another major factor inhibiting change is that legacy systems are commonly complex, undocumented, and structurally tangled. Because of this, there is no guarantee that change will not result in severely disrupted operations. Closely related to structural problems within an application is the fact that there are often multiple application system interdependencies. Changing any one affects others, often in unpredictable ways. Highly skilled developers have been known to throw up their hands and claim there is no way to conduct adequate tests. Such uncertainties present crippling risk or expense factors.

Entanglement.   The problems with legacy information systems are profound and pervasive. Structurally, legacy software is rigid and convoluted. These structural problems prevent timely quality improvements to the business process. Systems depend on obsolete technology. Costs are extravagant, not uncommonly in the hundreds of millions of dollars for a large business. Businesses spend 50 percent to 90 percent of their computing budget on maintenance. High maintenance costs limit investments in modern technology. Users are dissatisfied and must work around the system. Well-intentioned system owners try to upgrade, but are stymied. Current systems are too entangled to know where to begin to upgrade. Such profound problems directly impair business basics— cost, schedule, and quality.

When we look at where major computing expenditures are commonly made—operating the system, support and maintenance, and modest system enhancements—we see little value added from those expenditures. There are many other areas where investments would bring large value-added results—linking information systems to business objectives, discovering important business opportunities, system implementation planning, implementing new systems and processes, improving decision-making, obsoleting unneeded systems, and generally integrating information systems.

Racing to Keep Abreast.   Supposing that information system expenditures are redirected towards large value-added areas, the information systems professional is challenged with the complexity of making the transition from legacy systems. Information professionals struggle to be experts across any degree of breadth of technology. Technology is evolving too fast for business experts to be technical experts at any level of detail. Although the marketplace is laden with new and promising information technology products, the professional is faced with the question "how to get there from here?" Established businesses have an enormous investment in their existing information technology base and are heavily dependent on smooth and effective evolution, despite the rapidly changing technology and business environment. Often new information technology products are inexpensive; it is the deployment that is expensive. It takes substantial time to evaluate, integrate, and train people to incorporate new products. During that time the technology has often improved, causing a perpetual sense of confusion.

For example, one large company began to evaluate a new operating system and attempted initial deployment of it. It took several months to realize that it was not a mature enough product to deploy for mission-critical applications. Meanwhile, many people had been trained, project plans had been developed, and scattered projects had been started based on this operating system. In addition, significant software had been developed that depended on this operating system. Two years later, money was still being spent converting the software to another operating system. It was a perplexing problem because, at the beginning, a major business program was under way and needed significant information technological support. The existing legacy information systems could not provide the flexibility needed, but some elements of the available new technology were missing. The discovery of these missing elements late in the planning and trial use of the new technology could have been avoided. A system architecture must identify the critical and commonly used elements so that their availability is known and compensating actions can be taken to work around unavailable elements.

1.3   RECONFIGURATION OF THE ELEMENTS

Legacy systems are intractable, yet the demand and the opportunity for change is urgent. A solution lies in the application of a mixture of common sense and radical change. The commonsense approach asks people to draw on their understandings and feelings about what they do every day, first, to note the patterns of events that recur regularly and, second, to articulate and identify patterns of successful solutions. Some of the successful solutions are just beginning to appear as information technology and business undergo surging changes.

A number of successful patterns are appearing. Companies use off-the-shelf software for both office automation and line-of-business applications. It is becoming commonplace to see full network connectivity among computing resources. Client/Server architecture is used to achieve a broad sharing of information. Suites of information service components and service frameworks cover a broad range of functions. Software is beginning to use metadata to define and govern the information system. Companies that are highly dispersed, such as Bellcore, are establishing policy frameworks that encourage cooperative operations while allowing autonomy.

Implementing some of these solutions requires a "paradigm shift" or a fundamentally new way of thinking about things.[3] These great shifts demand a shift in conceptualization. For example, we have thought of tools as extensions of humans. Technology has evolved so greatly during the last few decades that we can now begin to see tools as extensions of business organizations themselves. In their book *Paradigm Shift*, Tapscott and Caston characterize the enabling effect of information technology in the following way:

- Work-group computing enables the high performance team which results in business process redesign.
- Integrated systems enables the integrated organization which results in organization transformation.
- Inter-enterprise computing enables the extended enterprise which results in recasting external relationships.

Information technology for a distributed environment has brought with it many new and profound concepts. Tapscott and Caston describe several technology shifts that are revolutionary in scope. Network computing will not only pervade the business, but also will be extremely common due to the advent of small and powerful processors that communicate and interoperate over high-speed networks that connect all businesses and homes. Software is becoming standardized and available as a commodity. Information processing operates more appropriately for human intelligence based on multimedia rather than on record-based information structures. Businesses are forming partnerships with technology suppliers, displacing the "account control" relationship of the past. Software development is becoming an engineering discipline rather than a craft. Monolithic applications are giving way to application frameworks that promote integrated systems. Software operations are becoming highly intuitive, such as graphical user interfaces based on metaphor. For example, the concept of transparency engineering is the notion that the user should not have to participate in the esoteric operations of the underlying mechanism, but should rather use the technology in an intuitive way. This concept originated for the requirement that distributed computing requires that a collection of separated components interoperate as if they were a unified single system. Communication mechanisms were invented to achieve this unification in a manner that virtually hides the complexities of communications among diverse computers. The notion that computing complexity could be hidden has been generalized to hide a variety of other kinds of complexity.

Secondary effects of migrating to a distributed environment are important also. Because computing systems can be networked so effectively, there is an enormous improvement in collaboration among disciplines; this results in cross-fertilization. A wide variety of technology becomes available in a distributed environment. For example, object orientation, logic programming, relational database technology, graphical user-interface technology, and other advances all contribute to a new information technology base. These technologies bring important new concepts that enable the transition from a high-investment legacy environment to an effective distributed environment. For example, Client/Server architecture, object orientation, and relational database technologies bring operational intuitiveness that results in greatly improved flexibility, reduced training, and improved system integration.

Two parallel evolutionary threads have emerged. On one hand, business enterprises exploited economies of scale to become highly efficient giant organizations. On the other hand, computing technology evolved into a general form of information technology and, thereby, became a mainstay of the business environment. The evolving business strategy began to separate policy from operations into an approach that centralized policy-making and decentralized operations. Throughout this parallel evolution, business computing has depended on centralized, host-based computing resources and centralized development and administration to support centralized large-scale operations.

The arrival of networked small computing resources enabled the beginnings of decentralized operations. However, as networked personal computers and departmental computers proliferate, it becomes clear that businesses need an infrastructure to integrate and manage decentralized information technology. The promises of work-group computing will not emerge simply from saturating the workplace with personal computers on a network. Integrated systems will not emerge from continued point-to-point file transfer of data extracts between systems. Inter-enterprise computing will not emerge by simply hooking up to the network and exchanging electronic mail.

Businesses need an architectural basis to guide the development of such an infrastructure. An architectural approach fills several gaps in earlier approaches to system development. Architecture introduces a systematic way to link technology with business strategies. Contrast this with an approach where business executives and system developers hammer out major technology decisions in the heat of problem-solving. Architecture encourages understanding the theme underlying the client's needs. Without architecture, system developers and users gather requirements like a shopping list with no integration principles to guide an overall business solution. An architectural approach assures that managers and developers consider information technology solutions from a variety of viewpoints. Without such an approach, solutions tend to be top heavy with solutions biased by the skills or interests of the designers and planners at the time.

Development requires several points of view: the enterprise perspective concerned with strategic social, managerial, and financial issues; the information perspective concerned with generating, communicating, and protecting information; the engineering perspective concerned with the design and implementation of mechanisms to achieve transparent distribution of functionality; and the computational perspective concerned with assembling and structuring information service components.

Distributed systems provide wonderful opportunities to create processes that exploit parallel work efforts where individuals, groups, even computer systems can collaborate. As a collaborative environment is created, it becomes imperative that workers are able to communicate and share information and knowledge throughout a business process. Information technology must leap beyond the record-oriented data processing approach. Legacy systems were not able to process information objects such as a shop order or a contract in a whole, integral manner, so business workers began to take for granted that information comes in files of unrelated data elements. With emerging technology it becomes possible to use that technology to process information, knowledge, and communication rather than data records. This allows information technology to participate in the communication and information-sharing required for collaborative work. Being more effective at the human level means that information technology facilitates innovation of a business process.

If we were to simplify recent information technology history, we would say that the 1970s was the decade where we learned that computers could process many simple data records much better than a person. In the 1980s, we found that we could work "online" where many people could concurrently process many simple data elements and do so at incredible speed. Banks and airline reservation systems exemplified this use of information technology.

During the 1980s, small-scale efforts, from inventor's garages to universities to high-tech startup companies, prepared for the 1990s with a vast array of new information technology. Such technologies as powerful processors, object-oriented programming, logic-based systems, and distributed processing have now matured. During the 1990s the large data center will go the way of the railway system with the introduction of trucks and airplanes. It won't disappear any more than the railway has, but it will become less relevant for many purposes.

Data and information processing will become highly distributed. Distribution brings with it a revolution in the way that people think of data. Distribution brings autonomy. Autonomy brings diversity and many new ideas. This wealth of diversity and innovation changes how we characterize information technology. Instead of focusing on the introduction of new products that make a difference to the business, we will focus on the introduction of new abstractions, new concepts that make a difference to the business.

Information technology changes our style of working. Today, it is easy to use electronic mail to work with people located in dozens of countries during a single working day. An order placed anywhere in the world could be propagated to affected departments of a company scattered in other parts of the world, the order worked, and the results delivered within hours or days through express mail.

This kind of thinking is not at the level of making a host database work faster or even making application development happen faster. Data distribution happens at the level of assembling intelligent modular components—modules that use machine-usable knowledge to govern their operations. The relational database is, perhaps, the best known example of the technology of the 1990s. There are three major elements of a relational database—a language, a fact base, and an inference engine. The user expresses a statement in a language that uses relatively ordinary concepts. The relational database contains data that has been organized according to knowledge about a domain. The relational database uses an inference engine to interpret the language-based request against the facts stored and satisfies the request in an intelligent way. Previous database technologies did not abstract away the intricacies of the underlying implementation details, nor did they display such abstractions as logic, language, or knowledge.

Legacy system applications were built to try to achieve this power. Most were not very successful because businesses cannot spread out the development costs over a large user base and they cannot apply an appropriate skill base for similar reasons. The 1990s bring a type of information technology that is architected as a series of layers of increasing system organization, with each layer perfected in its own right and shared with all that want to use it. Analogously, it is like the difference between a simple organism and a complex one. A complex organism has layers of increasing system organization from molecules to cell systems to tissues to organs. Simple organisms are a monolith. Legacy systems are monolithic and have no hope of providing the capabilities and adaptability needed for the evolving business environment.

Business enterprises will make the transition from legacy systems in a variety of ways. There will be elements of what has been termed "greenfield" and "brownfield." That is, in some cases, the transition will be made by leaving old systems behind and introducing new technology fresh—greenfield. In many cases, though, a mature company has much too much invested in legacy systems and existing data to "slash and burn" the old systems. There are ways to make the transition gradual and to regenerate existing data suitable for the new technology of the distributed environment—brownfield.

CHAPTER NOTES

1. Brodie, Michael L., and Michael Stonebraker. *DARWIN: On the Incremental Migration of Legacy Information Systems*. Technical Memorandum of Electronics Research Laboratory, College of Engineering, University of California, Berkeley, 1993.
2. Redman, Thomas C. *Data Quality: Management and Technology*. New York: Bantam Books, 1992.
3. Tapscott, Don, and Art Caston. *Paradigm Shift: The New Promise of Information Technology*. New York: McGraw-Hill, 1993.

2

Architecture and the Distributed Environment

2.1   BEGINNINGS IN DECENTRALIZATION

Our focus is the evolution of business computing from a centralized mainframe environment to a distributed computing environment. This transition began to happen in earnest during the 1980s as networked computing and desktop computing technologies developed. This first decade, however, created a legacy of decentralized resources that were an unprincipled scattering of mainframes, midrange servers, and personal computers.[1] Unprincipled or not, networked computing provided a leap forward in the ability for users to share computing resources. At first, devices such as printers were shared; then later more abstract resources such as file systems and mail systems were introduced.

As networked computing evolved, more sophisticated approaches began to appear, such as networked file systems and distributed computing systems. Networked file systems introduced a new concept called location transparency. Before this innovation, a user needed to know where a file was located on the network and had to specifically request the file. Distributed file systems managed location dependencies for the user. With a distributed file system, the user had access to all files in exactly the same manner, whether they physically resided on his local computer or resided remotely on the network. Distributed computing systems extend the capabilities of location transparency beyond file sharing by allowing collections of networked processors to interact through message exchange rather than shared memory. That is, the granularity of communication shifted to include arbitrary messages. With message exchange, however, the design of interacting computers quickly becomes quite complex. The term Client/Server architecture refers to a common form of a distributed computing system in which the design is greatly simplified because components play an assigned role of client or server. That is, one component always requests, the other always replies.

In the early 1990s, signs of chaos began to appear in the companies with growing networked computing environments. Personal computers began to proliferate on the network. PCs, departmental computers, and mainframes were each designed and built differently. Consequently, they did not interoperate well. The centralized MIS computers, department computers, and the PC network operated independently. Departments deployed different and incompatible hardware systems. The phrase "islands of automation" became popular. The unprincipled nature of early networked computing began to take its toll. To counter the chaos, some companies adapted a monoculture computing technology where a single major vendor, such as IBM, Novell, or Digital, supplied nearly all the technology solutions. A monoculture, however, stifled competitive advances, leaving large gaps in capabilities. Other companies deployed technologies from many vendors to acquire a broader range of capabilities, but the heterogeneity resulting from the mix of vendors created so much diversity that maintenance became slow and costly.

Networked computing and distributed computing systems clearly promised a breakthrough for businesses, but what was missing was an infrastructure that provided integration and management. *Distributed computing systems* are those whose components are separated. *Client/ Server architecture* is one form of a distributed computing system that simplifies the roles the components play, though there are other approaches, such as the actors model. *Cooperative Processing* further generalizes the environment with an effective technology infrastructure where there are additional elements, such as integrated heterogeneous networks, established standardization policies, and mediating services (middleware). Even more elements need to be added to the discussion such as the concepts introduced in the Open Distributed Processing (ODP) approach, which includes such concepts as federation, viewpoint models, transparency engineering, and object modeling. Also, information technology needs to be linked with strategic business objectives. In this book this broad situation that includes engineering, architecture, and business linkages is termed *distributed environment*. The relationship among these concepts is shown in Figure 2.1.

Lelann[2] suggested that the most important objectives of distributed system design are extendibility, increased availability, and resource sharing.

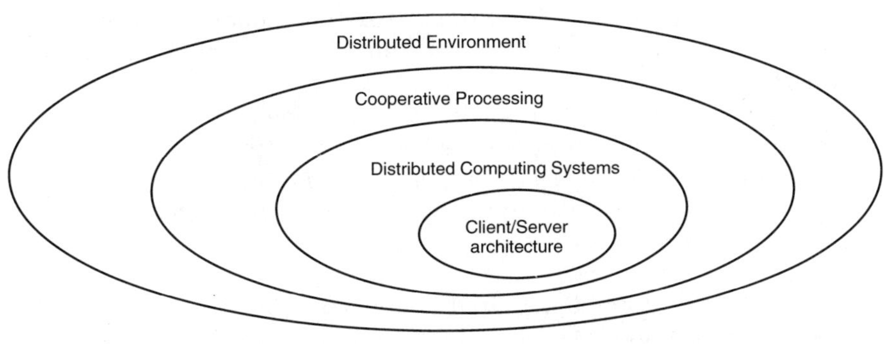

Figure 2.1   Scope of a distributed environment.

Coulouris and Dollimore observe that a distributed system, by virtue of component separation ". . . allows the truly parallel execution of programs, the containment of component faults and recovery from faults without disruption of the whole system, the use of isolation and interlocks as a method of enforcing security and protection policies, and the incremental growth or contraction of the system through the addition or subtraction of components."[3]

John Gantz suggested that the main features of cooperative processing include the following[4]:

- Client/Server or similar architecture to allow processing of a program across two or more processors
- Heterogeneous networks
- Open systems, with a qualification on the meaning of open
- Common user interfaces, generally graphical and windows-based
- Distributed application development tools and integrating subroutines
- Lots of middleware, or software programs that aid in distributed system, network, and storage management
- Distributed database management
- Object-management technology

The Open Distributed Processing (ODP) draft ISO standard, scheduled for ratification in 1994, provides a formal reference model for distributed processing. The ANSA project, a research consortium, has been a primary contributor. The ODP architectural model has the following key elements[5]:

- An object-modeling foundation
- Federation concepts that define a basis for cooperative processing in a heterogeneous, autonomous information technology environment
- Viewpoint models and languages that provide a means to describe information systems from selected perspectives including enterprise, information, computational, engineering, and technology
- A number of key distributed processing concepts such as transparency engineering

These definitions of distributed systems provide the basic scope for cooperative processing. As we examine the needs of migrating legacy systems to a distributed environment, we will expand the scope with more emphasis on business strategic issues, architecture, and a focus on data management.

2.2   NEED FOR ARCHITECTED INFORMATION SYSTEMS AND THE IDEA OF LINKAGE

Businesses are becoming more collaborative and adaptive to operate in a changing, complex world. Information systems are undergoing a corresponding change. They are shifting from rigid and centralized systems to systems that are reusable, distributed, and abstract. However, this shift is making it apparent that computing systems represent major commitments for businesses, and thus require a shift in the design approach from crafted systems to architected systems. Information technology architecture must be based on concepts and principles and must forge a link among three fundamental dimensions of the business—business objectives, business processes, and information technology. Business objectives establish targets at which business processes aim. The selection and configuration of information technology components needs to be done expressly to help the business approach become fully aligned with business objectives. However, operating within this broad scope requires people from all levels of the organization, from the senior management to the analysts, to establish common goals and approaches.

2.3   ARCHITECTURE PRINCIPLES FOR BUSINESS

Plans and designs are formulated repeatedly throughout the year to supply and improve information technology for business processing. It is not practical to engage continually in a dialog among all reaches of the organization during this process. However, it is essential that information technology and business processes are guided to achieve business objectives in the large scope. To ensure that architectural solutions meet requirements in the large scope, a company can formulate architectural principles expressly for its overall situation. For example, a business that is geographically dispersed should articulate a principle stating that shared data has standard data designations.

AT&T is developing what it calls a Global Information Systems Architecture (GISA). This architecture places strict limits on the number of different software systems in the company's plants worldwide. The company demands standardization to keep this large scope manageable. The following characteristics of AT&T's GISA development projects would be good candidates for principles to ensure linkage between information technology and business objectives[6]:

- Standard data designations and format
- Standard interfaces to common external systems
- Minimal size of local development groups
- Avoidance of redundant software development/searches
- Multiuse licenses for the same software
- An experienced team to coordinate global implementations
- Coordinated customization and upgrade maintenance
- User groups to share ideas and experiences
- Backup among multiple users in same area
- Improved communications between locations

Such principles are necessary for several purposes. As a first step, they provide the leadership to overcome the inertia of organizational change. Second, these principles provide critical pathmarks or a framework for standards to coordinate a large scope of the business. Third, by formulating these principles a pattern language is being developed that enables the community to better express their ideas concerning what works and doesn't work.

2.4 ARCHITECTURE AS A PATTERN LANGUAGE

"There is one timeless way of building."

Christopher Alexander, 1979

In an era of complexity and esoterica that surrounds information technology, architecture is sometimes seen as a dark science, an activity that a few experts must complete, so that ordinary activities can proceed. Christopher Alexander recently presented a new approach to architecture, building, and planning that treats architecture as everyone's business.[7] In this approach he encourages people to draw on their basic understandings and feelings about what they do every day. To explain his approach, he describes systems of patterns that recur throughout the history of building. He notes how these patterns serve to resolve conflicting forces that occur in a given context. For example, he notes how the design of ordinary barns follows a consistent core of patterns that are proven ways to best solve the problems of farmers.

Patterns exist in large or small details. A room in a house is made comfortable with windows on two sides and sitting ledges near the windows. A large community room needs alcoves at the periphery to accommodate the need for moments of privacy. A good fireplace has a place to put logs and a mantle to place small objects. A building needs a transition space between the street and the inside to give a person a moment to shift between the different ambiences, such as the glare and publicness of the street and the calm and intimacy inside the house. Visitors to Washington, D.C., will note the effective use of transition spaces between the outsides and insides of historic structures. For example, the Lincoln memorial uses a reflection pool and a massive sequence of steps leading to a building with massive columns containing a statue of Lincoln. The manipulation of one's emotional state by these design patterns to achieve a feeling of awe is unmistakable and effective.

Architecture, in Alexander's view, is a generative pattern language. It is not simply the depiction of the outcome of design efforts. Architecture can be a repertoire of answers to what works, in what contexts, to resolve what conflicting forces. To achieve the timeless and aliveness quality in what we build, ". . . we must begin by understanding that every place is given its character by certain patterns of events that keep on happening there."

Builders, planners, architects, and users alike help create our things and places. They are the ones that need to help development unfold according to the patterns that make the surroundings alive. As Alexander says, "To work our way towards a shared and living language once again, we must first learn how to discover patterns which are deep, and capable of generating life."

Good architecture, he observes, does not need drawings. It needs people to uncover their understandings and feelings about basic problems to solve and the configurations that provide the solutions. As people conceive of buildings and towns emerging from many autonomous elements following sequences of individual patterns, ". . . groups of people can conceive their larger public buildings, on the ground, by following a common pattern language, almost as if they had a single mind."

As people study, plan, and implement information technology to enable better business processes, Alexander's approach calls for the people to continually discover and articulate the patterns that work. That is, an important part of the job is to step back from the details that always differ from project to project to formulate a language that expresses the patterns that remain the same. Chapter 3 describes the process of developing abstractions.

2.5   THEME AS REQUIREMENTS—LISTENING TO THE CUSTOMER'S VOICE

On thousands and thousands of information systems projects, the approach was to gather lists of requirements—all of the requirements that could be generated. Hence, massive requirements documents line the shelves of the information system professional. Usually, however, it was impossible to meet the requirements with off-the-shelf products. Consequently, a culture of software craftsmen developed. Astoundingly complex legacy systems were the result. The lesson learned—system design is not an additive model of requirements. The architect must design to a theme, a system of patterns.

The architect doesn't need to begin with a shopping list of detailed requirements. The architect is creating a multipurpose artifact. The architect creates a framework to suit the client's basic purpose; the client furnishes and configures it to match the business process.

The business context is in a constant state of change, so the architect must design to a theme that covers an anticipated thread of evolution. For instance, in the 1990s the enterprise value set is shifting from the "organization man" who operates in a rigid hierarchical command and control setting to the customer-oriented professional who operates in an open, networked, dynamic, team-oriented setting.[8] In this setting information and collaborative information tools are key resources. The employee is empowered to make decisions. The scope of work is cross-functional and interorganizational.

The architect operates in a context. Given this context, the architect must assume a number of generic requirements from the outset. In the 1990s the trend is toward smaller enterprise units that have decentralized operations with centralized policy control. Operating units are given maximum autonomy and must assume maximum responsibility. In this context, the architecture probably will call for thematic elements such as reuseability, data independence, transparency engineering, and cooperative, distributed systems.

The central premises are that (1) the information professional must operate with a profound understanding of the customer's purpose and the everyday patterns and conflicts, and (2) both the business process and the information technology must continuously undergo improvement. Therefore, computing architecture must not only support new system development, but must also protect major investments in well-established systems.

The architect must *propose* requirements based on an understanding of the whole context. The architect must listen to the customer's voice as if it were music or a poem, and hear the theme. He must go back to the customer over and over to get it right.

2.6   ARCHITECTURAL OBJECTIVES OF INFORMATION SYSTEMS

Having witnessed the rapid growth of computing as a integral part of everyday business and having suffered the resulting chaos as computing became distributed, it becomes clear that information systems must be subject to disciplined design. What makes a good architectural solution for a business process? A good architectural solution produces systems that are functional, adaptable, and appealing. A community of users measures success along all three dimensions.

First, an information system must do the job. Thus, an information system must be functional. The system must meet objectives that are set. The system must be fit for the purpose at hand. It must produce results that are in the right form. It must display correct properties—timely, safe, reliable, consistent, and complete. It must not display dysfunctional behavior.

Second, the system must adapt to a changing environment. Adaptable systems allow continuous improvements in a diverse environment. Improvements may require changes in suppliers, products and tools, users, markets, or business processes. Users must have the right tools that can access and operate in diverse situations—multiple data sources, types of data, and multiple operations on data.

Third, the system must appeal to its users. Appealing systems stimulate delight in the users. Appealing information systems are intuitive. Failures and degradation are graceful and recoverable. Appealing systems match the user's style of problem-solving. Its operations are easy to learn and use, and display reasonable default behavior. Appealing systems help the user achieve business basics—on schedule, within cost, and a high-quality process.

The purpose of architecture is to guide the building of systems that satisfy a client and a community of users' purposes in the face of major commitments. In some sense the community of users are builders. Clients of a computing system design range along a continuum from operational users to business stakeholders. Clients come from different functional areas of an enterprise; they are responsible for various levels of the organization or have various relationships to the company.

At one extreme the individual user must be satisfied. At the other extreme, enterprise objectives must be satisfied. An information system must serve work groups, work between functional groups, work across stages of a process, and work between organizations and enterprises. Thus, as we consider architectural criteria, we should ask if the solution promises to meet objectives for the individual, the work group, between work groups, between organizations, and so on.

One important design objective concerns the cost trade-off between man and machine. "In prior technology eras, users optimized the machine—the expensive resource, and suboptimized the end user—the less expensive resource. In so doing, computing architectures were designed to keep machine cycles consumed at the expense of users at terminals."[9] That principle is turned on its head now. Machines are cheap; information workers are expensive. The architect must focus on the information worker—the user.

One study[10] showed that there are three dimensions of user satisfaction. Each dimension has a number of criteria on which to judge the user's satisfaction as shown in Table 2.1.

A large proportion of software design is directly concerned with user interaction. Since the mid-1980s there have been great advances in design for user interaction with software. In John Chisholm's "The Art of Software Design," Alan Cooper describes a series of principles to follow to ensure that software is user-centered.[11] Cooper's grand principle is that software design should be a "tactioneering" (touch or con-

Table 2.1   Dimensions of User Satisfaction

Information satisfaction	System satisfaction	Support group satisfaction
Availability	Ease of use	Technical competence
Accuracy	Ease of learning	Attitudes
Timeliness	Flexibility	Responsiveness
Precision	User control	Services
Reliability	Response time	Development schedule
Currency	Error control facilities	Charge-back methods
Completeness		
Output format		

tact) discipline. By that he means that the focus should be on measuring the quality and intensity of the interaction between the human and the system. Good software has high-quality taction. Cooper describes a number of design principles to achieve high-quality taction:

1. *Efficacious.* The software does the right job and satisfies the user's needs.
2. *Conceptual Integrity.* The software conforms to a unifying concept; the design makes the product seem natural and avoids appearing as a grab bag of features.
3. *Grammatical.* The system is easy to learn. The software is based on a few primitives and systematically extends them into higher order constructs. The so-called WIMP user interface is a good example. It is based on windows, icons, menus, and a pointer device. All else is built on that framework.
4. *Well-Mapped.* The objects and relationships that the user sees readily suggest their purpose and function. Good topological positioning and suggestive icons help improve this quality.
5. *Trustworthy.* The appearance and behavior of the system should engender trust by responding accurately and consistently. Failures should be graceful, allowing simple recovery.
6. *Engaging.* The software should abide by ordinary human emotion. It should be appealing, gracious, appropriately humorous, and generous. Brenda Laurel suggests that computers take lessons from the legacy of theater.

2.7 FUNDAMENTAL ARCHITECTURE CONCEPTS FOR INFORMATION SYSTEMS

Information systems that perform cooperatively with people need to be intelligence amplifiers. One definition of intelligence notes three frequently recurring concepts of intelligence: the ability to deal effectively with tasks involving abstractions; the ability to learn; and the ability to deal with new situations.[12] These qualities apply both in individual and social settings. This seems to bear on the fact that information systems that meet the objectives just described demonstrate three essential concepts—abstraction, integration, and extendibility.

Abstraction. An intelligent agent is able to solve problems when a situation can be classified as something it already knows about and knows how to deal with. That is, general features of the situation are abstracted from specific situational details, then action is taken with respect to the general features.

The concept of abstraction guides a design towards a system that appears simple and intuitive to the user. The appearance and behavior of the system match something familiar and basic to ordinary problem-solving. Esoteric operations of the information technology are made relatively *transparent*. The operations of the system closely match the operations of the user and the business process.

For a designer, abstraction provides critical *independence* between the specification of a system and its implementation. Abstraction is achieved by designing system functionality in layers of increasing system organization. For a user, independence allows improvements to occur with minimal impact.

Integration. The parts of a system must be able to share information and knowledge in order to combine their efforts towards a common solution. The concept of integration guides the designer to provide opportunities for cooperation—cooperation among machines, individuals, and groups within the same or different contexts and stages of a process. Integration guides a design towards implementation of the metaphors of communication, sharing, and coordination.

Cooperation among participants requires that they *interoperate*. This requirement has many implications for standards and suggests why the most important standards are concerned with interfaces, protocols, languages, and naming, all subjects that are the basis for interaction.

Extendibility. Due to the continuously evolving nature of computing technology, a computing architecture can never be a snapshot in time. The computing system needs to be continuously extendible. A system must be able to undergo incremental growth in form and function. Extendibility guides the design towards adaptability. A good design identifies adjustable system variables and constraints with respect to objectives. As system users and designers encounter new situations and learn from old situations, information system elements can be added or reconfigured to reflect what was learned. Extendibility enables a design to attain desirable system properties through use of the right structural elements and parameter settings that affect those properties.

Such an architectural framework is fundamentally parametric in nature[13] as shown in Figure 2.2. The architecture, as a matter of principle, addresses the right choice of the parameters to balance the set of overall business requirements in the current context. The setting of the knobs denotes the current trade-offs with respect to requirements, cost, technology, and other factors. Adequate extendibility of the system enables adaptive, nondisruptive changes to the system.

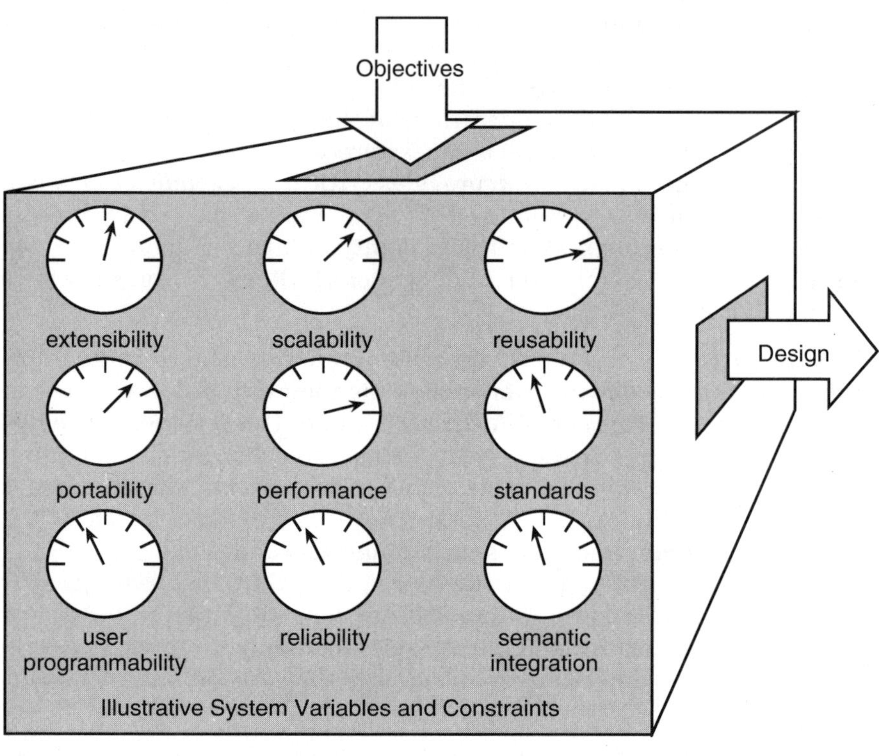

Figure 2.2   A good design balances variables and constraints to meet objectives.

Of all the architectural issues for the transition to distributed systems, there is one that draws out extraordinary passion from professionals—the balance between *local effectiveness* gained through autonomy versus *global integration* gained through interdependence (see Figure 2.3). Legacy systems are characteristically autonomous regarding their design approach. A department has a job to do and so they do it without letting other departments interfere. After all, the person in charge is rewarded for his or her local department function, not the company's overall well-being. The problem is, of course, that departments are often not profit centers. Profit comes from coordinating the company's process from end to end.

Business architecture principles are needed to explicitly establish

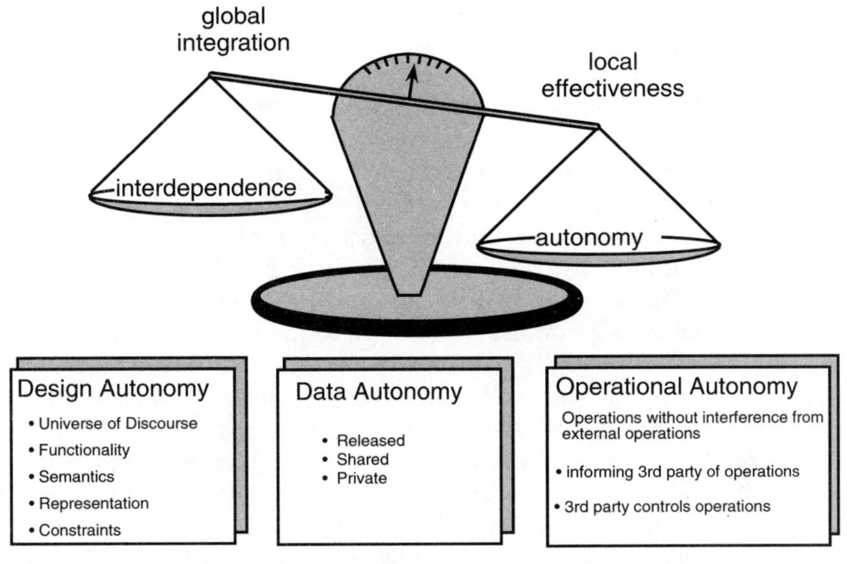

Figure 2.3   Autonomy versus global integration.

guidelines for this trade-off. Experience shows, though, that principles alone will not accomplish the mission. Qualities of the results must be measured from a broad business process perspective. Otherwise, people in charge are paid to suboptimize.

A second fundamental factor governs the autonomy integration balance. The old saw "if you want something done, do it yourself" is in effect. Centralized computer support is notoriously slow and unresponsive. Departments want autonomy so that they have control over development and maintenance.

Consequently, if global integration is the goal, at least two cultural factors must be changed. First, the agency in charge must be in charge of a macro process, not a narrowly defined function or organization. The agency in charge must be motivated to develop and maintain computing systems that improve the overall business process. The "agency" is not necessarily a person, alone. Companies are beginning to shift towards a process orientation that requires a team orientation instead of a hierarchical management orientation. We discuss more of this in Chapter 3. Second, to achieve global integration, the development and maintenance bottleneck must be eliminated. A support infrastructure must be developed that guarantees fast system improvements to support business process improvement.

A distributed computing environment intensifies the need to coordinate computing operations. Coordination results from managing interdependencies between activities performed to achieve a goal. If there is to be a balance between autonomy and global integration, the goals, activities, actors, resources, and interdependencies must be relative to the end-to-end process, not relative to a bureaucratic structure. Business goals must be identified. Activity ordering and assignment to actors must be relative to the end-to-end process. Resource allocation and activity synchronization must be relative to the end-to-end process.

A strategic approach is required to provide a standard framework and the practices for the coordination of computing processes, information management, and human use of computing. This requirement is particularly important because information systems consist of many active components. Because of the business trends in the 1990s, the basic goal of information technology is to support cooperative autonomy. Autonomy is necessary because the command and control is shifting to smaller enterprise business units. Coordination is required because the units cooperate in a larger process to achieve collective enterprise goals.

2.8   ARCHITECTURAL VIEWPOINTS

Information systems introduce fundamentally new dimensions to design. There is no doubt that a a hydroelectric dam, high-rise building, or a planned community is a complex design challenge. However, each of these artifacts is designed to a specific, fixed purpose. Business information systems can be as complex as any of these artifacts; but, additionally, an information system must be intelligent to assist human users and adaptable in order to track changing market conditions and increased global competition. If a system is based on the key concepts already described—abstraction, integration, and extendibility—these unique characteristics can be achieved by manipulating components:

- Replacing obsolete components with modern technology
- Adding new modular components to improve functionality
- Reconfiguring or upgrading existing components
- Improving communications between components
- Increasing the intelligence of components
- Increasing the knowledge available to the components

Interestingly, what we may mean by components depends on the applicable level of system organization. Figure 2.4 shows four levels of system organization. Components occur at each level in an assembly/subassembly or client/service relationship.

A system architecture that describes the computing platforms and network shows one viewpoint. As information technology matures, more layers of system organization are formally differentiated. During the 1970s and 1980s, the second layer, shown in Figure 2.4, began to mature. (Refer to the time chart in Figure 2.5.) Consequently, information

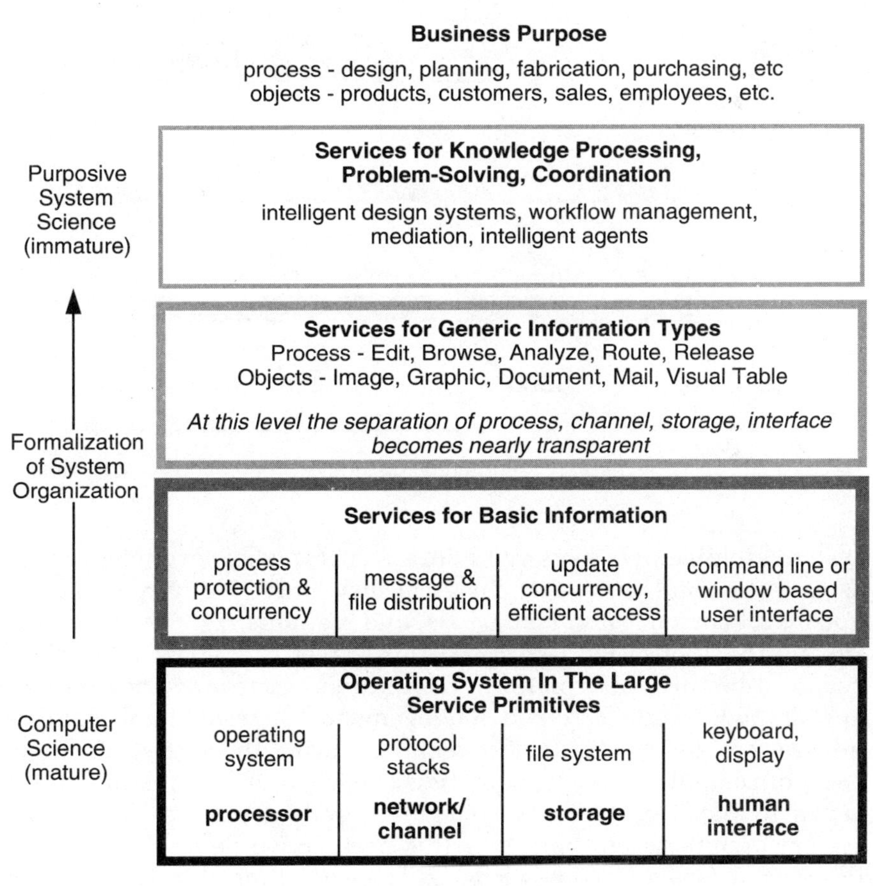

Figure 2.4   Formalization of higher levels of system organization.

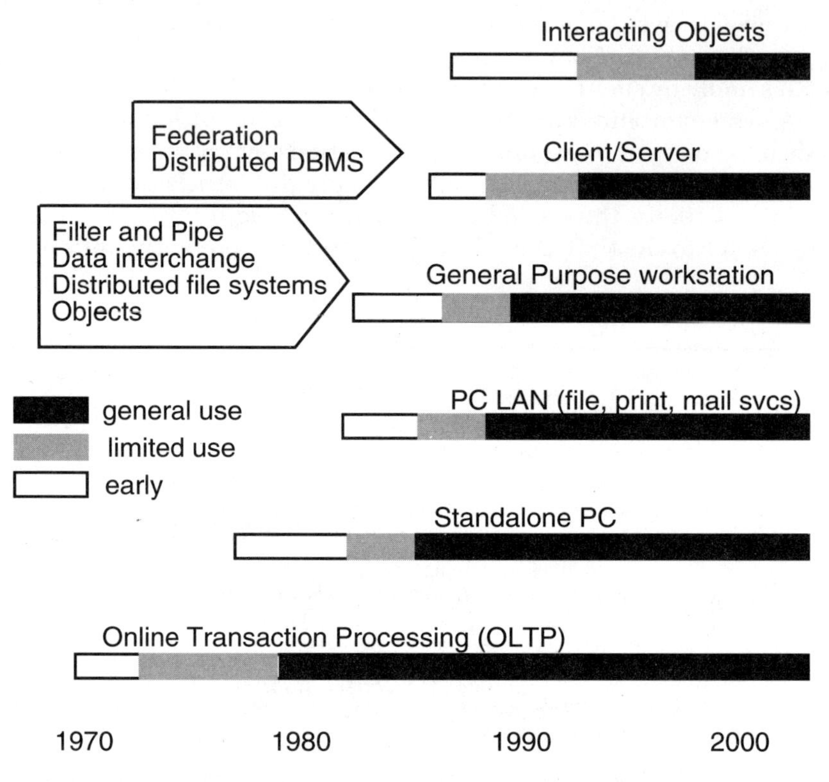

Figure 2.5   Evolution of commercial distributed computing infrastructure.

system architectures began to address such higher-level abstractions as protection and process concurrency, distributed file systems, storage update concurrency and fast access, and metaphorical user interfaces. During the 1980s and 1990s, the third layer of system organization began to mature. Information system architectures are beginning to appear that depict document management, electronic mail, database integration, and general object servers. During the 1990s, certain aspects of computer science, cognitive science, and information science began to converge to create purposive system science. Information system architectures that show this perspective depict systems that incorporate formalized knowledge, intelligence, and abilities to support collaborative work efforts.

The transition from legacy systems to a distributed environment requires critical appreciation of multilevel architectural viewpoints. At one extreme it is essential that an architecture not be limited to a computer platform and network perspective. To achieve as flexible and powerful a system as possible it is desirable to include the higher levels of system organization into the architecture. At the other extreme, the higher levels of organization do not have mature technology or system design expertise to support unlimited deployment. Figure 2.5 suggests the general level of maturity of evolving commercial distributed computing infrastructure corresponding to the lower two levels of system organization shown in Figure 2.4.[14]

Now that the infrastructure for distributed computing has matured enough for commercial deployment, the architectural focus is shifting to give more attention to cooperation issues such as inter-machine communication and information-sharing. However, it is important that the architectural focus be broader than just delivery system design issues.

Architectural design standards to support a broader focus are beginning to appear along several dimensions. An international standard effort known as Open Distributed Processing (ODP) has defined five viewpoints from which design can be generated and evaluated—Enterprise, Information, Computation, Engineering, and Technology:

- The *enterprise* viewpoint is concerned with the social, managerial, financial, and legal policy issues that constrain the human and machine roles of a distributed system and its environment.
- The *information* viewpoint concentrates on information modeling and flow, plus structure and information manipulation constraints.
- The *computational* viewpoint focuses on the structure of application components and the exchange of data and control among them.
- The *engineering* viewpoint concerns the mechanisms that provide the distribution transparencies to the application components.
- The *technology* viewpoint focuses on the constraints imposed by technology and the components from which the distributed system is constructed.[15]

Admittedly, the choice of these viewpoints may be somewhat arbitrary or vague; as a matter of fact, they have been criticized as such. However, without some heuristic that encourages a broad view of an information system, it is highly likely that an architectural design will be biased according to the participants' current specialized knowledge and responsibilities. Within each of these suggested viewpoints, there exists a body of design standards and guidelines concerning design forms, specifications, and products that the architect draws on to produce a design. Taking all the viewpoints together, the architect is much more likely to achieve a broad-based design than without them. As a matter of fact, if Alexander's model of architecture is followed, many people participate in the role of architect by virtue of identifying successful patterns to solve problems.

Achieving the transition from legacy systems to an distributed environment requires a design that satisfies objectives and constraints from all the five stated viewpoints. Making this transition can be an enormous challenge for all involved, especially since every point of view has its own set of objectives, variables, and constraints.

For example, the persons responsible for the technology viewpoint may focus on the evolution to networked PCs and powerful workstations, but may procrastinate concerning which products to commit to in a rapidly changing context. A technology support organization is probably charged with providing support for a vast array of products. Their constraint may simply be that they cannot keep up with the needed expertise and acceptance testing process.

The persons responsible for the engineering viewpoint may focus on the tradeoffs to make such an approach scale to the needed size or to achieve the required level of reliability. The engineering viewpoint may be operating to the documented requirements, literally; yet these requirements may not accurately reflect objectives, variables, and constraints from other perspectives.

The persons responsible for the computational viewpoint may focus on how to reengineer and repackage existing functionality to a new technology environment and a new information environment. During the transition from legacy systems, the costs of the new system components may place an extraordinary constraint on the budget for adjusting the existing systems to work with the new systems.

The persons responsible for the information viewpoint may be charged with the objective to define the system cross-functionally. Their main constraint relates to gaining cooperation from people narrowly responsible for specific functions within the enterprise. Finally, the persons responsible for the enterprise viewpoint may focus on which of many systems to migrate at what point (portfolio analysis), trying to determine how to stage a massive change.

Clearly, one of the critical objectives of the architect is to help orchestrate these different viewpoints during a complex problem-solving process.

2.9   ARCHITECTURAL METHODOLOGY

Given a discipline based on principles and a repertoire of design standards and patterns, the architect relies heavily on a process of classification and parameterization that encourages the use of highly refined, reusable components. This is preferred to compiling a shopping list of requirement details and developing a nonreusable, hand-crafted design.

Besides a design discipline, the architect adapts a methodological approach that allows incremental development and reusability. The architect promotes ongoing communication among system development participants concerning models and design rationale in relationship to the business purposes driving the process.

Such a constructive approach helps govern the kind of major commitments for business process changes required of the customer. It ensures that complex new systems can be built up and complex old systems can be migrated in stages as implications of requirements and design become better appreciated.

Architecture is a design discipline as is planning. Some people ask, "What is the difference between architecture and design?" Traditionally, architecture is viewed as style-centered while design is seen as more concerned with engineering details. However, the major distinction between architecture and design is a matter of scale and commitment. Architecture, like formal planning, becomes an essential part of the design process as the amount of applicable resources becomes a large commitment. Commitment may manifest itself as a judgment that once policy is promulgated, resources are marshaled, or construction is started, there is no turning back to a different approach. Planning, another design discipline, is concerned with the *process of construction,* whereas architecture is concerned with ensuring that the product structure serves the *process of using the product.* However, often the role of an architect is to be intimately involved in the construction process, if not a principal planner and supervisor. Figure 2.6 shows a typical context in which the architect must operate.

Developing information technology architecture has at least the following four process components:

1. Understand the business and technical environments.

    Identify principles that relate business strategies to technical approaches. Understand the customer's core competencies because this will be the foundation for long-term commitments. Determine the technology environment, including current technology investments and technical standards. This part of the process produces customer-oriented policy that developers use as guidelines to achieve strategic business objectives during the information system life cycle.
2. Understand the business process.

    Classify the process functional requirements. Identify the qualitative parameters. Identify the objectives that the system must meet.

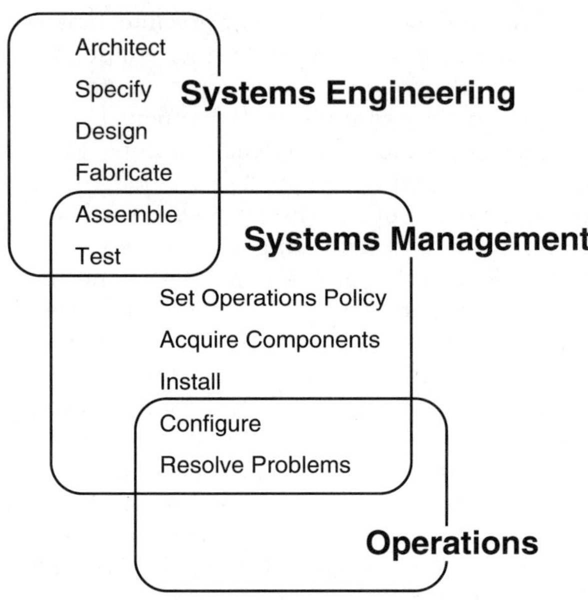

Figure 2.6   Architecture process context.

Identify the general events that recur. This part of the architectural process develops the set of patterns that define the customer's
situation.

3.   Integrate the patterns.

Partition the problem along various dimensions. Identify the conflicting factors. Formulate the key concepts that integrate the business strategies, everyday events, and feasible technical resources.
Promote a shared understanding of the context by developing functional models to show what functional elements are required, roles
played, and relationships among functional elements. Develop part-
whole (subsumption) models to show the layers of components to assemblies, service to client, mechanism to policy. Develop a general
construction strategy. Identify development and implementation phasing and geographical or functional partitioning approaches for large
systems. Develop models to build a consensus among the participants.

4.   Engineer solution details.

Promote general solutions and discourage ad hoc solutions.
Develop concrete or physical design. Allocate products, standards,

Table 2.2   Illustrative Qualitative Design Model

Quality	Mechanism
Transparency	Client/Server model, 3 schema architecture, distribution services, abstract data types
Reliability	Recovery mechanisms
Availability	Replication management
Efficiency	Parallelism, bandwidth, caching
Validity	Specification conformance, sole authority data sources
Security	Authentication, authorization, and data confidentiality mechanisms
Coordination	Concurrency mechanisms, protocols, shared policy and knowledge

or appropriate technology to functions. Develop qualitative models by identifying system qualities and design approaches (see Table 2.2). Specify interfaces. Define a framework of information classes.

Gain experience and validate concepts, methods, and parameters. Set up an integration and piloting test bed for large projects. Develop simulation metamodels by identifying relevant objectives, variables, and constraints. Simulate or prototype to adjust variables to meet objectives within bounds of the constraints.

CHAPTER NOTES

1. Raman, Khanna (ed.). *Distributed Computing: Implementation and Management Strategies.* Englewood Cliffs, N.J.: PTR Prentice-Hall, 1994.
2. LeLann, G. "Motivations, Objectives and Characterization of Distributed Systems" in B. W. Lampson, M. Paul, and H.J. Siegart (eds.). *Distributed Systems—Architecture and Implementation.* New York: Springer-Verlag, 1983.
3. Coulouris, George F., and Jean Dollimore. *Distributed Systems: Concepts and Design.* Reading, MA: Addison-Wesley, 1988.
4. Raman, Khanna (ed.). *Distributed Computing: Implementation and Management Strategies.* Englewood Cliffs, N.J.: PTR Prentice-Hall, 1994.
5. Brenner, John (ed.). *OPENFramework: Distributed Application Services.* International Computers Limited, 1993. Prentice-Hall International (UK).
6. "AT&T Adapts a Global Manufacturing Architecture." *Manufacturing Systems.* January 1994.
7. Alexander, Christopher. *The Timeless Way of Building.* New York: Oxford University Press, 1979.

8. Tapscott, Don, and Art Caston. *Paradigm Shift: The New Promise of Information Technology.* New York: McGraw-Hill, 1993.

9. GartnerGroup RAS Services. J. Schulman and C. Miller. "The SMS Scenario: The Impact of Change in Information Architecture." *Software Management Strategies, Strategic Analysis Report, R-003-121* (February 26, 1993).

10. M.H. Alai Tafti. "A Three-dimensional Model of User Satisfaction with Information Systems." *International Journal of Information Resource Management,* vol 3, no. 2 (1992): 4–10.

11. Chisholm, John. "The Art of Software Design." *Unix Review* (March 1994).

12. English, Horace B., and Ava Champney English. *A Comprehensive Dictionary of Psychological and Psychoanalytic Terms: A Guide to Usage.* New York: David McKay, 1958.

13. Credit goes to Ashutosh Tiwary for emphasizing this point in many fruitful discussions.

14. Brenner, John (ed.). *OPENFramework: Distributed Application Services.* International Computers Limited, 1993. Prentice-Hall International (UK).

15. These viewpoints are described in a number of reports, several of which are identified:

Dobson, John. *An Architecture for Multi-vendor Systems.* N.p., n.d.

Herbert, A. J. *The Advanced Networked Systems Architecture.* N.p., n.d.

Nicol, John R., C. Thomas Wilkes, and Frank A. Manola. "Object Orientation in Heterogeneous Distributed Computing Systems." *Computer* (June 1993).

Sloman, Morris. *Management for Open Distributed Processing.* IEEE Order Number: 0-8186-2088-9/90/0000/0533. 1990.

Tschammer, V., and D. Strict. *Principles and Models for Integrating Distributed Systems from Existing Components.* Tokyo: IFAC Distributed Computer Control Systems, 1989.

3

Distributed Systems Are a New Paradigm

"...color blindness was nowhere noticed until John Dalton's description of it in 1794."

Thomas S. Kuhn, 1962[1]

The transition to a distributed environment from a host computing environment, or even a pool of desktop computers, brings with it a number of radical shifts in frames of reference. These shifts are not simply due to operating in a distributed or networked environment. Rather, great diversity and innovation of information technology accompanies distributed computing which, in turn, brings new models of the world and new ways of solving problems.

In 1962 Thomas S. Kuhn published his now-famous book, *The Structure of Scientific Revolutions*. He describes two senses of a paradigm: (1) " . . . the entire constellation of beliefs, values, techniques, and so on shared by the members of a given community," and (2) "concrete puzzle-solutions . . . employed as models or examples." Several years after his book was published, Kuhn became convinced that the deepest significance of paradigm shifts concerned the emergence of new exemplars or model solutions that enabled a community to see the same thing when witnessing the same situation and to see differences when the situation was different. One of the prime objectives of the next few chapters is to show several different faces of distributed information systems to convey a new paradigm.

However, before exploring the dimensions of information technology in a distributed context, we should note that the community whose constellation of beliefs, values, and techniques is at issue here spans business and information technology disciplines. Distributed systems represent a paradigm shift for this broader community.

There was substantial evidence collected in the 1980s to indicate that application of information technology to business problems had much less impact on a company's bottom line than might be expected. For many people this is counter-intuitive. Great new tools should help business health. Thomas Davenport's reply to this paradox is that businesses have deployed information technology as an afterthought, an add-on. He makes the case that the value of information technology for businesses is in its role as an enabler of process innovation.[2] The concept is deceptive. Davenport suggests avoiding the following approaches:

1. First, think only about the technology and then think about how to design the business process (technology push).
2. First, think only about the process, then think about what information technology to use (business pull).
3. Focus on systems and technologies that implement a process (translation).

Davenport's argument is that information technology doesn't *implement a business process,* but that it *enables process innovation.*

The context that information technology serves spans an immensely broad scope. Information technology may be applied to successive levels of business transformation as shown in Table 3.1.[3] The argument is

Table 3.1   Successive Levels of Business Transformation

Level of Business Transformation	Description
Local	Using information technology to improve a particular part of a company, perhaps by automating manual processes
Internal Integration	Integrating information technology within the company
Business Process Redesign	Using information technology to enable business process redesign
Business Network Redesign	Transforming inter-company cooperative networks for competitive advantage as a group
Business Scope Redesign	Using information technology to redesign the company's business scope

that if distributed information system technology is to make any difference, then it must serve new ways of doing business. However, that in turn requires new ways of thinking about how business must be designed, the topic of the next section.

3.1   THE INVITED REVOLUTION—BUSINESS PROCESS ORIENTATION

"It is time to stop paving the cow paths."

Michael Hammer, 1990[4]

Business process as bucket brigade.   In the global 1990s, companies are beginning to look for dramatic improvements in the way that they do business. As Hammer points out in a pithy article on business revolution, businesses have followed the original Henry Ford model of business. According to that model work is organized as a sequence of narrowly defined tasks. Complex control mechanisms and bureaucratic management schemes are used to ensure that tasks are rigorously performed as planned. This approach resembles a bucket brigade, where work is handed from person to person.

Hammer describes the consequences of this business model: "Conventional process structures are fragmented and piecemeal, and they lack the integration necessary to maintain quality and service. They are breeding grounds for tunnel vision, as people tend to substitute the narrow goals of their particular department for the larger goals of the process as a whole. When work is handed off from person to person and unit to unit, delays and errors are inevitable. Accountability blurs, and critical issues fall between the cracks. Moreover, no one sees enough of the big picture to be able to respond quickly to new situations."

A bucket brigade is rarely the best way to quench a fire. Similarly, there is often no need to use people merely as information channels. Information is an electronic phenomenon; with low-cost information channels saturating the workplace, information can be everywhere at once. Workers can have many facts at hand at any point in time. They can coordinate their work during the process rather than at the end. Workers can organize their work around outcomes instead of tasks. One person can oversee the process of moving an order through the entire process. Managers can shift their function from control to removing roadblocks.

Hammer describes how the Ford Company more recently used information technology to radically simplify their goods acquisition process. They used to pay the supplier when they received his invoice. This approach required a complex, bucket brigade-like accounting process involving purchasing, accounts payable, and receiving departments. The new approach is to accept all shipments if there is an outstanding order and pay when they receive the goods. This revolutionizes the process because they no longer have to route invoices through many steps of accounting processes. They simply accept and pay on goods received against an outstanding order in a central database available to all participants in the process. The central database changes the concept of an information channel from a bucket brigade to a common well of information.

The transition to distributed information systems changes the focus from departmental integration (narrow organizational objectives) to a focus on business integration to achieve end-to-end objectives.

Islands of data.   An interesting line of psychological research showed the effects of different interaction patterns in a community. The experimental setup was simple. Two apartment styles were studied. One apartment complex was designed so that all the mailboxes were separated. The other was designed with mailboxes in a centralized location. The results of the study showed that many of the apartment dwellers who shared a mailbox location became friends and helped one another. Those who did not share mailbox location were much less likely to do so. The principle is simple enough: Frequent interactions facilitate collaboration; isolation facilitates isolation.

The traditional company forms functional organizations—marketing, research and development, manufacturing, sales, support. Each organization is headed by a vice president. Each vice president has several levels of management responsible for parts of the functional organization. Every one in the functional organization is responsible for understanding that functional organization's goals and objectives and is expected to contribute to that functional organization's effectiveness. Here's the rub. How do the functional organizations coordinate their activities? VPs work out strategic coordination, but are very careful to do what the president wants. Middle-level management works out tactical coordination, but are careful to do what their boss wants. Workers, who work out operational coordination, are careful to do what their boss wants. Success in the hierarchical organization requires skills for satisfying the boss. The theme is efficiency, control, and avoidance of failure. The hierarchical organization erects brick walls. Departments throw their product over the wall, bottlenecking human intelligence.

Where is the customer in the hierarchical organization? How can the workers do a really good job if they have little visibility of what the customer wants? Moreover, not only does the worker have little visibility of the overall process, the worker has little authority to make changes anyway. It is his boss who has authority, who in turn is mostly concerned with satisfying his boss. It gets worse. Not only is there no visibility and no authority, the worker must throw his results over the wall to the next functional organization. There is no mechanism to collaborate with all of the other workers in other organizations—that's the job of management.

The hierarchical organizational style has already begun to crumble. A process-oriented approach is displacing the traditional hierarchy. The process-oriented approach uses multidisciplinary teams to solve a problem reaching from the end customer to the delivery of the product and beyond to the customer using the product. The traditional hierarchical structure relegates customer satisfaction to the marketing and sales department. The process, team-oriented approach considers the customer throughout the process. The fundamental innovation of the process management approach is to link everyone in the organization with the customer. The structure of the organization is described as lateral links from customer needs to customer satisfaction.

Lateralization of the organization requires a multidisciplinary team approach. Managers don't lose their jobs; they become refocused on removing roadblocks, ensuring that there is good training, helping to establish standards, and managing resources. Teams focus on the objectives needed to ensure effective collaboration. Teams are responsible for streamlining communications and business processes. They search out and eliminate unproductive activities in the process. They collaborate to improve elements of the process such as documents, specifications, designs, and code. They identify and deploy work roles and timely participation by the right individuals. They brainstorm. They alert one another to important situations. The team improves decision-making.

The network as the computer. The computing environment should support a team-based business. The first step is to transform the computing network into a computer. Consider some work group that uses a central mini-computer that serves as a file server, print server, and communications server for a network of several dozen workstations.[5] In a legacy environment this would be so many terminals connected to a departmental computer. But, where the terminals are each themselves computers, this is a system of several dozen computers. If the workstations use a sophisticated operating system with a network file system, such as UNIX, then devices, such as disk storage, that are attached to a workstation are easily shared across the network. Such a setup represents a gigantic increase in processing power, storage, and communication capacity. A network of computers can easily total a 1000 mips (million instructions per second) and 10 gigabytes (trillion bytes) of disk storage connected by a moderately fast data channel (10 million bits per second, roughly the speed of disk storage). Such a departmental setup easily outstrips the power of a large mainframe computer for many purposes (though not necessarily for other purposes, such as OLTP).

In a network such as this one, many parts of the computing system are sharable resources. Public processors, printers, and storage devices are managed by the system administrator. The sum of the public components form a virtual data center. Devices such as printers or data storage are often plugged into a convenient workstation where they are configured by the system administrator to operate "in the background" unobtrusively to the user of the workstation. To the user, the workstation appears to be a private, autonomous resource.

From another point of view a user may actually be using a number of the computers on the network overlapping with other users using multiple computers. Using X window technology, a user may have several windows open, each the result of processing on someone else's workstation. "In a networked computing environment resources are shared, scattered, easily co-opted, and managed in new and unusual ways."[6]

The networked environment helps contain costs because of the device or resource sharing. But it also enables the next benefit—the network as the process.

Network as the business process—parallelism, collaboration, and follow through. Once the computer network is technologically one big computer, the next step is for the business to take advantage of it. Consider a business process where work flows from person to person, department to department, each adding some element to the finished product. With networked workstations this process is enhanced in a number of ways. In the simplest case, where the original manual procedure is computerized, the computing network would speed up the process since paper work information can be shipped around nearly instantaneously. However, consider more complex work than clerical work, such as design, analysis, or planning. With this kind of work, a paradigm shift can be achieved by allowing more work parallelism and collaboration and by allowing individuals to follow through with their activities during the entire process. Normally, manual processes are highly serial in nature. Each step is completed in isolation from the others, with each subsequent step waiting for the previous. Two problems arise from this serial process. First, it wastes time since each step waits for the preceding step.

Second, it wastes intelligence because each step is performed without feedback and collaboration from other participants in the process. Parallelism can be achieved by subdividing tasks that can be worked concurrently and merged. Collaboration can be achieved by sharing knowledge.

For example, consider the process at one manufacturing company whereby internal policy documents are prepared through a process that involves several departments. Person A submits a suggestion for an improved section of a policy document. The submitted suggestion is judged by another person to require the attention of the expert who authors that class of policy documents. The expert prepares an update to the document. The update is routed through affected departments for concurrence. Markups are sent back to the author. The author incorporates the markups. The final draft is reviewed and approved by a review board. Management approves the final document. The document is published. Throughout these various steps, various publication activities have taken place, including such tasks as preparing text, drawings, and revision pages. The work items in this process may have touched dozens of desks and required dozens of memos, meetings, and phone conversations. The time to incorporate a relatively simple policy document change can easily take months to complete.

Clearly, the more information that participants can share instantaneously over the network and the more subtasks that can proceed in parallel, the faster the process can be completed. Perhaps, even more importantly, individuals can carry a project through the various steps in the process, thereby using the integrating capability of human intelligence to ensure integrity from start to finish.

3.2   REFORMATION OF INFORMATION

Originally, the concept of data was a fairly narrow notion referring to raw measurements and observations of atomic facts. Observers would share data, but normally analysis is required to make meaning of it. Commercial computers during the last thirty years have used the concept of data not only as the basic unit of memory, but also as the basic unit of communication; data in, data out. Business processes, however, share information—data that has been interpreted within a context and compiled into relatively complex forms. Since computers could only work at the raw data level for most of the last 30 years, businesses made a compromise and began to build data processing systems that reduced human information to machine data. A shop order in a useful human form, for example, is a complex object that compiles many pieces and forms of data into a structured object. A shop order that comes out of a legacy application reporting system is flattened into a series of rows of cryptic data fields. It is not that it is impossible to format ergonomically effective output information within a legacy environment. The problem is that there is no commonly available infrastructure to do it economically and flexibly.

The compromise made to accommodate computerization was to disassemble information objects into data chunks suitable for data processing as shown in Figure 3.1. With computerization, workers now had to reassemble the data manually into information objects. Often this became incredibly awkward. It is common to witness workers rekeying data from one paper report into another data system. Computing systems were specialized according to the kind of data or processing appropriate to available algorithms. Such specialized computing systems would not interoperate—word processing on one type of system, graphics on another, financial transactions on another, inventory transactions on another, mail on another, and so on. This made it even more difficult to reassemble information from the data.

The transition to distributed systems enables the assembly of a spectacular diversity of information technology developed over the last two decades. The mainframe environment, however, nurtured narrowly defined forms to achieve highly efficient processing for narrow purposes. During the 1980s, a wide variety of information technologies were developed. Distributed computing environments facilitate assembling information technologies, like building blocks, into more and more intelligent forms. The enterprise shift to macro-process enhancement will begin to draw on these possibilities. Our experience has shown that there are a few fundamental information technology phenomena that underlie these possibilities:

Representational and behavioral realism. Machines, using sophisticated software, are becoming more able to treat information in a realistic manner. The gap between human and machine forms of information is narrowing. Graphical user interfaces is one of the more obvious examples. Many readers will remember the first time they "dragged" a document into the trash on their computer. This is a far cry from the user having to know the correct command to recall from memory the exact system name of the data file to accomplish the same thing.

This is what is referred to as operating at a "low level." That means a low level of abstraction, where the representation of operations and the data are implementation-specific. Distributed systems incorporate information technology that operates on knowledge as well as data. The

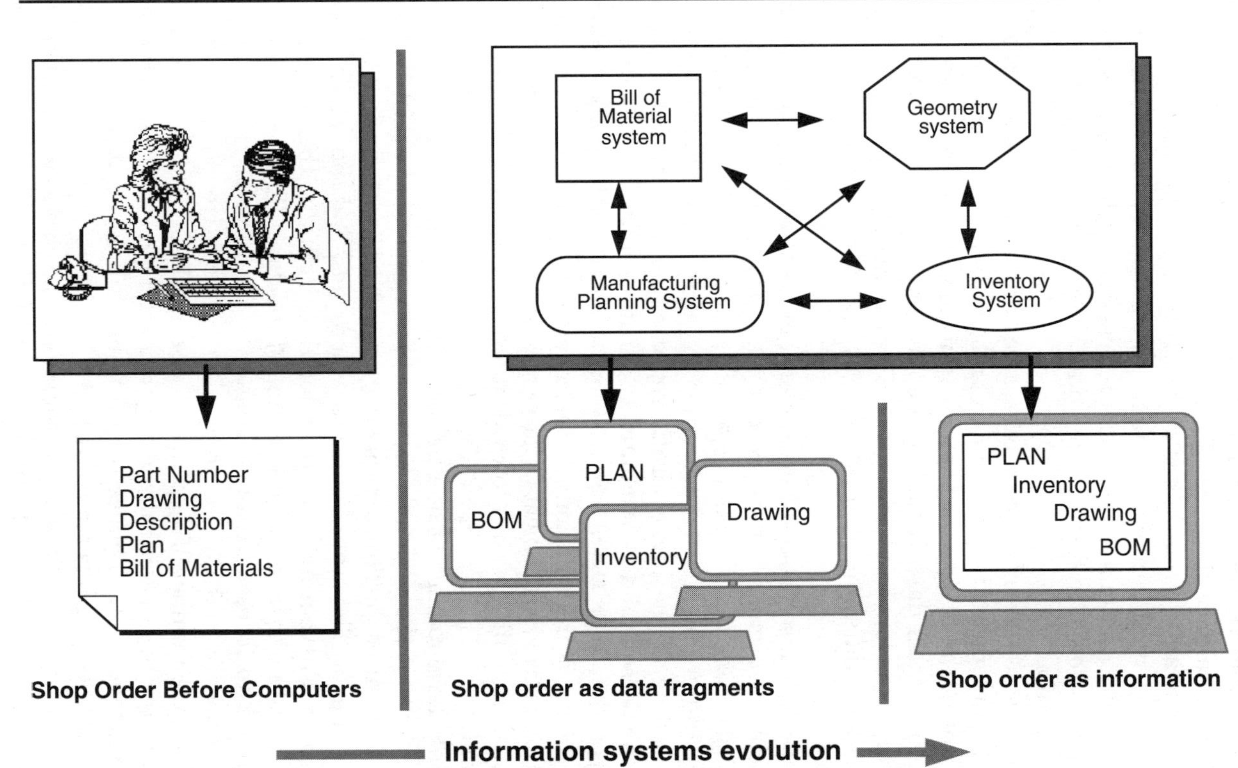

Figure 3.1   Data to information—recovering from the data compromise.

computer "knows" what objects it has and knows what operations it can do. The metaphorical user interface takes advantage of this machine knowledge and allows the user to recognize an object, then use a gesture to express an intent. This is a shift from the command, file, and data record-oriented behavior common to legacy systems. Using data and process abstraction techniques, it is possible for data to be created, stored, and shared in realistic forms—metaphors, objects, object behavior, relationships.

Legacy systems suffer from excessive information noise because low-level, implementation-specific representations are accumulated into monolithic data files. For example, during product development, it is common to pass data files from department to department. Each department adds low-level data to the file. The result is that there is so much low-level data, no one understands how the data relates to the macro-process.

Legacy databases also suffer this lack of abstraction. Where databases should be organized to represent realistic objects, they represent data records. For example, instead of information organized as employees, jobs, and organizations, personnel databases are likely to be defined according to the idiosyncratic representational scheme used to develop the personnel departmental application software. In a distributed system, however, there is much more opportunity for cross-departmental sharing of information. Departments outside of personnel need information on realistic objects, not personnel tasks. Thus, during the transition there will be a shift towards more realism in the organization of information.

During development of one project, the users insisted on using a special feature of the available terminal that presented a 132 character-wide presentation. This arrangement resulted in a form containing nearly 100 fields. The stated purpose was to get all of the information on the screen. Further analysis revealed that, actually, the user didn't expect the system to do much processing of the data. The user expected the computer to focus on transferring data file records to the screen where the user would do the processing himself. However, to do so required a large number of data items to be available. This is similar to the situation found in centralized, legacy system environments, where every department has a paper recycling bin full of massive printouts and desks stacked with reams of reports. In distributed computing environments, in contrast, it is not uncommon to be chided as a tree killer when a user habitually prints out a few pages.

In a mainframe environment the user often perceives the computer as having very little adaptability. The transition to distributed systems brings a tremendous increase in adaptability for a number of reasons. One of the more important factors is the degree of abstraction offered by the emerging technology as exemplified by new approaches to documents.

"The New Document"—so reads the title of the feature section of the August 1994 *Byte Magazine*. *Byte Magazine* is a reliable bellwether of information technology transferring from the lab into industry. *Byte* claims that computers are primarily document processors, and reports that one expert says, ". . . at least 80 percent of corporate electronic information is in the form of documents, as opposed to structured database records."[7]

The so-called new document is distinguished by being managed as a composite of object types, including text, image, logically tagged, spreadsheet, vector graphic, audio, video, fonts, and so on. Document processing becomes a framework of services for editing specialized types, routing documents (work flow), managing document repositories, integrating ordinary database data into documents, and so on.

Documents are full of surprises for technology. One large manufacturing company had to confront the complexities of moving to a distributed document management environment when they embarked on a program of modernizing the publishing and distribution of their product and process standards policy documents. The problem had two main requirements. First, complex, technical documents needed to be viewable at remote workstations located at several locations throughout the world. Second, a remote expert system also needed to be able to retrieve certain parts of the documents for computer processing.

The documents were converted to a markup language form (SGML, standard generalized markup language), so that the documents could be treated as composites of abstract elements down to a certain level of granularity. For those not familiar with this concept, a markup language is used to mark or bracket off several types of document parts. For example, titles, paragraphs, paragraph headers, enumerated lists, and footnotes are elements. A grammar is used to define a document type.

For a simple example, we could define a memo in the following way (read the arrows as "is defined as," the plus signs as concatenation):

memo —>	date + opening + body + closing
date —>	mm + dd + yy
mm —>	ASCII character string where the value is in the range 1-12
opening —>	to person + subject + references

to person —>   ASCII character string

body —>   one or more paragraphs

etc.

This definition is a "grammar" that defines a type of document. This is analogous to ordinary language grammar that defines how words can be structured into sentences. The document markup language used to define the grammar, SGML, is an industry standard; there are numerous commercial document processing products that can easily work with such a definition.

Using this markup language approach, document objects are hierarchically defined from the overall composite object down to the level of printable characters. Such an approach provides many benefits. It is a standard and open approach, so that many different kinds of applications can use the same source data. Clean, easily definable rules can be applied to manage the integrity and content of the document. The document can contain many different kinds of objects such as graphics, tables, voice annotations, and charts as well as ordinary text. (As an aside, formatting information that determines the presentation view of the material is partially contained in attributes for each of the objects. However, formatting presents a number of fairly complex issues which are not discussed here.)

Each type of object requires associated editing and viewing applications. Typically, publishing and word processing applications supply most of the functions needed. In our example, the company defined a dozen or so document types to cover the various document structures and content constraints that applied. A commercial document publishing application was purchased. The Information Systems (IS) department, with the help of an outside vendor, assembled additional products to form a document distribution system.

The lessons learned on this project were quite extensive. Even though the company had carefully defined policies for writing product standards documents, the conversion to a grammar-defined document revealed many surprises. The company found many otherwise unknown inconsistencies, omissions, and ambiguities. Also, because not all of the process elements were technologically mature, the process flow turned out to be challenging, containing a number of interim workaround solutions. For example, some data tables contained in the documents were so large that it was difficult to shrink them to a displayable size while still maintaining enough visual resolution to read the tables at a video display terminal. But the tables could not easily be segmented because then column and row headings must be provided in a special way.

Surprises were discovered concerning the business process also. Normally document versioning was done by republishing individual hard copy pages containing updates. The updated pages were manually replaced at each document station along with front matter that recorded the correct version of every changed page. With the new system, a "page" is a dynamic concept depending on the size of the display device. The business process for document versioning had to be carefully reexamined.

The second application requirement for this system, document element access by expert systems, is not a conventional application requirement. Furthermore, one of the main kinds of data in the documents was tables of technical data. It was natural for the company to explore the relationship between tables of technical data found in the documents and normalized relational data tables. However, it quickly became clear that there was a complete body of information processing theory that was either missing or just touched upon in the literature.

Data tables in documents contain an enormous amount of information in highly specialized visual structures. Consider two examples. First, visual tables often use complex column and row headings. The same data is captured as cell data in a relational table. For example, a top column heading may read Supplier Name. Under that may be material type for each supplier. Under that may be stock dimensions for each material type.

Second, data cells are commonly highly structured, violating the first principle of relational technology. Although the analysis was never published, it turned out that there were a number of relatively straightforward transformations that could be applied to convert back and forth between visual and relational tables.

One interesting surprise was found. Visual tables can be surprisingly compact. Some tables, when converted to canonical relational form went from a few dozen rows to several thousand rows. One reason is that data cells can contain combinations. So, for example, if one row contains a cell that contains *"supplier x or supplier y"*, and another cell in that row contains *"part a or part b"*, then normalizing the table expands into four rows containing the combinations x/a, x/b, y/a, and y/b. If there are many columns containing many disjunctive values, the combination grows quite rapidly, occasionally to the point where processing and storage resources become a major factor.

As we will consider in another chapter, the more recent experience with multidimensional databases and decision support has a close connection to the kinds of technical data tables found in the documents just described.

3.3   INVENTION OF TRANSPARENCY

Distributed systems are, by definition, collections of components separated in various ways, particularly by location. There are many benefits to be gained from a separated collection of components—parallelism, fault-tolerance through redundancy, protection through isolation, and extendibility. Distribution also brought the necessity to invent ways to integrate components into a coherent whole. This concept developed by the ANSA project is called *distribution transparency*, one of the great abstractions in computer science. The commercial computer supplier, Sun, coined the phrase, "The network is the computer" to promote the concept that all networked computing resources can be treated as one coherent whole simultaneously available at each desktop.

Distribution transparency.   Many experts consider transparency to be the most important property of well-designed distributed systems. Coulouris and Dollimore[8] define transparency as ". . . the concealment of separation from the user and the application programmer, so that the system is perceived as a whole rather than as a collection of independent components." They describe transparency from several perspectives. For the user, distribution transparency provides a unified interface to a collection of computing resources using the same names and operations regardless of their location. Services are guaranteed to be delivered wherever the user is located. The system manager enjoys flexibility of configuration and simplified extension as the system scales up or down. The application programmer avoids having to re-invent difficult software that links distributed software components together and to existing services. The system programmer can add components to the system without having to interrupt system operations. The business manager enjoys lowered cost and fewer skilled experts to integrate complex systems.

Transparency engineering.   Distributed data services mask process complexity and implementation diversity through transparency engineering. Transparency engineering is the approach by which complexity and diversity is masked. Several modes of transparency form the design goals for a distributed service environment. Each form of transparency has a number of mechanisms available to achieve the design goal. Transparency goals are meant to simplify and improve the usability of the system. They are not meant to hide relevant details from the user. The diversity and complexity that are part of the meaning of the information sought by the user or that the user must be aware of should not be hidden. Transparencies are relative and require trade-offs. For example, in some circumstances, replication transparency may be achieved only at the expense of the copied data being several hours or days stale. But, like a phone book, such staleness is acceptable in the face of the costs required to maintain instant updates.

The following describes basic forms of transparency and common design approaches to achieve the transparency.[9]

Location Transparency provides consistent appearance and behavior independent of the location of data storage, processor, and other mechanisms. For example, conceptual names are used to refer to services and objects rather than implementation-specific names. Naming Services provides such a level of indirection so that implementation specifics can be changed during maintenance without impact on the user.

Access Transparency enables local and remote objects and services to be accessed using identical access operations.

Failure Transparency enables the concealment of faults. The system provides self-corrective system actions. Computing failures are undone or repaired without requiring human intervention. All-or-none semantics are deployed where appropriate.

Scaling Transparency allows performance characteristics to be maintained despite changing system load. The system can be sized according to site requirements at proportional costs.

Replication Transparency ensures that the viewing and operating characteristics of copied data are consistent with original data within declared limits. This effectively improves availability of data and management of resource loads. Currency is relative. Users are willing to live within stable and known limits of data staleness. Effectiveness of less than total transparency depends on the type of data, the user's inherent ability to recognize and compensate for errors, and the consequences of errors. Getting the wrong phone number is not too bad. Getting the wrong bank balance is more serious.

Migration Transparency allows objects and services to change location without visibility to user.

Concurrency Transparency allows multiple users to operate on the same granule of data without mutual interference. Different approaches are used for small granules, such as a banking transaction, and large granules, such as a design or planning document.

3.4   LIVING IN AN ABSTRACT WORLD

One of the characteristics of a paradigm shift is that it can be very hard to become aware of it. The necessary change in conceptualization may not be along the lines that a person is expecting. We all experience that inability to see what may be obvious for someone else in a certain situation. To experience the shift in that situation, we must adapt a new framework or frame of reference. Normally, it takes several exposures to a new model of the world for a person to significantly alter a constellation of beliefs, values, or techniques. Cognitive psychologists have numerous illustrative examples to guide a person through a minor "Eureka!" experience. That is, there are exercises that allow a person to experience difficulty in "getting it" and then, by following directions, to experience the right cognitive framework and suddenly understand something in a new way. For example, in Figure 3.2 there is a matrix of nine dots. Your task is to connect all nine dots with four connected straight lines.

The task at first seems impossible because most of us see the matrix as a box whose boundaries coincide with the outside dots. The solution, however, requires one to adapt a new frame of reference as shown later in Figure 3.4.

We introduce this section with a brief discussion of cognitive psychology because one particular shift in conceptualization that is often difficult to "get" is thinking about problems and solutions at multiple levels of abstraction. By abstraction, we mean hiding details of implementation while providing a capability. This is different than merely providing the capability. During the 1990s, several areas of computing began to produce extremely effective multilevel abstractions. A few ex-

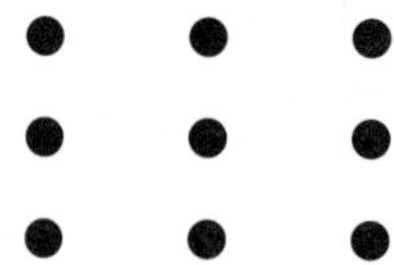

Figure 3.2   A puzzle to exercise reconceptualization.

amples would include graphical user interfaces, document processing, databases, and data communications. For example, one major multi-level abstraction that is still being developed and one that is extremely important to information processing is the concept of a document. One can say that applications operate on files or one can say they operate on documents. Word processors, spreadsheets, and some information retrieval applications treat documents as compound objects containing other abstract objects such as diagrams, tables, or indexes. The underlying data storage mechanism is often a file, but doesn't have to be. That is many objects may be conveniently stored as one file or, vice versa, many files may comprise one object. The point is that such implementation details should usually remain out of context or awareness. This forces the system to be more flexible and powerful. In Chapter 4, we will go into layers of abstractions in more detail.

It is our experience that making the transition to distributed systems requires the architect, the planner, the manager, and others to see that the concept of abstraction is itself a tool. That is, it is not sufficient to simply understand one or another particular abstraction such as metaphorical, icon-based user interfaces. What is necessary is the systematic search for and even invention of more and more new abstractions. In other words, every time a user or a software developer has to worry about details of the implementation, there should be an effort to identify an abstraction to hide those details.

Developing abstractions.   According to Mary Shaw, "The essence of abstraction is recognizing a pattern, naming and defining it, and providing some way to invoke the pattern by name ..."[10] Shaw describes the development of abstractions as follows: (1) The evolutionary cycle begins with ad hoc problem solving; (2) Experience then selects the better solutions. (Architects accept the inevitability of what they call the "parti shift"—throwing out a dead-end design concept and starting fresh); (3) Once useful solutions have been established, they are studied and codified; (4) Models then are developed to support automatic implementation; and (5) Theories are developed that enable the extension and generalization of the solution; (6) Subsequently, the more sophisticated level of practice results in harder problems to tackle in an ad hoc manner. The cycle then repeats itself. As abstractions evolve, they hide more detail and complexity while providing more results.

Legacy computing systems are typically built within a highly proprietary and closed architecture context. Within this context, the abstraction development cycle tends to fail at the fifth stage. That is, solutions are not generalized and extended, the very essence of abstraction. On the other hand, the emergence of distributed computing brings a great increase in diversity of suppliers. Suppliers begin to cooperate by adapting common frameworks of generalized concepts, because no one vendor can supply a total solution. There are several good examples of this—X windows, TCP/IP communication protocols, World-Wide Web, several popular operating systems, object-oriented programming, and relational database technology.

One of the main shortcomings of legacy applications is that there is limited abstraction. It is not surprising for a staff who is steeped in mainframe technology to first consider reengineering the existing software as a strategy for modernizing a legacy system. As the marketplace produces a wide array of applications, the reengineering approach often loses its appeal. However, let us explore this approach to examine an interesting (but, admittedly, somewhat vague) abstraction. Reengineering a legacy system requires two tactics: rewriting the code for reuse and unbundling monolithic applications. The goal would be to unbundle monolithic legacy applications by factoring out modules forming well-defined services (i.e., abstractions). What remains is just that logic necessary to orchestrate the services or to formulate the policy for the use of mechanism components as shown in Figure 3.3.

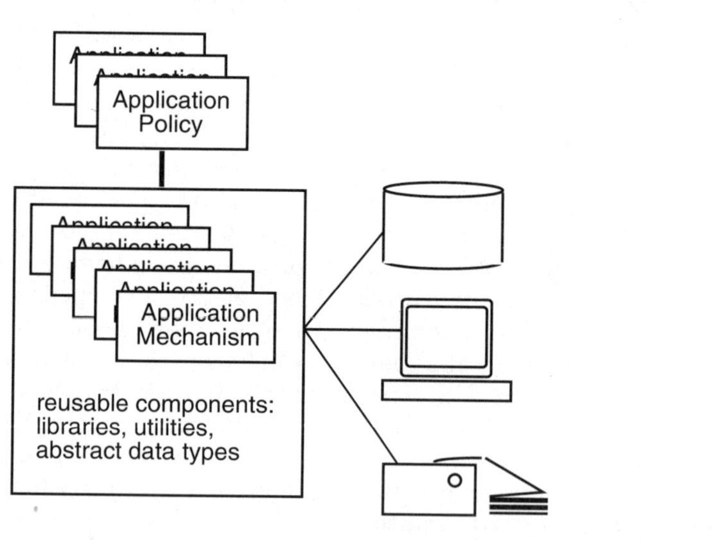

Figure 3.3   Separation of mechanism and policy.

System components can be classified into two important categories—*policy* components and *mechanism* components. Policy components establish purposeful behavior. That is, policy is represented by those components which define or describe the interaction among these components in order to implement a system. Mechanism components form the infrastructure used to accomplish a task. The mechanism represents the reusable components. Thus, policy is the use of reusable components, in a given context, to solve a class of problems. In this sense, policy can be equated to "user logic" in an application or to the concept of "user level abstractions."

Such a separation of a "system" into policy and mechanism components has many benefits, analogous to those gained in an ordinary organizational or social setting. Policy establishes what is to be achieved. Mechanism implements the policy. Similarities can be drawn to game-playing. The rules of a game are the mechanism and the moves in a particular game are the policy. In the computing context this separation enables simpler change and expansion of the system with greater reuseability of existing components.

For example, this separation of mechanism and policy has allowed the user-interface standard, X windows, to be used for implementing several networkable windowing systems and toolkits such as Motif.

To avoid confusion in the use of this concept, it is important to point out that classification into mechanism and policy components is relative. One person's application is another person's policy. For those familiar with software engineering of user interfaces, consider an application consisting of a user interface written in Motif running on top of X windows. From the perspective of the windowing system, X and its libraries (Xlib) provide the basic mechanism, while Motif implements a specific style and policy of 3-D widget appearance and windowing. From the point of view of the application, the presentation (display behavior) component of the application comprises the policy which, in turn, is implemented using the Motif toolkit as its mechanism.

Frameworks. For software development efforts of any significant size, it becomes critical to acquire or develop what has been called a design framework. "A framework is a collection of abstract and concrete classes and interfaces between them; just as an abstract class is the design for a concrete class, a framework is the design of a subsystem."[11] Frameworks have been related to Alexander's pattern language.[12] From a computational perspective, a framework is a collection of building blocks (classes in object-oriented vernacular) that forms a system of policy-governed, interacting mechanisms. The components

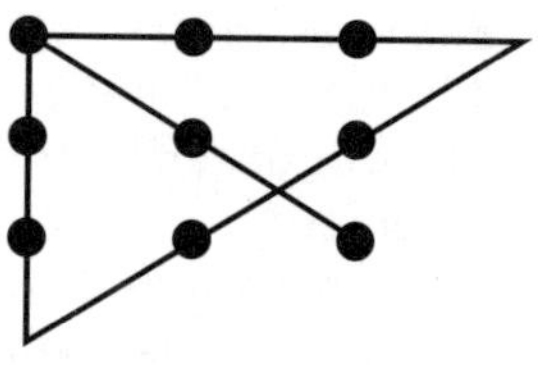

Figure 3.4   Solution to the puzzle to exercise reconceptualization.

can be highly parameterized and customizable, but yet display default behavior to achieve simplicity.

From a business viewpoint, a framework embodies the basic concepts and knowledge about some problem domain. The business importance of frameworks is that they promise to enable greatly reduced cycle time to develop solutions and therefore increase user satisfaction and system flexibility, while they reduce development and maintenance costs.

Broad frameworks based on large problem domains are largely in the future. A common tactic for development is to develop or acquire suites of subframeworks that are specialized for a particular domain.

3.5   SOFTWARE AS A COMMODITY—A SHIFT FROM LABOR TO CAPITAL INTENSIVENESS

The emergence of abstraction and abstraction layering as a paradigm has created a marketplace for what is called "open systems." An *open system approach* to computing systems promotes the assembly of computing systems from standard, common products. It minimizes custom building to proprietary standards. This approach is expected to improve cost management, response time to implement upgrades, and overall quality. Adopting this approach requires a change in attitude as suggested in the following quote:

> It has been commonplace to say that, within a few years, we will no longer speak about "object-oriented programming" any more than we do now about structured programming—it will have been completely absorbed into the programming culture. However, object-orientation goes beyond structured programming, or even programming in general. What is truly different is not that we can bundle data and operations, or that we can define new classes from old by inheritance, or even that dynamic binding

and polymorphism enhance the reuse potential for software. Rather, what is different is that, in order for an object-oriented approach to be applied effectively, *we must change the way we think about software development as a labor-intensive activity in which each application is hand-crafted from individual requirements, to a capital-intensive one in which we invest more in the development of reusable components that can be plugged together to produce standard 'line' of applications.*[emphasis added][13]

For many people, the concept of open systems is too vague to serve as a specification. However, as a design philosophy, it is an essential feature of a distributed architecture. In the following we offer a variety of definitions of open systems to convey this philosophy.

Three design principles characterize an open systems environment:

- Highly modularized structure
- Abstract and generalized interfaces and functionality
- Products and technology that conform to non-proprietary, industry standards

The X/Open Consortium defines open systems as "systems and software environments based on standards which are vendor-independent and commonly available."

Another definition of open systems is:

An open system is one in which the components and their composition are specified in a non-proprietary environment, enabling competing organizations to use these standard components to build competitive systems.[14]

The Institute of Electrical and Electronics Engineers (IEEE) technical committee on open systems (TCOS) defines open systems with respect to standards:

A comprehensive and consistent set of international information technology standards and functional standards profiles that specify interfaces, services, and supporting formats to accomplish interoperability and portability of applications, data, and people.

An open systems environment that conforms to the above design principles exhibits a number of properties important to the support of business objectives:

Independence.   Because of the modularity and generality, major facets of the system can be decoupled to operate independently. The business process should be decoupled from the application software. Within an application itself, the user interface and data operations should be decoupled from the application logic. Such independence allows process improvement to be achieved through assembly and reconfiguration of components rather than through modification of application source code.

Interoperability.   Open systems accommodate some degree of diversity by providing inter-operability among diverse vendor implementations. Interoperability allows applications to have greater access to data from diverse sources across the network.

Portability.   Software becomes portable. Portability provides flexibility and responsiveness to needed upgrades by simplifying the movement or rehosting of applications and data to different computing environments.

Scalability.   Businesses with distributed operations need to use the same applications in different situations, though the operational units may have varying needs for performance and size. Because of modularity and abstractness, open computing systems can scale up or down to meet operating needs.

Reuseability.   Each of the characteristics above contributes to achieving a large measure of reuseability for the system components. From the specification point of view, the primary form of reuseability refers to well-formed things that are general and thus can be used *as is* in multiple situations. Properties of reusable things include: (1) well defined and understood interface, usage, and behavior or form; (2) generality; (3) quality. A secondary form of reuse refers to reusing material from existing items to refashion a new item (salvaging). Reuseability does not refer to monolithic packaging of many capabilities to gain use in multiple situations, but rather to the generality of a unified capability. Reuseability includes both *tangible* elements such as software and hardware as well as *intangible* elements such as concepts within specifications.

Adapting an open systems approach requires a total change in the way that information systems are developed. Instead of several large projects focused on specific functions in the organization, companies must develop an infrastructure based on reusability.

CHAPTER NOTES

1. Kuhn, Thomas S. *The Structure of Scientific Revolutions.* Chicago: University of Chicago, 1962.
2. Davenport, Thomas H. *Process Innovation: Reengineering Work through Information Technology.* Ernst & Young. Center for Information Technology and Strategy. Boston: Harvard Business School Press, 1993.
3. Scott-Morton, Michael, S. (ed.). *The Corporation in the 1990s.* New York: Oxford University Press, 1991.
4. Hammer, Michael. "Reengineering Work: Don't Automate, Obliterate." *Harvard Business Review* (July–August 1990).
5. A number of ideas in this section are from an insightful paper by C. Klabunde, "System Administration Services," unpublished.
6. C. Klabunde, "System Administration Services," unpublished.
7. Reinhardt, Andy. "Managing the New Document." *Byte* (August 1994).
8. Coulouris, George F., and Jean Dollimore. *Distributed Systems: Concepts and Design.* Reading, MA: Addison-Wesley, 1988.
9. ANSA
10. Shaw, Mary. "Toward Higher-level Abstractions for Software Systems." *Data and Knowledge Engineering* 5 (1990). North-Holland.
11. Chen, D. J., and David T. K. Chen. "An Experimental Study of Using Reusable Software Design Frameworks to Achieve Software Reuse." *Journal of Object Oriented Programming* (May 1994).
12. Johnson, Ralph E. "Documenting Frameworks Using Patterns." *OOPSLA* (1992). Also see James O. Coplien. "Pattern Languages for Organization and Process." *Object Magazine* (July–August 1994).
13. Tsichritzis, Dennis, Oscar Nierstrasz, and Simon Gibbs. "Beyond Objects: Objects." *International Journal of Intelligent and Cooperative Information Systems,* vol. 1, no. 1 (1992).
14. Nutt, G. *Open Systems.* Englewood Cliffs, N.J.: Prentice-Hall, 1992.

Information in Transition

In Chapter 3 it was noted that business process innovation often is enabled by information technology and that a current major innovation is a shift to a business process orientation. This chapter examines the transition from an information point of view. The major requirement that process orientation levies on the information perspective is that individuals and teams must be able to share information and knowledge. Thus, the transition requires a shift from a data management focus, typical of a legacy system environment, to a communication and shared-knowledge focus, favored in a distributed environment.

The primary problem to be faced in a distributed environment is integrating the many individual information systems used by a company in the face of the diversity that exists among them. It is impractical to expect applications and databases to be recast into a unified, consistent data design and operations form. Integration must be accomplished by being able to compensate for differences in implementation or, even better, by not being affected by implementation issues.

In order to make the transition, it is necessary to apply principles of data abstraction. Data abstraction allows the meaning of stored or communicated data to be separated from its implementation complexity and diversity. In particular, we must make the structure and meaning of the information explicit in the form of metadata, that is, formalized knowledge about the meaning of data.

4.1   REPRESENTING THE MEANING OF INFORMATION

At the heart of information processing is the idea that data represents the world with respect to the people using the data. These three dimensions of meaning are illustrated in Figure 4.1.

The first dimension of meaning is the world, itself, that provides the subject matter for the information with which we are dealing. This dimension of meaning could just as well be labeled object or subject, whatever term designates the actual reality being represented as information and interpreted by an agent. Business applications may be focused on banking, oil drilling, telephone, medicine, and so on. The subject matter can have various process aspects such as design, planning, building, testing, selling, accounting, and so on. In this discussion, we are considering information in a way that is applicable to any and all subject matter.

The second dimension of meaning concerns the intelligent observer of the world. Information exists by virtue of an agent (machine or person) who interprets and processes signs, symbols, and language that represent the world. The agent dimension of meaning presents several factors that we must consider.

For example, the fact that businesses are shifting to a process orientation from a hierarchically partitioned orientation has implications on how we treat information. In the extreme hierarchical model with weak computing support, there are many unskilled, heads-down workers tending to fixed, relatively mechanical processes. At the other extreme there are many ". . . better educated workers who mix structured work with opportunity-based initiative and individual responsibility for quality and customer satisfaction."[1] These two extremes require two models of information. The heads-down model requires information that needs little interpretation. The information worker model requires that workers have access to an information model of their situation; that is, information that tells them what information is available, how to obtain it, and how to

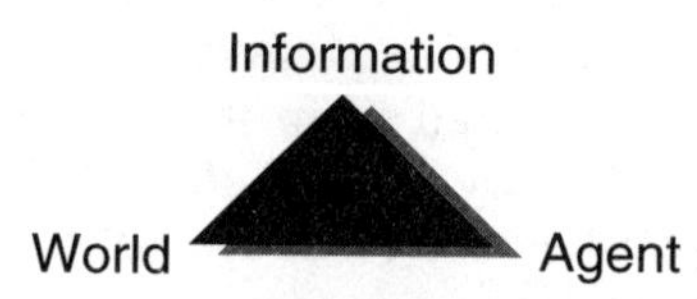

Figure 4.1   Three dimensions of meaning.

interpret it. There are many variations on these contrasting models. Given the general evolution towards smarter, more involved workers, and teaming relationships, a general principle emerges—the better the information, the better the process works. Workers are able to make use of more of the meaning of the information made available to them. It thus makes sense that all the workers should have access to a broad and general model of the entire business process to better share information and knowledge.

There are many variations on the skills and knowledge that workers have or need for a given process. There are many variations on the diversity and distribution of the information and the workers. These variations require different models of the agents and the information concerning a process.

The third major dimension of meaning concerns information as signs, symbols, and language, which is the main focus of this chapter. Information itself has three key facets to consider which may be characterized as form, function, and fit for purpose as discussed in the following sections. *Form* concerns the various structures and medias that manifest information. *Function* concerns the content, semantics, and relationships of representations to the real world. *Fit for purpose* concerns how information mediates purpose and lawfulness of agents operating in the world.

4.2   INFORMATION FORM

Information technology applies to a variety of forms ranging from atomic data to simple and complex data structures. It has been suggested that information management is becoming more focused on documents. As we noted earlier, 80 percent of business electronic information may be in the form of documents. These more complex structures typically have additional properties, such as visual formatting for human use. However, the structural complexity is not simply due to visual aspects. The concept of a document has also become more general, becoming more like a container of subobjects such as graphics, tables, and other forms. We should expect that these improved capabilities to handle document structures should spin off increased capabilities for automated processing of complex data structures in general, such as a bill of materials or a design object. Automated processing of data structures provides such benefit that the overall balance of requirements for technology is probably evenly divided between formal data structures and human-oriented documents. During the transition to a distributed environment, we should consider a broad framework that covers the range from simple

Table 4.1   Information Dimensions

Information Dimension	Description or Example
structure complexity	data records versus complex data models
visual formatting	plain versus publication standards
media types	text, image, video, audio
structure types	text, tables, graphics, charts
generic application forms	mail, news, calendar, schedule
replication properties	currency (up-to-date), consistency

to complex, from computer-oriented structures to human-oriented forms. In general, there are a number of major dimensions along which information services are needed as shown in Table 4.1.

It is easy to understand why document processing is such a major requirement for information technology. For example, Figure 4.2, suggested from an unpublished study in the computer manufacturing industry, implies that well over half of an engineer's time is spent using a language.

What happens as a company's information technology base migrates towards a distributed environment and a process orientation? Isolated

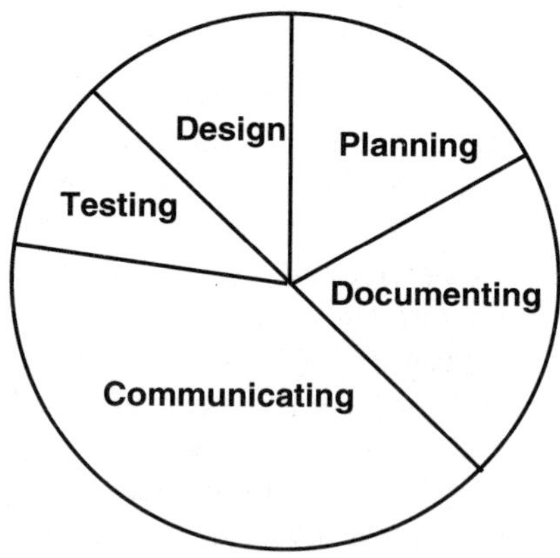

Figure 4.2   Engineers spend most of their time using language.

databases and file systems won't support the transition. The cost of building and maintaining interfaces among the applications in these centralized systems is prohibitive. Industrial publications report that software interfacing issues represent a major component of software expenses, reaching into the range of 40 to 60 percent of the computing budget. The transition to a distributed environment will only increase the need for interfaces.

This transition forces the realization that good communications are vital. It always was, but in the hierarchical organizational model, the solution was to rely on information absorbers in the form of management levels. With the advent of process-oriented organizations, it becomes clear that a new view of communication is essential. The experts, the operators, and the managers must all participate as a cross-functional team.

To achieve process objectives, often the team must share information at the subtask level where they can share knowledge of the situation. As shown in Figure 4.3, if subtasks are able to exchange knowledge,

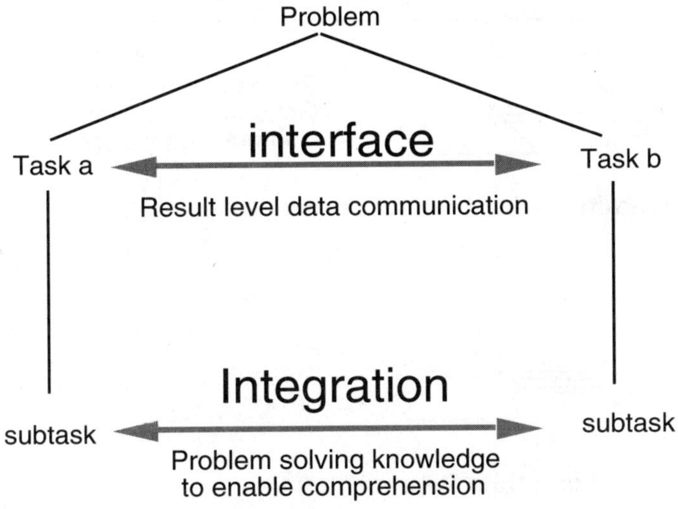

Figure 4.3   Task integration depends on sharing knowledge.

solutions can be easily integrated. However, if subtasks have an interface simply based on result data, integration is more difficult. Data does not carry its own interpretation, as do facts and knowledge. Therefore, the interfaces should be based on the exchange of some representation of the knowledge of the task and not just data produced by the task.[2]

4.3   STRATIFIED INFORMATION MODEL

The collection of stored information for a company is often a strategically important part of the company's knowledge base. Information technology has gone beyond the limited notion of "data processing" and has now begun to reach the level of a knowledge and communication metaphor. One can think of databases and associated information services as representing the communication process of "asserting" facts into a repository. To achieve such data abstraction requires that we stratify the system. That is, different problems exist at different levels of abstraction, and can be thought of as stratifying them out along a spectrum. The two main kinds of strata to be discussed are shown in Figure 4.4. First, we consider data abstraction by separating concepts at different levels of system organization. Second, we consider data abstraction by separating meaning from form.

(a) Stratifying Abstraction Levels

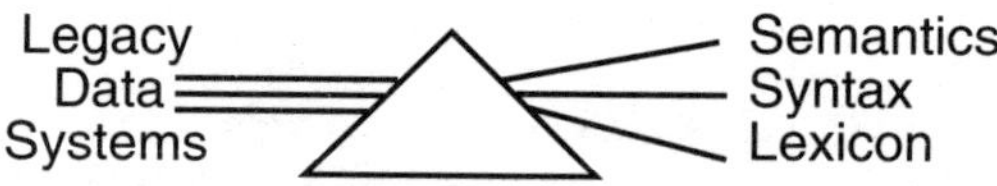

(b) Stratifying Data Representation

Figure 4.4   Knowledge stratification.

4.3.1 Levels of Data Abstraction to Match Levels of System Organization

A critically important design philosophy is to represent information at an appropriate level of abstraction. To achieve this requires that the computing system be organized into multiple levels of organization, where each level manages an appropriate level of abstraction or generality. Even though they are large, multifunction applications, legacy systems tend to have a two-level abstraction architecture—application and data storage. To accomplish the simplification of the representation of information it is necessary to increase the number of levels of system organization. Additional levels of organization then accommodate appropriate data abstraction as shown in Figure 4.5.

Data and application are confounded when there are insufficient levels of organization, because additional levels of abstraction are implemented in an ad hoc manner with consequent uncontrollable interdependencies.

Applications and human users employ data representations that are abstractions of real-world concepts in the application domain. For example, "shop order," "financial model," and "employee" are concepts used by typical applications. Storage representations, in contrast, are optimized for performance and capacity. This requires the database design to be based on data structures that have been factored into atomic elements such as tables and attributes.

Table 4.2 illustrates how multiple levels of abstraction are used to represent information. Abstractions at lower levels are "implementations"; at higher levels they are "specifications." For example, an order

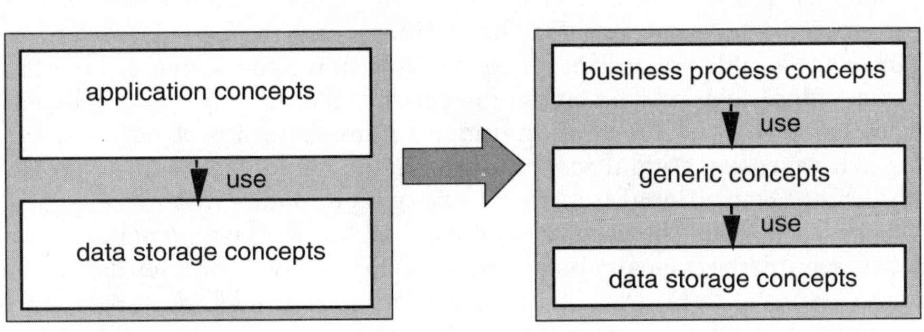

Figure 4.5   Levels of system organization to match model generality.

Table 4.2   Example Levels of Abstraction

Level of Abstraction	Data Type Abstraction	Behavior Type Abstraction	Processor Type Abstraction
High-level, ordinary business concepts	Shop order (also: schedule, part, financial model)	Shop order can be scheduled, assigned, and completed	Order is processed by order taker, shop, workstation
Intermediate-level generic abstractions, becoming standard computing abstractions	Document (also: form, table, fact, geometric object, spreadsheet)	Document can be written on, drawn on, and filed	Document is processed by word processor
Standard low-level computing abstractions	Relation	Relation (table) can be selected, projected, and joined	Relation is processed by Relational DBMS
Very low-level abstractions	Files containing records containing fields	Open, read, write, close	File system within operating system

is implemented with a document. A document is implemented with lower-level computing components such as a data file or relational table.

Each level of abstraction can be thought of as a pattern of components that solves a class of problems. The class of problems that a document solves is how to collect a variety of pieces of information into a structured whole suitable for the ordinary person. The class of problems that a table addresses is how to show that a fact depends on a few independent factors. The class of problems that a file addresses is how to collect a body of information under a named storage object.

All representational information should be considered part of the data. Representational information may be implemented in a declarative or, as is often the case, procedural mechanism. Because data storage mechanisms typically have had no means to store complex definition components of data, such as a structured object, such definitions are commonly implemented in the application—moreover, in *all* applications that use the data. This usually results in unmanageable replication. In a large-scale, multiple-domain environment these object representations are typical. Consequently, data definitions are interwoven throughout many applications. This is a major source of entanglement that makes legacy systems a problem. To simplify the information, it is necessary to provide mechanisms to separate these extra-database representation components of data from applications and then manage them as components of data. Refer to Chapter 5 for more discussion on mediating components.

4.3.2　Wisdom of the Existing System

Legacy systems are extremely complex, partly because business and computation perspectives are confounded. Most of the approaches to migrating legacy systems focus on defining new mechanisms to compensate for the complexity. In this section, we take the opposite tactic and advocate methods to simplify the problem in the first place.

The most effective way to simplify is to raise the level of abstraction used by data management, technology, and programming. Relational database, logic programming, and object-oriented technology lift persistent facts and information from operational forms to logical forms. The key concepts that these disciplines use to lift the level of abstraction are classification and relationships. Recasting information systems into classes of objects and patterns of relationships among them allows development of generic services for a whole class of individual situations. Classification and patterning simplifies problem-solving by incrementally narrowing the solution search space. These same concepts should be used to understand the legacy system and to define the target system.

The crucial first step in designing the transition from legacy systems is to sort out what kinds of things the system is about and then to identify patterns in the structure and interaction. This very obvious step is understandably underplayed. There is only a minimal accumulated body of data abstractions. Information technology that operates as a high level of abstraction has been scarce. A large proportion of the technical and management workforce has been steeped in mainframe technology with little or no opportunity to retrain in emerging technology. Consequently, planners, designers, and coders often want to dive into the procedures and specification detail they feel necessary to migrate the data and recreate the applications that operate on the data.

Typically, the developers scoff at the wisdom of the existing system. What they should scoff at is the implementation of the system, not the concept of the system. Businesses operate profitably and the system supports the operation—else no one would be paying for the system migration. It may be hard to change the system or make it operate more cost effectively, but it works. The planners and designers must begin the transition by understanding the wisdom of the system. What are the real-world things that the system deals with? How are these things related? In other words, what are the basic patterns that underlie the information the system deals with. With a solid understanding of these basic questions, it becomes much easier to begin teasing out specifications from implementations.

The basic currency of computing systems is information. Information that the system deals with must be understood to migrate to new environments. In information systems there is a basic core of information that must be represented in order to understand the system.

4.3.3   Operational Form to Logical Form

Databases can store facts and information in logical forms, or they can store operational results in computational data structure forms. Newer database technology, such as relational databases, stores data as facts (at least simple data). Older database technology, such as IMS, stores data as computational data structures. Practically speaking, the biggest problem presented by the storage of data as data structures is that the operations that *define* the underlying information are mixed with operations that are *applied* to the information. In other words the rules of the business are mixed with the rules of the computing process.

Programming suffers a similar problem. A typical COBOL or C program contains mixed operations on business facts and operations on computational structures. Within any given subroutine, there may be a procedure to locate a substring out of a string of characters while at the same time there may be a procedure to confirm a hotel reservation. Again, operations that *define* the underlying information are mixed with operations that are *applied* to the information. Object-oriented, logic-based, and 4GL-based programming are evolutionary steps taken to avoid this mix of abstraction levels.

Consequently, a major task facing the transition of legacy systems to a distributed environment is migrating from databases and software built on computational forms to databases and software built on logical forms. This is a data reverse engineering task. To accomplish this, we need ways to recover specifications out of implementations. We need ways to abstract the logical information from the operational forms. Refer to Chapter 6 for more discussion of regenerating data.

4.3.4   Information Structure Abstraction

A major proportion of legacy system data is readily interpretable as a collection of relational tables. Some data, on the other hand, such as geometry, images, compound documents, networks, and circuit designs are not readily interpreted merely as relations. For relational-oriented data it is relatively easy to coerce arbitrary record structures into standard relational forms consisting of rows of simple data elements. Having done that, it is necessary to perform a second stage of data abstraction to put pieces back into objective form that the user or application can use. This is done by converting data tables into view objects using some sort of view mechanism as shown in Figures 4.6 and 4.7. Chapters 5 and 6 consider these issues further.

There are at least two major problems with this approach that must be solved. First, a surprising amount of legacy system data is too complex to easily fit into the relational model. Second, when the object model is used to capture structure complexity, it interferes with analysis processing since analysis processing tends to cut horizontally through object representations. Refer to Chapters 5 and 6 for more details.

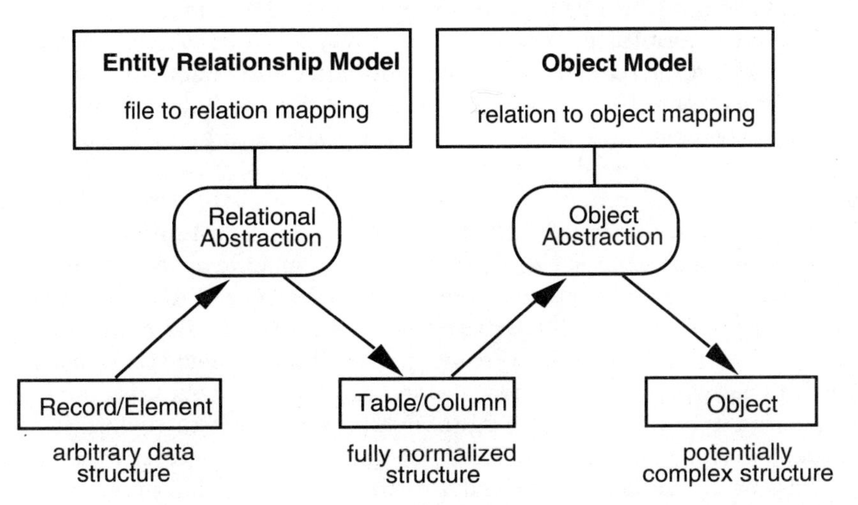

Figure 4.6   Regenerating legacy system data through two data abstraction stages.

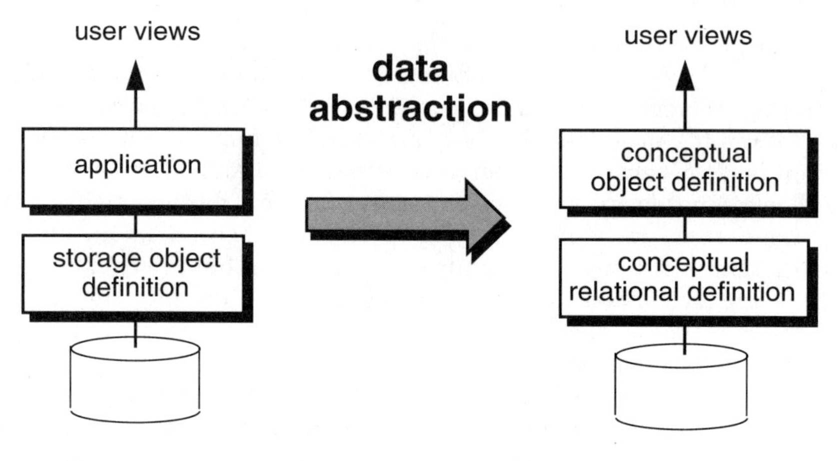

Figure 4.7   Data abstraction as a method of transparency engineering.

4.4   INFORMATION FUNCTION—MEANING AND REPRESENTATION

The meaning of data resides in many places. Some meaning is represented in the naming conventions for data types or database component names. Meaning resides in application code embedded in the operations that are applied to data. Meaning resides in visual forms used to display or report data. It is contained in titles and headings of forms, row and columns, and field labels. It is contained in dates, units of measure, and footnotes. A lot of the meaning of data resides in the knowledge of people who build, document, or use a system in the form of conventions, common sense, and contextual specific assumptions.

Semantic models capture some of the meaning of data by classifying data into a semantic structure that includes such elements as: data or object type; relationship types between object types; structural constraints between object types; names of objects, attributes, relationships, and operations; indexical information such as keys; definition of value domains; subtyping structure; composition structure; exceptions; dependencies; and operational definitions in the form of preconditions, post-conditions, and invariant conditions. This form of meaning can be explicitly represented in metadata that can be stored and communicated as data in its own right.

4.4.1 Stratifying Information along Linguistic Lines

When we are caught in the complexities of managing data in legacy systems, it is not easy to see that data can be interpreted as ordinary, simple facts. For example, suppose there is a table of data containing information about books as shown in Table 4.3. This table represents facts of the form:

> Book entitled X is about topic Y. It is published by Z. Publisher Z is located at W.

Since we can consider databases as containing asserted facts, then we can just as easily apply simple linguistic concepts to this data. We can identify three main components of data definitions along classical linguistic lines:

1. *Lexical* and vocabulary information defines how to parse and identify individual data items.
2. *Syntactic* information defines well-formed expressions or structures.
3. *Semantic* information associates expressions or structures to a model of the world.

Existing data systems differ in their treatment of these three aspects of data definition. Most data implementations depend on the simple metadata model shown in Figure 4.8. This example shows a structured data type that represents an ordinary address. The structure is simply an array of five attributes, each of which are data types.

4.5 METADATA

Metadata is the explicit form of definition. By representing the meaning and structure of data, metadata allows computational processes to interpret data and thereby determine which procedures to apply. Metadata is

Table 4.3   Example Table of Published Books

Published Books
book title
book topic
publisher name
publisher address

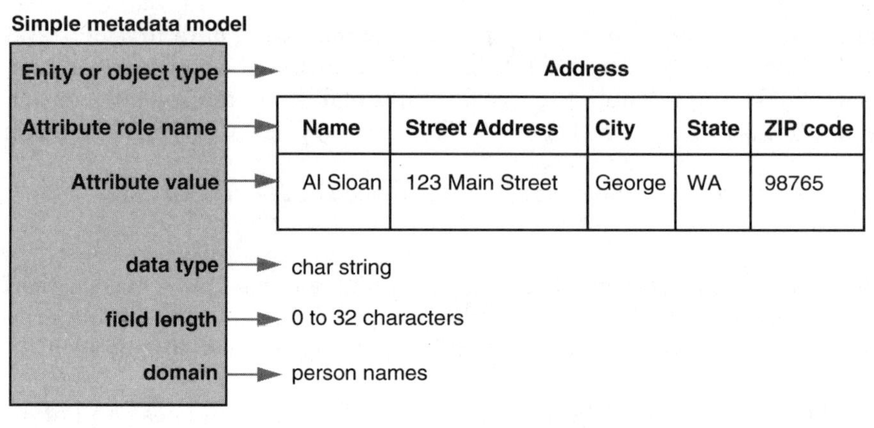

Figure 4.8   Common metadata components.

information that defines and describes the structure and meaning of data. It represents some of what we know about the data.

To illustrate typical metadata, consider a conventional address. Metadata would identify the parts of an address and for each part would specify the type of data. A conventional address has five basic parts as shown in Table 4.4: addressee, street address, city, state, and ZIP code.

The standard entity-relationship data-modeling approach considers an address to be an entity type with attributes. Other data-modeling approaches use designations such as object and service contract, table and attribute, record and field, or predicate and arguments. An emerging approach uses concept types and conceptual relations.[3]

As Figure 4.8 shows, information about a concept is narrowed down to primitive facts that have standard computational procedures that can be applied to associated data. For example, if a data item is identified as a zip code, then computational procedures use the metadata to determine

Table 4.4   An Ordinary Address

Al Sloan

123 Main Street

George, WA

98765

that it is appropriate to apply character string operations on a five-character field.

This metadata captures basic lexical and syntactic components of the definition. Given sufficient metadata management discipline, this is enough metadata to share information at the lexical level. It is not sufficient to share information at the syntactic level, unless there are mechanisms to capture structural components. For example, Street Address in Figure 4.8 may need to be represented as a substructure containing house number and street name.

Some of the semantic level of definition is captured by data types. Data types are typically defined recursively as compositions of other types until they ground out in the primitive data types of the programming paradigm being used. The highest data type depends on the programming paradigm being used, particularly the ability to extend types with user-defined types. For example, only some approaches provide mechanisms to define domains in terms of a type-subtype hierarchy. An important semantic area concerns part/whole relations.[4] Yet there are very few approaches that provide a systematic mechanism to represent these relations.

A formal model is one that treats this basic metadata systematically. One of the most important factors that formal models introduce is well-defined lexical rules. With these formal models, such as a relational database system provides, if one wants a data element, the only way to get that element is to use its attribute name. This helps guarantee access transparency. Database systems that use a weak model, such as IMS, allow data elements to be named by the application. Thus, lexical components of the data definition depend on the application.

Syntactic information is captured within each relation in a relational model by defining what attributes (domains) form a tuple. One way that relational database schemas capture semantic information is by requiring all data tokens for an attribute to be defined as one of a set of legal types within a domain.

A relational model captures some syntactic and semantic information about collections of relations by using view definitions. A view is, effectively, a query. Some important semantic information is captured through the normalization process and through the use of domains as the basis for attributes. However, other semantics spanning multiple relations are not well represented in relational schemas. To capture the definition of complex objects stored in a relational model, syntactic and semantic information must be augmented with an abstract data type, as done in an object-oriented approach, or with rules in a logic-based system.[5]

4.5.1   Representing Simple Data Semantics

Even though a formal model treats basic metadata systematically, more complex semantics may not be represented. Names capture semantics to the extent that they identify the class or type of the object being represented. However, classes or types are related and form a structure. One structure is a class hierarchy. For example, the sequence "thing > book > story book" forms a hierarchy. Another structure is formed by functional dependencies. Attributes of an entity form a simple functional dependency structure. A semantic model that shows entities, attributes, and relationships forms a more complex functional dependency structure.

Often data is misunderstood because the metadata contains only an unstructured collection of attributes, a sort of attribute soup, as illustrated in Table 4.7. Functional dependencies are poorly represented. Take the following example. Suppose organizations A and B have data on publications as shown in Table 4.5. If our objective were to integrate the two sources of data, it would be necessary to first understand the data. As can be seen in the table, the data element names are a limited source of information to help us understand the relationship between the two sources of the data. Without reverse engineering the software, data names within the context of a local oral tradition concerning data types are often our main source of data definitions.

If the data elements were named better, it would be easier to understand the data. Naming conventions normally supply modifiers only where necessary to distinguish names within a given context, as shown in Table 4.5. Enhanced naming conventions provide more information about the meaning of the data, as shown in Table 4.6. For example, "title" is better named "publication title" and "publisher" is better named "publisher name." This tells us that title is functionally dependent on the particular publication. That is, for a particular publication there is

Table 4.5   Data Elements to Be Integrated into One Data Source

Data source from organization A	Data source from organization B
title	title
code	topic
publisher	publisher name
keyword title	address
keyword code	using university
research area	state

Table 4.6   Data Elements with Enhanced Names

Data source from organization A	*Data source from organization B*
publication title	book title
publication code	book topic
publisher name	publisher name
keyword title	publisher address
keyword code	using university name
keyword research area	university state

one and only one title. Even with enhanced and fully distinguished names, we still don't know the meaning of some of the elements.

If we just have data element names, we need a description of each data element to just get a clue to the meaning of the data. For instance, unless the domain of knowledge is common sense, it is not obvious that publisher name refers to the publisher of a titled publication. It is not obvious, for example, that university name is associated with a book rather than a publisher.

Figure 4.9 helps show the meaning of the data elements more clearly. Two major kinds of information have been added beyond the

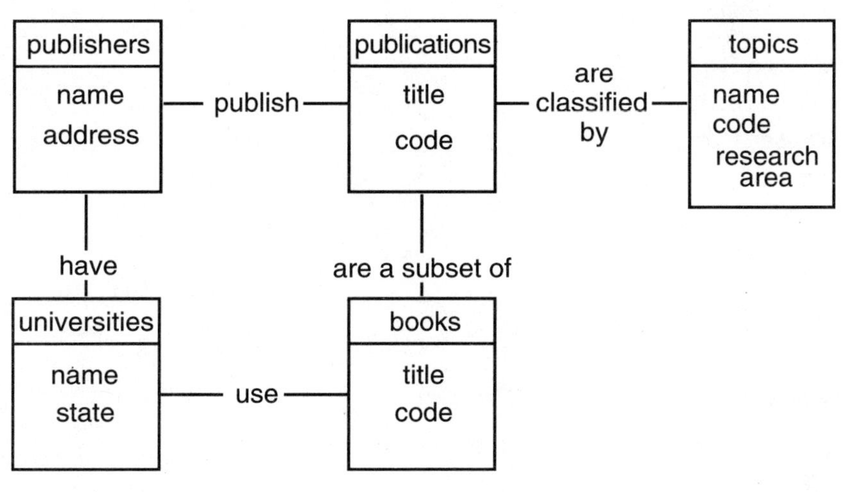

Figure 4.9   A simple semantic data model.

information in the previous tables. First, attributes have been grouped with the object to which they apply. Second, relationships among the objects and collections of objects have been shown. This model shows one of the most important semantic elements—mappings or functions. Attributes are mappings from an entity to some value domain. Relationships are mappings from some entity to another entity.

In legacy systems all of this information would typically be flattened into a single record, as shown in Table 4.7, creating attribute soup. The quick grasp of the data meaning is not possible without the data model in Figure 4.9. For example, is it clear from the data record that the following query is easily answered:

> list all universities that use the books that they publish.

By looking at the graphical data model, it can be determined that this query can be answered. Using the data model computationally, the query is a selection from the logical join across the relations or entities that cover the query:

> use [universities (name: U) , books (title: B)] and
> have [universities(name): U , publishers (name: P)] and
> publish [publishers (name: P), publications (title: PUB)] and
> equal [books (title: B), publications (title: PUB)]

Table 4.7   Flattened Data Model That Obscures Data Meaning

record element
publication title
publication code
publication topic
name
code
research area
publisher name
publisher address
type of publisher
type of publication
using university
using university state

In this pseudo-language query, single-letter names (U, B, and P) are like pronouns providing a way to co-reference objects. In English the query would read as: "Find all cases where a university U uses a book B, and the university U has a publisher P and that publisher P publishes a publication PUB and that publication PUB is the same as book B."

4.5.2   More about Metadata

There are a number of theoretical and standardization problems with metadata. One problem is that the meta information that describes how to operate on attributes is not standard. Most databases support common data types such as date, time, integer, character, and float. The ANSI relational database standard, however, does not prevent incompatibilities. Two relational databases, where there is good standardization, do not agree on data type definitions. Examples that are particularly troublesome include real numbers, dates, text, and objects such as graphics.

The concept of an attribute name is often confused with the concept of a domain. For example, in the address example one of the attributes is addressee, yet the attribute is often called "name" which really refers to the allowable domain of values. This is equivalent to someone asking someone's age by asking, "how many years are you." The other attributes in the example suffer the same problem; each assumes knowledge of their purpose. Each attribute in the address example really refers to a geographical destination.

Some characteristics of attributes are properties of the combination of the attribute and the implementation context in which it is used. Field length, for example, really depends on how the data value will be displayed. Consequently, such a characteristic should be qualified, such as maximum or default field length.

Metadata versus embedded procedure.   In contrast to using metadata in declarative, factual form, computational procedures can embed data definitions. In the previous example, application code could be constructed that implicitly assumes that zip code data consists of five characters. However, the declarative, factual form of metadata is preferred, wherever possible, over definitions embedded in application code. There are a variety of reasons to avoid procedural definitions, including lack of reuseability and difficulty in the validation of embedded definitions.

This is not to say that all metadata is nonprocedural. Metadata may supply a procedure or function to be used to operate on the data.

Two common cases for this are either (1) to transform the data into a convenient form for computational or display purposes, or (2) to extend the primitive operations on data, as is commonly done in object-oriented programming approaches.

Standard or sharable definitions. To realize the benefits of data definition, however, each of the components of definitions just described must either be based on standards or there must be mechanisms that apply transformations to translate nonstandard definitions. As the data environment becomes large or complex, data takes on variations in usage, format, implementation detail, or performance requirements. Consequently, the requirement for standard data definitions becomes more important, but also, more difficult to achieve in large-scale environments.

Making definitions public. These definition elements may be made public in one of two ways. Some definitions may coexist with the data. For example, punctuation creates self-defining data by delimiting words. Markup language (such as SGML) delimits and identifies text object types in documents. Other definitions are externally applied through machine-usable data declarations such as in dictionaries, database schemas, and software data declarations.

4.5.3   Definitions Depend on the Formalism

A requirement for sharing data is the use of public data definitions or "contracts" in an object-oriented formalism. Using public definitions, applications can share the same data as long as they share data definitions. Sharing data definitions has turned out to be one of the most difficult and perplexing problems facing business systems. The transition to a distributed environment, however, demands effective data sharing.

By a data definition we mean the information that conveys fundamental characteristics of the thing being defined, including its relationship to associated things. The nature of the definition depends partly on the language brought by the computing paradigm or conceptual framework being used.

Older information systems operate on a weak formal model. Information definitions are formed from custom procedures (i.e., application code) operating on data types and record structures that represent computing artifacts. Specifications are in the implementation details. More modern approaches to definitions separate specifications from implementation detail.

One type of approach to operational definitions uses a global or generic reasoning model to provide behavioral characteristics:

- Relations and domains (attributes) in a relational model
- Predicates and terms in an untyped predicate logic model
- Predicates and types in a typed predicate logic model

Another type of approach to operational definitions uses local, custom procedures to provide behavioral characteristics:

- Object classes and methods in an object model
- Functions and types in a functional model

Structural definitions such as database schemas or programming data structures define attributes and their structural composition. The atomic unit in these models is the value container—attribute, element, term, or data type. The definition of this atomic unit includes:

- Attribute role name
- Domain of values the attribute ranges over
- Concrete representational type (character, integer, etc.)
- Value if the unit is bound to a value

Compositions of this atomic unit are defined as structures of atomic types in such forms as sequences, trees, and sets.

Behavior definitions can be defined declaratively or procedurally. Procedural definitions are usually not very effective for a variety of reasons. A declarative definition of behavior depends on the paradigm. Where there is a local reasoning engine, such as object- or function-oriented systems, behavior definitions specify preconditions, post-conditions, and invariant conditions on structural components. Where there is a global reasoning engine, such as a logic model, behavioral definitions can be interpreted from a program of rules and facts. In the relational model, though, a behavioral definition is more difficult to interpret.

4.6   METADATA-DRIVEN DATA INTEGRATION

The transition of legacy systems to a distributed environment often begins with two needs: First, the data that is virtually locked up in transactional (i.e., line operations) information systems must be extricated and made more generally available for decision-support information systems. Second, as new and strategically important software packages for line operations, decision support, or whatever becomes commercially available, these software packages need access to the data locked up in the existing legacy systems.

In this section we discuss an approach and process for regenerating legacy system data into a distributed architecture to satisfy the needs for improved data availability and interfaces to newly acquired software.

To regenerate legacy data into a distributed architecture, several types of metadata and system data will be gathered. This information can be categorized into the following classes:

- Data definitions
- Data mappings
- System utilization and administration

The classes of specifications are shown in Figure 4.10. The cloud on the right-hand side of Figure 4.10 represents specification information. This specification information is intended to be a functional component of the system, not just input for system development. It exists in three forms: documented specifications; queryable information about the data and the system; active specifications that directly configure the system. Refer to Chapter 5 concerning the services that can be used to implement the services shown in Figure 4.10. The following kinds of specification and system data will be gathered during the transition.

Data definition.   Data definition models specify the conceptual and design views of data.

- User views capture the intended meaning of the data from a specialized user or application perspective. These definitions are in business-oriented terminology. They define what the end user or application requires from the information services. This view is needed to capture variations on basic data definitions.
- Generic views capture the basic intended meaning of the data from a unified and cross-functional perspective. This model may evolve as additional user views are incorporated if the user view introduces new data meaning. Generic views contain both atomic definitions as well as derived, aggregated, and other complex information structures.
- Database schemas capture the data storage designed view of data definitions.
- Presentation and display models capture how information is structured and formatted for human use.

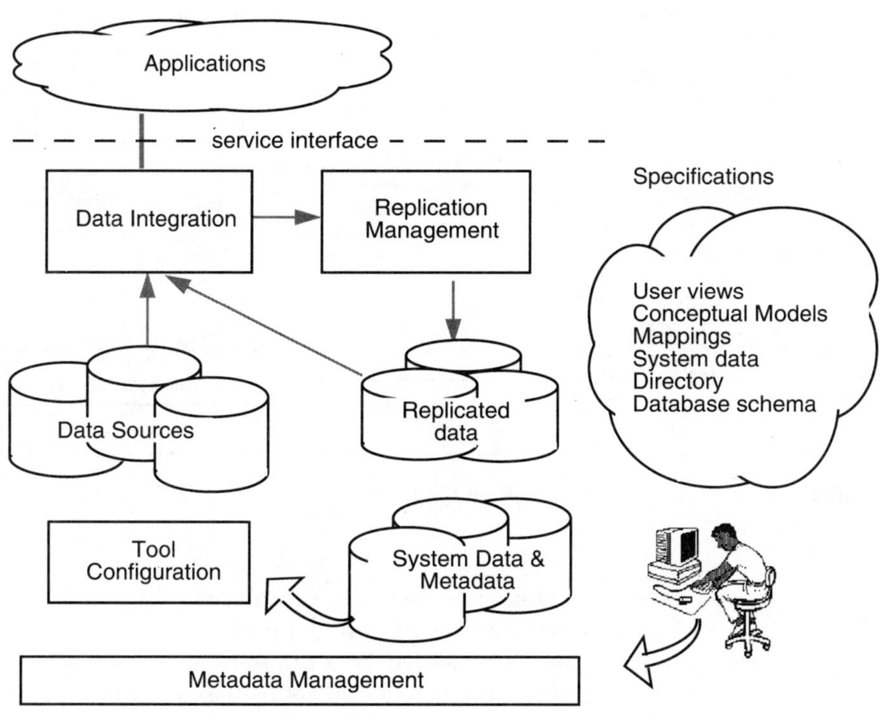

Figure 4.10   Metadata-governed data integration.

Data mapping.   Data mapping models specify how data definitions correspond among the data models. This information is used to manage multiple versions, copies, or derivations of data. Transformations required to fully specify the mapping between objects are often added to the mapping model. Figure 4.11 depicts the general correspondences among the major sources of metadata.

- User view to generic concept view: This mapping serves to relate terms in the user view to terms in the generic conceptual view. There are often many user terms that relate to the same generic term. Since most file systems derive their data definitions from applications that use the data, applications are a source of user views.
- Concept to design or generic conceptual view to database schema: This mapping serves to relate terms in the generic conceptual view

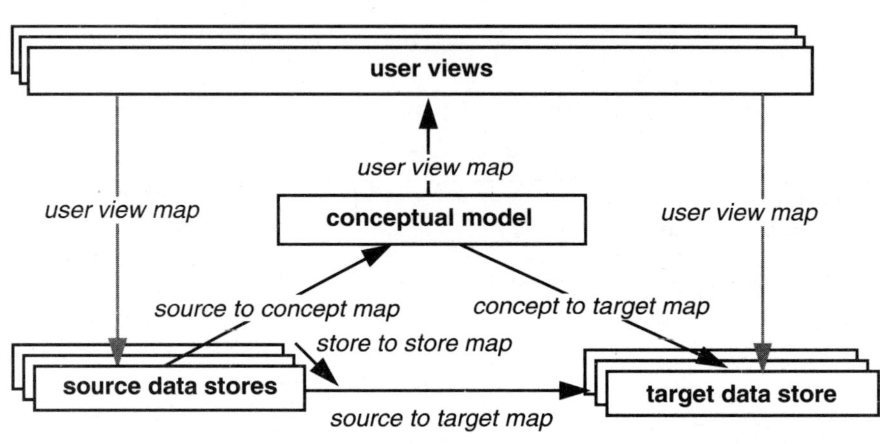

Figure 4.11   Unification model for data integration.

to terms in database schemas. There are often many database elements that map to the same conceptual element.

- Resource manager schema versions: This mapping relates multiple database definitions of common data objects. Normally unstable, it should be used primarily during analysis phases to derive the conceptual to schema mappings. However, this mapping is often used (or misused) to establish a concrete contract between autonomous systems. This is a primary source of "legacy system-itis" due to the proliferation of point-to-point data exchanges and the extreme expense of maintenance of system-dependent translations. The preferred approach is based on unification through the generic conceptual view.

- User view versions: This mapping relates multiple user views to one another, but is normally unstable, as is any implementation-specific definition. However, this mapping is useful for users to translate between functional areas, much like a glossary. More importantly, user view versions derive from applications that are the source for file system definitions. That is, in legacy systems, where there is sometimes little generality in data definitions, the application data definition serves as a user view rather than a resource manager schema definition.

An Example of Mapping.   Consider a scenario in which the business process needs information on pets and their owners. One user needs to view the data with respect to the population of different types of pets in different regions. Other users need other views of the data. One source of data contains veterinarian clinic visit logs containing pet names, pet type, and owner names. Another source of data contains owner names and address information. The conceptual model contains concepts covering all user views. A new database is created to integrate the source data to satisfy all the potential views of the data. Table 4.8 shows an example of a subset of the mappings needed to specify how the various data elements correspond to one another.

The names and mapping information in the table constitute a sample subset of the specifications. Notice that names for similar data are different and that some new data elements are created as derived data. Experience has shown that name aliases are a critical source of confusion. Careful management of aliases is a highly valued result of this mapping process. Additional specifications would need to be gathered to complete the table. For example, Sources 1 and 2 must be joined on owner and customer name to derive the target pet owner name and address. A declarative specification of the join would be added to the metadata. By declarative, it is meant something like an SQL expression that *selects* result data *from* a source *where* applicable constraints hold. Additional mechanisms are needed. For example, if region were to be a coded area that included more than one city, then a translation table would need to be defined.

The typical legacy system approach to supplying user information is to gather this metadata, create the new database intuitively, code up requested reports, and then drop the metadata. The approach advocated here stores the metadata as data in its own right, to be used by both

Table 4.8   Example of Data Mappings

User view 1	Conceptual model	Source 1	Source 2	Target 1
Pet type	Animal type	Pet type		Pet type
Region	City		Address	City and State
Region	State		Address	City and State
	Animal Owner	Owner Name	Customer Name	Pet Owner
Animal Count	Animal Census			
		[count by type]		Number owned

developers and end users. The metadata is in declarative form as much as possible to avoid dependence on particular implementation methods. End users can use the metadata to query about what information is available and how to interpret it. The developers use the metadata to maintain and test the system.

System administration and utilization.   System administration models specify the configuration of the system for system management. Utilization models specify performance and resource utilization during operation of the system.

- The most important type of administration model is a directory. A directory contains information that maps object names to system addresses. A directory allows system objects to be identified without undue dependence on how those objects are implemented. For example, the directory provides location transparency.
- Another important collection of administration information is security and account information used to manage authentication, authorization, and access control, and to administer fair allocation of resources.
- Administration models contain information to specify replication synchronization policy. This information specifies how often to refresh remote copies of data.
- Utilization models capture measurements of the use of the system.

This is the kind of information that populates a data dictionary or metadata repository. To make this information effective, it is necessary to formulate this information in both human and machine form. That is, it is necessary to use a "metamodel" that defines the kinds of specifications (metadata) that are required. Unfortunately, standards for metadata models are sparse. Consequently, there will probably be few dictionary or repository products available to rely on for the comprehensive suite of metadata and system data that is needed for a particular migration effort.

Metamodels must be defined for all these specification models in a use-neutral form so that the process can be implemented using any commercial product. When implemented, the metadata may be actually distributed inside the various commercial products. The use-neutral specification models may be populated with data by accessing the internal metadata of all the component commercial products involved. Until greater standardization is achieved, it will not be uncommon for metadata to be housed among multiple tools.

Control and conformance to requirements.   A simple system is often described as three components: input, process, output. Normally, data is shared by sharing the process output. In complex processes, however, the system is better defined as data and control parameter input, process, and data and control parameter output. In other words, control parameters are an important element to be shared as well as the data itself.

Often it is effective to develop tools that unload control parameter settings (i.e., metadata) from software so that a complete configuration management process can be used to control conformance. Input specifications can be compared to unloaded specifications to verify that information tools are configured correctly.

4.7   FIT FOR PURPOSE

"Managers must shift from a plan to produce specific offerings
. . . to a structure for responding to change."

Haeckel and Nolan 1993[6]

Just as the fly-by-wire pilot is flying an information representation of his or her plane, an employee is running an information representation of his or her business. As information technology evolves, a business person has many information tools to do the job. However, it is not enough to do the job right; the tools and the information must help do the right job—that is, meet business objectives. A typical business has many information sources, business units, and multiple relationships among these elements. Business units are faced with astounding information complexity. Helping them stay on track with business objectives requires a map of the business, one that can be shared among the people and information tools. This requires that businesses develop models of their business information. In the previous section conventional information modeling was described. However, conventional information modeling has focused on representing the form and function of information. This section examines issues concerning the suitability of information and information tools for doing the right job. Haeckel and Nolan point out that conventional modeling tools have limited ability to capture certain business requirements. Consequently, there is some issue of whether a company's information will be fit for the purpose. For example, modeling approaches and information tools exhibit the following limitations:

- Specifications not linked to business objectives
- Commitment and human accountability not incorporated
- Not dealing with unstructured work and ad hoc processes
- Taking months and years to map the information model to computer code
- Being paradigm-bound

4.7.1   Linking Specifications to Business Objectives

An information model should span business objectives and specifications. Current tools and methods often leave these facets of business information disassociated from one another. Cultural factors are also to blame. There is commonly a big gap between senior management and the line workers regarding language, knowledge, and communication modes. This gap must be narrowed to improve the business. Two ways to do this are: (1) limit scope of an enterprise data model to key, highly prioritized subjects, and (2) develop an abstraction ladder.

An abstraction ladder is developed by articulating multiple levels of abstraction as shown in Table 4.2. Where a senior manager wants to coordinate global inventory, an information worker thinks in terms of integrating part nomenclature, and a database technologist is concerned with inter-operating between diverse database models. The problem must be stated at all of these levels concurrently.

At a high level of abstraction, the information model must capture the business expert's understanding in strategic business terms. At intermediate levels of abstraction, those strategies must be specified in tactical terms. At a low level of abstraction, those tactics must be specified in operational terms. At the lowest level of abstraction, the strategies, tactics, and operations are implemented with concrete mechanisms.

The success of an enterprise information model depends on developing this abstraction ladder so that there is a continuity of understanding from top to bottom. Consequently, the actual implementation is a valid and faithful rendering of the higher levels of abstraction and, inversely, the higher levels of abstraction can actually be implemented.

In practice, there is a strong class struggle throughout the chain of authority. Each level of authority tends not to speak the language of other levels. Worse, there is usually no attempt to bridge the gap. Creating an information model requires bridging this gap. Typically an information model is created by a modeler or "knowledge engineer" who functions low in the chain of authority. Consequently, information models tend to be focused on operational levels rather than on tactical or strategic levels. Also, information models, for similar reasons, tend to not cross discipline boundaries. For example, information models are often limited to either an entity-relationship methodology, a decision-support methodology, an operations research or strategic planning methodology, and so on.

Developing a coherent abstraction ladder is a good task for prototyping methodology. It is important to rapidly develop executable code that demonstrates the implications of the less tangible strategic and tactical visions.

4.7.2   Incorporating Commitment and Human Accountability

Information models can be bland or vivid. A bland information model may simply represent information objects—for example, orders and shipments. A vivid information model identifies quality and performance objectives to bind general ideas to real-world implications. For example, rules should be articulated that specify expected performance—"Shipments are sent within a specified time of order receipt." Furthermore, the information model should identify work roles that are accountable for business performance. To make this work, however, employees must be given broad visibility of the business process so that they can participate and improve each step of the process. The information model helps provide the necessary visibility.

4.7.3   Dealing with Unstructured Work and Ad Hoc Processes

The information model should capture the structure of the business process, not the step-by-step procedure. Flow charts are often used, mistakenly, to represent a business process as a specific procedure. This technique portrays the sequence of actions and decision points to carry out a procedure. The problem with flow charts is that they do not permit multiple levels of abstraction. Consequently, the representation must be changed with each improvement in the *implementation* of a process. Furthermore, much of a company's work is relatively unstructured and ad hoc. Flow charts are not able to capture the essence of unstructured work. A good representation of a process does not change as long as the process concept doesn't change, even though the actual implementation of the process may change.

Recent developments in object-oriented information modeling propose that work be modeled in a logical or declarative fashion instead of a procedural fashion.[7]

Successful information modelers understand that they are programmers at a different abstraction level. Programming uses, and information modeling should use, contracts as the most important concept. In programming terms, a contract may be visualized as a procedure call protected by constraints, that is, surrounded by a precondition, a post condition, and existing within an environment (context) characterized by an invariant.

Contracts define operations unambiguously by identifying customer expectations as the final state or post-condition of the operation and the operation's requirements or preconditions.

4.7.4   Mapping to Computer Code in Days or Weeks instead of Months or Years

During the 1980s, it became a well-known phenomenon that a major information system effort would take three to five years to complete. In itself, that may not be so bad; after all bridges, highways, dams, and skyscrapers take years to build. The problem is that with legacy systems, nearly all changes seem to be major undertakings. With a dynamic marketplace, the business must be able to modify its process quickly to remain competitive. We can identify three key ingredients for quickly adapting systems:

- Well-articulated objectives and specifications
- Reusable elements or configurable building blocks
- Executable specifications

The key to reconfigurability is reuse of generic building blocks within a patterned framework, that is, being able to adjust parameters and assemble a system to order. Attorneys use standard forms and fill in the blanks. Writers use word processors and adjust the formatting parameters for the job at hand. Standard business practices have highly reusable commercially available components such as product data management, payroll, point-of-sale, and application systems. Reusable components have been built for these well-known processes.

However, to use these commonly available reusable packages, it is necessary to supply the particular knowledge of the business. Word processors must be configured to enable information sharing and coordinated work. Configuring larger scale software such as product data management or payroll requires a well-developed information model.

In those cases where the business problem is not as well understood or standardized, reusable and generic building blocks are still required to achieve nimble, adaptable company responses to market conditions. Modern technology supplies many tools to build reusable building blocks, including relational databases, object-oriented programming, forms-driven code generators (4GL), and the information service components discussed in Chapter 5. However, inventing reusable abstractions is difficult and is not an algorithmic activity. Inventing reusable abstractions requires inventors and people skilled at developing abstractions.[8] The process of developing abstractions was discussed in Chapter 3.

4.7.5   Using a Spectrum of Modeling Methodologies

An information model is primarily a structural representation of the business as opposed to a procedural or algorithmic representation such as flow charts. By far the most common information modeling methodology is the entity-relationship approach or variants such as NIAM. Object-oriented and logic-based methodologies are beginning to become established. For certain purposes, mathematical modeling is used.

All methodologies are based on one or more of the following logically primitive constructs to represent the world: individuals, predicates (classes), relations, functions, structures, and a system of expressions (linguistic, algebraic, or other) combining these constructs.

All of the common data-modeling approaches have weak means to represent structures. Each of the common modeling approaches tends to have a weakness in one or more of these characteristics. Entity-relationship modeling has a weak ability to form logical expressions concerning individuals, so that many kinds of constraints cannot be expressed. Early object-oriented modeling had a weak ability to formulate logical expressions, so that relations and rules could not be expressed. Recent developments in ontology standardization and formal specification techniques may improve this limitation. First-order logic systems have a weak ability to express a system of types without extreme clutter. Because of the incompleteness of specific modeling approaches, it is necessary to use multiple systems in a toolkit.

A second major problem is becoming apparent concerning modeling methodologies. Each methodology provides a raw language system with only a bare handful of concepts. Any given applied model of the world develops fairly high-level concepts that must be invented each time a modeler develops a model. What is missing is an accumulated, standard catalog of reusable concepts for modelers to draw upon. This catalog is sometimes referred to as an "ontology." Some standardization efforts are beginning to address this problem, such as the DARPA knowledge-sharing effort[9] and STEP (an international effort to define manufacturing product data). STEP, for example, is developing what they call application protocols that define a basic catalog of concepts such as a geometric point, line, and curve. From that layer additional concepts can be constructed that standardize more abstract concepts such as part, assembly, or bill of materials.

These two problems, paradigm specificity and a lack of standard concept catalog, must be recognized. Having acknowledged modeling limitations, a broad range of employees can set aside their language and cultural differences and set out to formulate an information model that spans the full gamut from business objectives to software code.

4.7.6   Multidimensional Tables versus Relational Tables

Shifting to a distributed computing environment brings a great diversity of information processing approaches. Transaction processing (OLTP), operational reporting, and analysis processing (decision support) have been recognized as very different processing domains. Data modeling and data management practices for these situations tend to differ in many ways. However, as we better understand information processing theory, we see that such diverse domains have important unifying factors.

Developments in decision-support processing have recently emphasized the difference between the relational data model appropriate for transaction processing and the multidimensional data model appropriate for online analysis processing.

Multidimensional tables represent an important extension to the relational approach that began to emerge during the early 1990s. In a relational database, primary keys may contain multiple components. For the example in Table 4.9, the primary key is the first four columns: material type; use type; size; and effective date. The fifth element, price, is dependent on the combination of these keys.

Multidimensional tables make use of the case where the primary key components are orthogonal. Each of the primary key components

Table 4.9   Stock Price Data in Relational Format

Material Type	Use Type	Size	Effective Date	Price
copper	military	1 inch	Jan 1	$.09

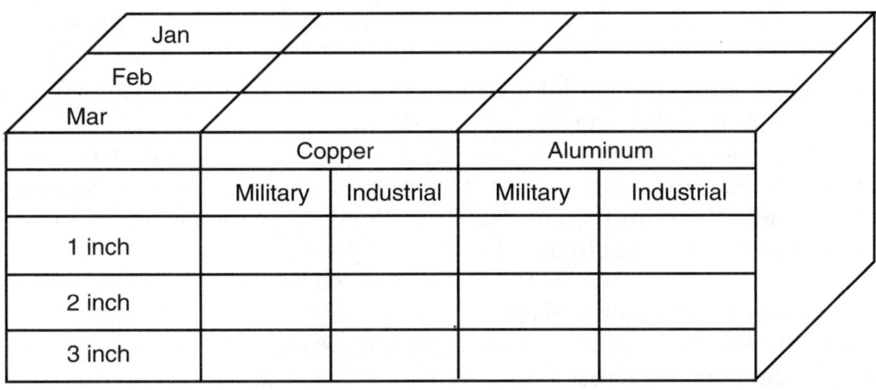

Figure 4.12   Cubical presentation of data using hierarchies to present additional dimensions. Here there are four dimensions—Date, Size, Material, and Use.

forms an axis. That is, in our example, Material Type, Use Type, and so on can be put on different axis with price data in the corresponding cells. For that matter, the keys can be hierarchically arranged to capture the dimensions as shown by the usage type under material types in the top row of Figure 4.12.

One major difference the multidimensional approach brings is that it transforms data values to attribute types—from cell values to column headings. For example, in Figure 4.12 copper and aluminum were data values in the relational model, but are column headings in the multidimensional model. Any data value subset can be used to represent a category. For example, if a data attribute or column contains color information, then all the rows for a given color form a subset or category. In Figure 4.12, dates are treated as intervals so that January dates form one category, February dates form a second category, and so on.

In many cases, to use this extra information it is necessary to identify functions such as sums and cross-tabulations of scalar values to create data for multidimensional matrix cell entries. Entity-relationship models tend not to show derived data. Consequently, many data functions are not modeled. The multidimensional approach suggests that summaries should be modeled for all important dimensions (potentially all primary key attributes) and cross-tabulations for each combination of dimensions. Taking this principle to the next level of generality, there should be automated functions that can generate these arithmetic operations on any attribute that is functionally dependent on any orthogonal data attributes (primary key components). Functions should also be modeled to automatically create interval data, such as summaries, by time period, unit of measure, geographic coordinate, and so on.

When using data values, however, the name of the category is not in the data. For instance, a column may contain types such as copper, ferrous, and aluminum. The name "material type" may not be in the data and must be supplied by the user or domain expert.

The example shown in Figure 4.13 demonstrates several kinds of data relationships required for analysis processing. These relationships are often not modeled for transaction processing. Each actual or budgeted sale of a product in a market is an event. Similarly, expenses are events. These Dollar Events are subcategorized in two ways. A sale or an expense may be either an actual event or may be simply planned as a budget item. This creates the two subtypes shown in Figure 4.13. Recall that in entity-relationship diagramming, a subtype may be

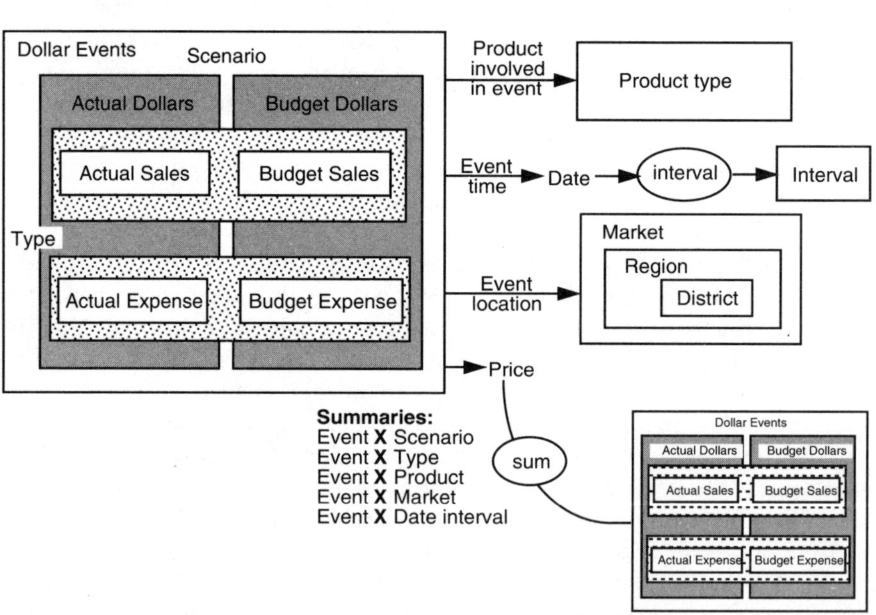

Figure 4.13   Richer modeling needed for analysis processing.

shown as a (subtype) box within a (supertype) box. Commonly, sales would be modeled so that transaction programs could capture Sales transactions. Budget concepts would merely be represented by an analyst at his local workstation.

Since events capture scalar data values, a number of summaries and cross-tabulations may be derived. This is shown in Figure 4.13 by the oval that represents the application of an arithmetic function. (A declarative specification, by the way, not a procedural definition!) Also, dates can be intervalized into days, weeks, months, and so forth, as shown by the interval function.

By selecting the dimensional parameters to the sum function, a variety of multidimensional models can be derived as shown in Figure 4.14.

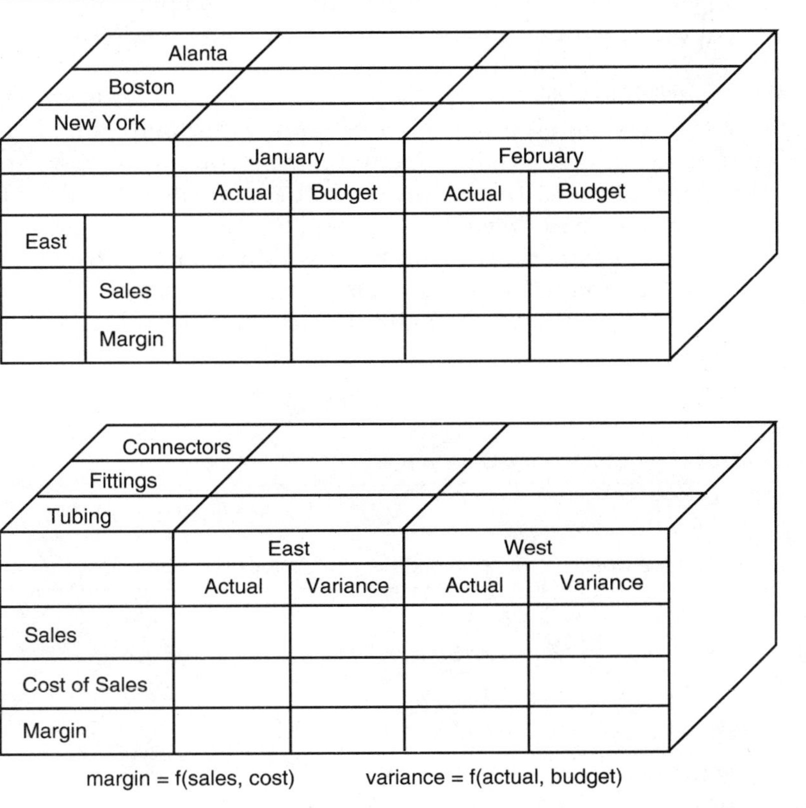

Figure 4.14   Two multidimensional views of the data modeled in Figure 4.13.

Relational database systems are designed according to a well-known and standardized model. A theoretical basis for the multidimensional data model has not yet been well developed. Each commercial multidimensional database system has its own approach. Consequently, one of the problems with multidimensional databases is that programmers commonly have to manually set up the dimensional relationships, thereby making the analysis environment static and dependent on the programmer.

4.7.7   Presentation Tables versus Relational Tables

Compare Tables 4.10 and 4.11. Table 4.10 is a visual presentation table. Table 4.11 is a relational table. It would seem straightforward to transform one form into the other. However, as we examine the transformations necessary, we see that there is additional semantic information in the visual table, not normally captured in the relational table.

1. The material types (copper, ferrous, aluminum) are column headers in the visual table, but cell data in the relational table. In many similar tables, the heading "material type" would not even appear in the visual table. Instead, it would be implicit in the knowledge the user has of the domain.
2. Visual tables sometimes contain explanatory notes, such as unit of measure or explanations of unusual or missing entries. This kind of information would be normalized into separate tables in a relational scheme.

Table 4.10   Stock Price Data in Presentation Format

			material type (note 1)		
Size	*Use (see note)*	*Effective Date*	*Copper*	*Ferrous*	*Aluminum*
1	**Military**	Jan 1			
1	**Industrial**	Mar 15		*Price*	
1	**Home**	Feb 2		*Data*	
2	**Military**	Jan 1			
2	**Industrial**	July 12			
2	**Home**	Oct 1			

Note 1:   Price data is in U.S. currency.

Table 4.11 Stock Price Data in Relational Format

Material Type	Use Type	Size	Effective Date	Price
copper	military	1 inch	Jan 1	$.09

3. Cell data may contain compound values such as a list of values. The compound values may represent an implicit logical expression. If a cell contains the expression "red, blue" it may mean "red or blue" or "red and blue." For example, Table 4.12 shows such a case. Based on knowledge of the situation, the user may read this table as:

Connectors are supplied by both Acme **and** Pacific

Connectors conform to **either** spec 6056 **or** 8088

Additional implicit information is contained in cell data. For example, in Table 4.12, Milspec 6056, 8088 is meant to mean that both numbers designate a specification. That is, the term "Milspec" distributes over both numbers as follows: Milspec 6056, Milspec 8088.

4.8 FROM DATA TO INFORMATION

The theme of this chapter is that information technology helps business processing when it implements the metaphors of communication and knowledge. Managing the storage and presentation of data is only the beginning of information technology. Considerations of how data represents the world must be added to the discipline of information management.

The first key principle is that information technology helps by providing mechanisms to achieve data abstraction, hiding the details of how the technology is implemented. The second principle is that information must be managed along several dimensions—form, function, and fit for purpose. The many forms of information require an array of mechanisms suited to each form. The function of information was examined with respect to how its meaning or semantics can be captured

Table 4.12 Logical and/or Expressions in Data Tables

Part	supplier	specification
connector	Acme Inc, Pacific	Milspec 6056, 8088

as data itself or metadata. Finally, since information serves different purposes, these purposes need to be identified, and a variety of modeling and processing approaches applied to serve those purposes.

CHAPTER NOTES

1. Medina-Mora, Raul, Terry Winograd, Rodrigo Flores, and Fernando Flores. *The Action Workflow Approach to Workflow Management Technology.* CSCW 92 Proceedings (November 1992).
2. Stephen C-Y Lu. *Knowledge-Based Engineering Systems Research Laboratory.* Annual Report, 1991.
3. Sowa, John F. *Conceptual Structures: Information Processing in Mind and Machine.* Reading, Mass.: Addison-Wesley, 1984.
4. Simons, Peter. *Parts: A Study in Ontology.* New York: Oxford University Press, 1987.
5. This set of properties of the relational model is the main reason end users use SQL directly only for simple representations. More complex representations require view mechanisms. On the other hand, SQL is powerful and popular because relational models do capture lexical and simple syntactic and semantic information very well.
6. Haeckel, Stephan H., and Richard L. Nolan. "Managing by Wire." *Harvard Business Review* (September–October 1993).
7. Kilov, Haim, and James Ross. *Information Modeling: An Object-Oriented Approach.* Englewood Cliffs, N.J.: PTR Prentice-Hall, 1994.
8. Cunningham, W., and K. Beck. "Constructing Abstractions for Object-Oriented Applications." *Journal of Object-Oriented Progamming,* vol. 2, no. 2 (1989).
9. Ramesh, S. Patil, Richard E. Fikes, Peter F. Patel-Schneider, Don McKay, Tim Finin, Thomas R. Gruber, and Robert Neches. "The DARPA Knowledge-sharing Effort: Progress Report." In Charles Rech, Bernhard Nebel, and William Swartout, eds., *Principles of Knowledge Representation and Reasoning: Proceedings of the Third International Conference.* Cambridge, Mass: Morgan Kaufmann, 1992.

5

Service-Based Architecture

In this chapter we examine the concept of a service. A service is like a micro-application whose job is to perform a narrowly defined function in a general way, operating on a well-defined type of data. Services, so defined, become reusable building blocks that can be composed in a variety of ways to operate on data, itself composed of multiple layers of abstract data types. Actually, data and function become unified by virtue of a typing or classification system.

In the preceding chapters a case was made that inventing appropriate abstractions is a key method for making distributed systems work. In Chapter 4, we attempted to raise the level of abstraction ordinarily used to describe business data by talking about information rather than simply data. In this chapter, we lower that level of abstraction to talk about services rather than applications. In the last few years, as information technology architecture became more commonly addressed, it was common to find systems partitioned into data (management), application, and delivery system. Our premise is that these concepts need to be refined.

In Chapter 2, Figure 2.4, we presented a simplified concept of levels of system organization in which the bottom two levels represented basic or primitive system services and information. In this chapter we examine these kinds of services in more detail. First, we briefly introduce idealized low-level services that are at the foundation of distributed systems. In the ordinary business context, the technical staff should be familiar with these services, but normally they do not develop or maintain them. Secondly, we describe higher level services with which, again, business technical staff should be familiar. These higher level services, however, have less commercial standardization and stability, so technical staff will often be required to at least integrate them, and occasionally to develop software to create them.

One purpose served by this technical discussion is that suggested by Thomas Kuhn. To participate in a paradigm shift it is necessary to explore exemplars and models that reveal various aspects of the new paradigm. The reader may want to skim the next section on low-level services and return to it as necessary.

5.1   REALLY LOW-LEVEL VIEW OF DISTRIBUTED SYSTEMS

Michael Schroeder describes a mythical, state-of-the-art distributed system with the purpose of laying out the basic issues with which distributed computing systems must cope.[1] His model describes the properties and services of an imaginary distributed system. The main characteristic of his system—that makes it more ideal than real—is the current lack of transparency across heterogeneous implementations of the services.

The system Schroeder describes is a heterogeneous collection of hardware, software, and data components. For example, the various processors may be running such operating systems as MVS, UNIX, MS-DOS, and NT. Its size and geographic implementation can vary over a large range. The system is connected by a network and provides a uniform set of services. The system exhibits certain global properties. The uniformity and globalness imbue the system with coherence.

The system exhibits the following properties:

- *Global names* means that the same names work everywhere to enable global sharing. Names apply to machines, users, files, distribution lists, access control groups, and system services.
- *Global access* is accomplished by functions that are usable everywhere. A document can be printed based on a file located in another country. A file update is immediately available to another person at some other site without special actions.
- *Global availability* is accomplished by providing replicated mechanisms and services. If one printer is down, another can easily be used.
- *Global security* is provided by being able to use the same authentication and access control mechanisms throughout the network.
- *Global management* can be performed by one person anywhere on the network. A remote machine can be configured or an administrative function can be applied to all the components within a large management domain.

To achieve these properties the following primitive services are provided:

- A *naming* service provides access to a distributed database of names and attribute values for machines, users, files, distribution lists, access control groups, and services.
- A *remote procedure call* mechanism provides a standardized interface and enables invocation of services anywhere on the network.
- A *user registration* service allows users to be registered and issues certificates permitting use of system resources.
- A *time* service provides globally consistent time.
- A *file* service gives access to files located anywhere on the network. Multiple file name spaces are connected by the naming service.
- A *management* service gives access to administrative functions and data of each system component.
- A *print* service provides standard printing capabilities.
- Additional services are provided for *mailboxes, terminals*, and *accounting*.

Actual systems can approach this ideal model. Issues of heterogeneity that provide the most difficulty can usually be worked around, though with significant expense. For instance, realizing a remote procedure call between a Unix and MVS mainframe interface can be accomplished with an additional service layer that provides transactional messaging services. This additional layer of services is described in the next section.

5.2 SERVICES AT A MID-LEVEL OF SYSTEM ORGANIZATION

The catalog of commercially available application software has grown quite large. Moreover, software manufacturers are beginning to adapt the best practices from all their customers and putting them into a system. By using this software, a company is reaping benefits from a large body of accumulated experience. Since accounting, manufacturing, and many other business practices are universal, companies are beginning to realize that they don't have to reinvent the software to perform these functions. Some companies are beginning to realize that the primary value of their MIS staff is assembling solutions and making interfaces work.

Interfaces, too, have a universal basis. With a large catalog of software and a wide variety of computing platforms, the design problem of distributed computing begins to shift towards a new set of goals—data independence, data abstraction, and transparency engineering. To achieve these goals in a universal way, there must be a layer of mediating capabilities between applications and data resources. Somewhere around 1991, the term middleware became popular. Middleware began as a sort of utility software that made it possible to begin to connect diverse sources of data remotely located from the application.

The transition from centralization to networked systems, and then to cooperatively distributed systems requires more than just connecting diverse resources. It is becoming apparent that systems should be architected into place. From an architectural perspective middleware provides services that applications use. What services should there be? A large company will find that where departments are just buying software packages, no one asked what services does the company, not just the department, need. If one department needs a data service, chances are that other departments need that service. To achieve cooperative processing, information technology must meet such design goals as data independence, data abstraction, and transparency engineering. The question becomes what services will meet these design goals.

Current distributed systems provide a number of service functions, some of which were described in the previous section, such as:

- Remote data access for both standard relational databases, as well as proprietary databases
- Distributed transaction management
- Network management
- System management
- Security, including authentication and access control
- Directory services
- Distributed file and database management
- Distributed user interface services
- Inter-application communications

These services form a mediating architectural layer between applications and computing platforms. In other words, middleware began as an increased capability to interconnect, but is now evolving towards capabilities to achieve a broader notion of cooperative processing. To use mediating services for the transition from legacy systems, we need a model that accommodates the diversity and complexity of legacy systems and the increased sophistication of distributed systems.

5.3   THE BASIC MODEL

The goal is that anyone should be able to use any data, anywhere in a form fit for the purpose. In a basic scenario, the user has an information tool that operates on data available from any of several sources. Sources may be local or not, on the same kind of computing platform or not, in a preferred format or not. To provide this broad range of capability, there must be many data services to mediate requests from the information tool. (Refer to Figure 5.1.)

These services provide the necessary capability to provide access to and operate on target data. Additionally, as we will see, these services provide a number of functions to assist in the process. Products that supply these services may employ other products to eventually provide a path of mechanisms to make the data available. The services are a set of capabilities that may be implemented with any of several designs.

The functionality may be actually part of an information tool or data source or it may be implemented as a separate component itself. Therefore, from an implementation point of view, a set of services may call upon another set of services to get the job done. The effect is that many sources of data are available to the information tool. But we also want to make this happen relatively transparently. It should not be necessary for the user to control and manage unnecessary mechanics of this process (refer to transparency engineering in Chapters 3 and 6).

In the basic model, shown in Figure 5.1, the data system can be treated as a black box that simply responds to a request to view or operate on data. The data system may be a database management system (DBMS) or a system application such as a calendaring or mail tool. We will often call such system capabilities "resource managers."

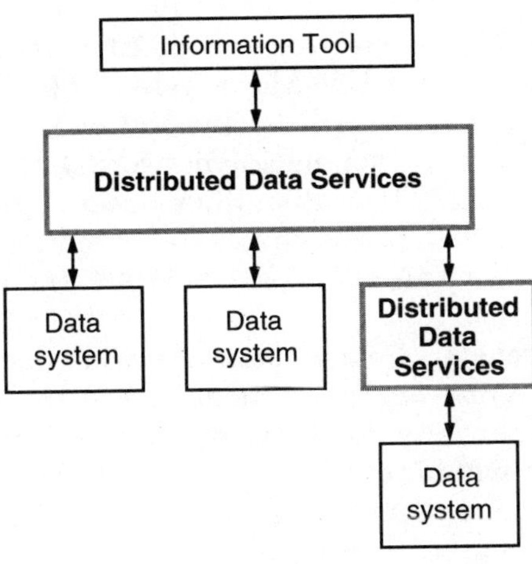

Figure 5.1   The basic distributed data services model.

5.4   THE WORLD-WIDE WEB AS AN EXEMPLAR

A spectacular example of a service-based architecture is the highly distributed system consisting of browsers (such as Mosaic), the World-Wide Web, and the Internet. This system provides information-sharing, discovery, and retrieval capabilities over the global Internet.

As we shall see, this system exemplifies the basic model, shown in Figure 5.1, in the following way: Mosaic is the information tool. A variety of document browsing or rendering services are the first level of services. Web provider services are the second level of services.

The *World-Wide Web* is a "wide-area hypermedia information retrieval initiative aiming to give universal access to a large universe of documents."[2] The Web effort began in March 1989 under the auspices of CERN (a European physics laboratory). In this context, documents must be thought of as containers of dynamic components such as images, tables, and indexes. They are dynamic because they carry with them executable code that allows them to render (display) themselves. There are a number of rendering programs that have been developed. Mosaic, the first popular graphical user interface software package, manages self-rendering services and thereby formed the first key human interface to the Web. Mosaic was released to the Internet community during 1993. Mosaic began under the auspices of the National Center for Supercomputing Applications (NCSA) shortly after the beginning of the Web initiative. Commercial suppliers are developing their own versions of Mosaic.

The *Internet* is an immense collection of interconnected computer networks based on the TCP/IP protocol. Project Internet started in the late 1960s. By 1980 there were only about 10 interconnected networks based on the IP protocol. In 1994 there were 34,000 NFSnet networks.[3] (NFSnet is a backbone operated by the National Science Foundation and is a major subset of all computing networks). In 1994, the Internet connected approximately 10 to 30 millions users in over 50 countries.[4] NFSnet statistics show that 1 terabyte (10^{12} bytes) per month was transferred over the Internet in June 1991. In 1994, the NFSnet carried 12 terabytes per month.

Note that the model of mass communication due to the Internet is significantly different from every model up to this point. Television, radio, and newspapers are broadcast from a central point to consumers. The consumer gets what is given by a few. With the Internet, the model is a network, where the consumer participates and seeks out and selects information from many sources.

The pieces of this system grew out of research efforts and are freely available to the public. The system that emerges from these pieces is, quite simply, revolutionary, rivaling the emergence of the printing press and broadcast in importance to social evolution. We emphasize that a key characteristic of this system is its emergent nature. This system differs from what might be called packaged or vertically integrated systems. Each of the major elements represent a general capability with an open, standard interface. The system is comprised of components provided by many participants. There were literally thousands of participating contributors in early 1994 and the growth rate is sharply rising.

From a simplified computational perspective, the system consists of the pieces shown in Figure 5.2. From an informational perspective, the figure also shows major information services available. There are three major elements to the system:

1. The client processor contains a collection of browser services that provide the capabilities to browse hypermedia documents, view images, read mail, listen to audio, view video sequences, and navigate through directories and indexes.
2. The system provides data access services that locate sources of information and transport the information from the source to the user.
3. The system components participate in the global Internet, providing interconnectivity between any two or more processors. This is

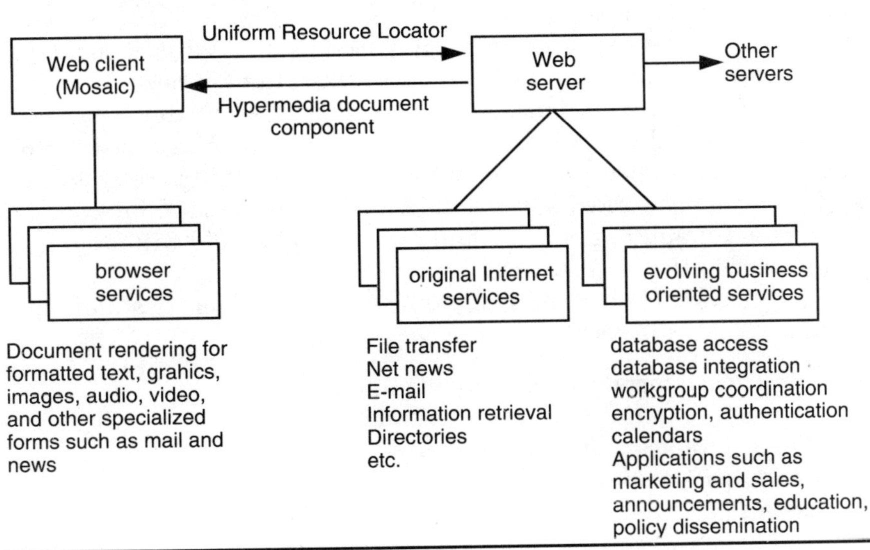

Figure 5.2   Functional architecture of the World-Wide Web.

enabled through the use of a suite of standard protocols. One such protocol, recently developed for multimedia access, is a directory protocol that uses what is called the uniform resource locator (URL). The URL names a resource with three pieces of information: the access method, target host address, and target information object.

A person using the system first sees a browser application running on a personal computer or workstation that appears much like the Macintosh Hypercard application. A home page that looks like a fully formatted document with hypertext capabilities is presented first. The user navigates through a hypermedia web of information by selecting ("pointing and clicking with a mouse") "hot" elements of the document, such as a word, icon, or picture. Each navigational event retrieves the linked piece of information (document component) and brings it on the screen for viewing. This piece of information, in turn, may be a hypermedia document, thus creating a web of information. The piece of information retrieved may be retrieved from any source on the Web, anywhere in the world. The search and retrieval behavior is virtually transparent to the user.

In practice there is a delay as one navigates through a document because information is flowing through the Internet. Experience has shown that this delay can be relatively minor relative to the benefits gained. For example, a document that is presenting a design approach may interconnect up-to-date information sources throughout the world, displaying drawings and specifications from documents in several cities in a matter of minutes.

With only the hypermedia display, the user could just as well be using an isolated personal computer or workstation connected to a storage device such as a hard disk or compact disk. That is, the dynamics of the system would be like using published books and databases. However, the system also provides online services located throughout the world. These networked services provide immediacy and interactivity among tens of millions of users and providers now, and will provide for many more in the near future.

In the system's beginnings, public domain capabilities alone provided the following services

- Libraries of formatted documents and data files
- Documents containing images, audio, or video
- Public databases and directories
- An interactive network news
- E-mail

Thus, network services include file and multimedia document servers, simple database access, news compilation, and mail exchange.

This system is in an early stage of development. Yet, it is already robust enough to be used commercially for limited uses. The commercial suitability must be enhanced by adding additional features to cover such concerns as security and performance.

Given that this approach will quickly develop into a robust, industrially viable system, consider some potential business uses.

- Delivery vehicle for integrating diverse databases
- Collaborative document development
- Work-flow management
- Online publishing of documents
- Directories
- Calendars
- Education
- Workgroup sharing
- News
- Marketing and public relations

The system is simple and ubiquitous so that even a mom-and-pop florist business can have its own home page and process orders from around the world. The system is scalable so that large companies can incorporate the system as an important element of an integrated business process. At the time of writing this there are a number of companies learning how to operate in business "cyberspace."[5] These pioneers report that "It's just like having an interactive billboard on the electronic highway." However, with this new paradigm, new concepts are emerging such as two-way marketing channels and network malls. Starting a business in this environment is tricky. For example, just getting a presence on the Internet has been likened to hanging up your shingle on a rural road.

5.5   MAJOR SERVICE ARCHITECTURES AND APPROACHES

In this section we examine a number of basic approaches that enable applications to operate on a variety of preexisting sources of data hosted in heterogeneous computing environments distributed at multiple sites. The purpose of these approaches is to logically integrate these data sources. Such integration faces many technical problems. The diversity means that implementation mechanisms do not readily interoperate. Data has inconsistent structure, format, and definitions. Operations in a diverse, loosely coupled, and large-scale environment require special considerations for interpreting data, maintaining data consistency, recovering from failures, and optimizing processing.

Software manufacturers would like to supply information tools and resource management tools that would interoperate in a diverse environment and would work for any situation. However, there is such a vast number of combinations that no supplier can possibly manage them. Information technology standards are in development that will greatly improve on the current situation. However, historical trends indicate that new information technology emerges much faster than standards.

There are several integration approaches that will support a distributed computing environment. Each approach supplies a system of data services for information tools to use. Figure 5.3 lists a number of approaches that can be layered on top of basic resource management services.

Some of these approaches are outgrowths of the legacy system technology. For instance, function libraries, the lowest common denominator, are not much more than improvised ways to package procedures to cope with specific problems. DBMSs and transaction managers have been extended to provide distributed processing capabilities. All of the major DBMS suppliers have extended their products in an effort to keep pace with the transition to distributed computing. However, as information technology grows more complex, DBMS suppliers recog-

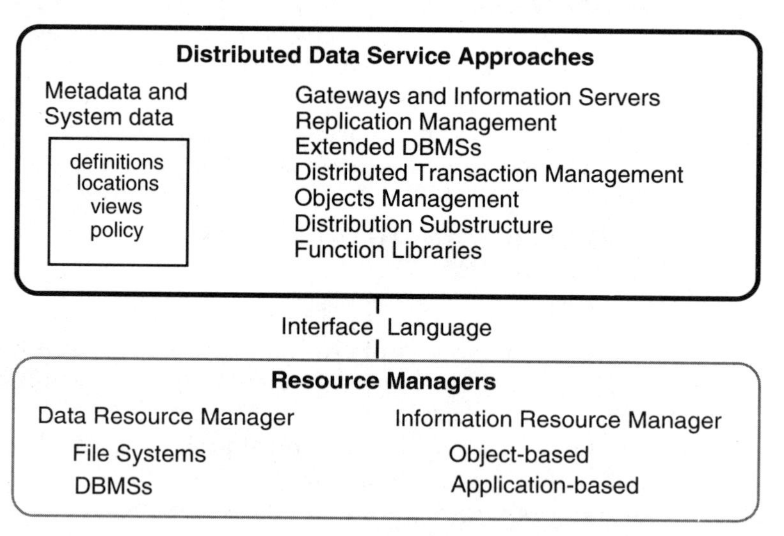

Figure 5.3   Distribution services layered on resource management services.

nize that DBMS can't and shouldn't try to provide all data services. For example, even though DBMSs provide transaction management, it has become apparent that distributed transaction management is a capability that stands on its own. Distributed transaction management must provide its services for an array of resource managers, where a particular supplier's DBMS is only one of many resource managers. In other areas DBMSs have tried to provide data services that stretch the concept of a DBMS. (For an example, see the discussion on stored procedures in section 5.6.4.)

Other architectures introduce a relatively new approach. Gateways and information servers introduce generalized interfaces to diverse information resources. Replication management introduces technology to distribute data in a disciplined way. Gateways and replication management approaches provide integration of heterogeneous data sources with the trade-off of weaker transaction management. However, once this trade-off is made, certain intractable legacy system transition problems can be overcome. One general strategy for the transition of legacy systems to a distributed architecture is to decouple update and query capabilities. By migrating parts of the system to a distributed architecture, a number of essential process improvements can take place that, among other things, facilitate the migration of the remainder of the system. For example, one important process improvement that occurs when query components are migrated to a distributed architecture is that data definitions become broadly shared and thus open to standardization. Once enterprise data definitions have been improved, it becomes much simpler to plan the subsequent migration of systems with update functions.

In a typical legacy environment there will be multiple processors hosting multiple databases. The processors will commonly be near processing capacity (particularly mainframes, since they are extremely costly to operate under capacity). In a legacy environment there are likely to be a variety of types of data management systems—relational, hierarchical, network, and file systems. Replication management is used to distribute the data to more convenient systems to improve data availability. In the process of replication, some amount of data integration may be achieved.

Another approach, distribution substructure, extends or layers on operating systems to provide basic capabilities for distributed computing. Such extensions include standard directory services, remote procedure calls, distributed system management services, network file systems, improved security, and so on. Object management is a sophisticated form of layered operating system and programming environment extensions that introduce a relatively new programming paradigm.

Each of these mediating approaches has its limitations. In the worst case, raw function libraries perpetuate the problems of legacy systems. Improvements in DBMSs provide some of the increased functionality that we seek, but depend heavily on the existence of a homogeneous information technology environment. Distributed transaction managers, like raw function libraries, introduce procedures with a relatively low level of abstraction. Gateways are like adapters in that they get the job done, but are not integrated into an overall approach. Use of raw distribution substructure provides the necessary tools for software manufacturers to create extremely sophisticated software, but, at the same time, provide the typical using company with high risks for developing just more expensive legacy systems. This could be avoided by waiting until commercial products incorporate this substructure as part of a more comprehensive distribution architecture.

None of these approaches, alone, provides all the data services needed to support a heterogeneous, distributed computing environment. However, the approaches can be combined to support most situations.

The newer technology approaches, such as information servers and object management, have the potential to provide breakthrough improvements in legacy systems. One of the reasons is that these approaches have begun to use a new paradigm in which policy and definition are in a declarative form. That is, information that specifies how the system shall function for a particular context is specified in the form of machine-usable rules and definitions. This information, metadata and system data, sometimes gathered into a dictionary or *metadatabase,* is available for shared use by the services and is easily changed and maintained by the support staff.

Metadata and system data are provided for a variety of levels of operation. Physical models enable machine conversion including basic data type translation. Directory models provide naming and location information across independent name spaces. System metadata provides operational policy such as access control lists. Synchronization metadata provides scheduling policy. Mapping metadata defines the conversions between storage paradigms, such as mapping between a hierarchical IMS data structure to a relational data structure. Conceptual metadata provides definition of real-world entities and properties such as value set or domain definitions. User metadata provides definitions of view variations or specializations on conceptual definitions.

5.6   MAJOR SERVICE ARCHITECTURES— A CLOSER LOOK

In this section we examine approaches to extending basic data services for a distributed architecture (see Figure 5.4).

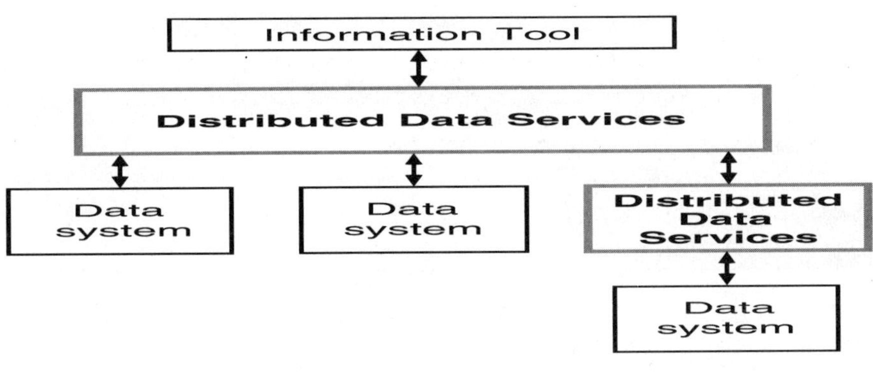

Figure 5.4   Major data service elements.

5.6.1   Language Mechanisms

As information systems scale up to serve very large business systems, they become composed of many highly differentiated, modular systems. Modularity of the system requires communication mechanisms among the modules to integrate the components.

> Computer applications will be based on communication between subsystems that will have been developed separately and independently. . . . There are no global objects. The only thing that all the various subsystems hold in common is the ability to communicate with each other.[6]

In the process of implementing communications between modules, we don't want to interweave communication protocols within the module code. The code in a module should be focused on a particular function.

The DARPA knowledge-sharing effort introduced a communication model that helps explain how to separate functionality. In their model, communication has three distinct levels. A message can be thought of as wrapped in two envelopes. The outer envelope is used to physically move the message from sender to receiver. The receiver removes that envelope to find the inner envelope that is used to classify the nature of the message inside. The message content is an expression in some language. This model is shown in Figure 5.5.

This model has a sound basis in ordinary life. When one writes a check to pay for goods, a message of three levels is being sent. A piece of paper is given to someone (the mechanics). A check is a social protocol

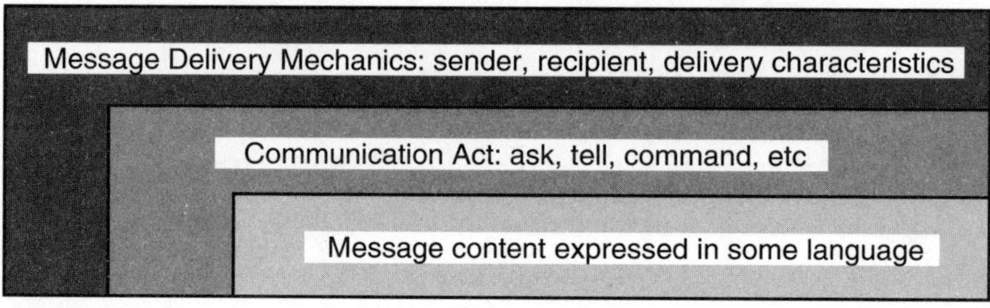

Figure 5.5   Levels of communication for a message.

that identifies an act of promising to pay (the communication act). The marks on the check that identify the payee, amount, and so on are the message content. Each of these components can be handled independently. The delivery, the promise to pay, and the payee or amount promised can be done by separate agents.

Message delivery mechanics.   The outside level of the communication model is responsible for the mechanics of messaging. This includes interpreting the destination designation, delivering the message to the destination, guaranteeing expected properties of the delivery such as invoking the target actor and guaranteeing delivery of the message, managing data storage, and recovering from operational failures.

Communication act.   The next layer of the communication model is a simple layer that is responsible for identifying the mode or intention of each part of the interaction. Linguists call this the speech act or performative. This level of communication identifies if the message is a query, command, or an assertion for example. In very sophisticated systems there may be many modes. Humans display such speech acts as judging, hypothesizing, sentencing, joking. In data processing systems a message is typically an act of asking, telling, commanding, or exception raising (issuing an error message). SQL allows the user to specify whether the SQL statement is an act of *asking* (SELECT), an act of *telling* (UPDATE or DELETE), an act of *commanding* (CREATE). A procedure call is a single communication act—invoking. The communication act resulting from a procedure call is either *telling* or *exception raising*.

Message content.   The innermost level of the communication model contains the message content, that is the expressions in a data language. This level is as complicated as whatever language is being used. For data processing, we could consider two language extremes. SQL is a data language that allows one to formulate queries, assertions, or definitions of great expressiveness. Application programming interfaces (APIs), in contrast, are rudimentary languages used to exchange function invocations and parameters.

Because appropriate abstractions are required, and SQL is appropriate for relational abstractions, it is adequate for handling relational data storage services. SQL is regarded as relatively poor in its ability to express most higher level abstractions.[7]

Two language approaches are used to achieve more independence than SQL alone can provide. First, application program interfaces (APIs) are used to employ service functions of the required complexity or abstraction. However, APIs have limited flexibility since they rely on predefined functions. A second approach is to use languages (graphical or linear) that incorporate more logic features than SQL supplies. Three such higher level languages that are emerging as standards are Conceptual Graphs, Knowledge Interchange Format, and the Semantic Unification Metamodel.[8]

5.6.2 Distribution Substructure— Messagepassing Mechanics

An essential property of distributed systems is that there are modules that must communicate and interact. Communication and interaction occur at many levels. The previous section described multiple levels of language— message delivery mechanics, communication act, and message content. In this section we will discuss additional levels of system organization. Transparency engineering requires that these levels do their job by hiding the implementation details of what goes on at lower levels.

In this section we discuss messagepassing as the communication basis for distributing computing. Such communication includes the responsibility for task management, such as waking or activating the recipient in order to invoke a response. There are a variety of modes and a number of key factors required to do that. In general, there are mechanisms to hide complexities and differences of communication whether two modules are on the same machine or different machines, or in the same software package or in different packages, and so on. This is an important foundation, because then we consider a different set of issues that could otherwise be confused with the messaging foundation. For example, we must consider mechanisms for applications to interact with remote databases. If we establish that there is an effective, well-encapsulated, messaging substructure, then we can go on to examine the other layers of communication without confusing them with lower level implementation detail. For example, exchanging SQL query language statements in a distributed setting has issues beyond the message exchange issues.

5.6.2.1 Degrees of Messaging Sophistication In a nondistributed, legacy environment, the message mechanics layer is usually relatively simple (transaction management system notwithstanding). The system architectural issues are few and concern the choice of a programming environment and operating system. In a distributed environment, however, the architectural issues become abundant, especially at the current stage of technology maturity. To understand the primary architectural variables we consider the following levels of messaging sophistication.

Call interface communication. The call-level interface, shown in Figure 5.6 a, is used by a programming language. This is the form of communication all programmers know well. Message mechanics are totally hidden by the language compiler. The intention or communica-

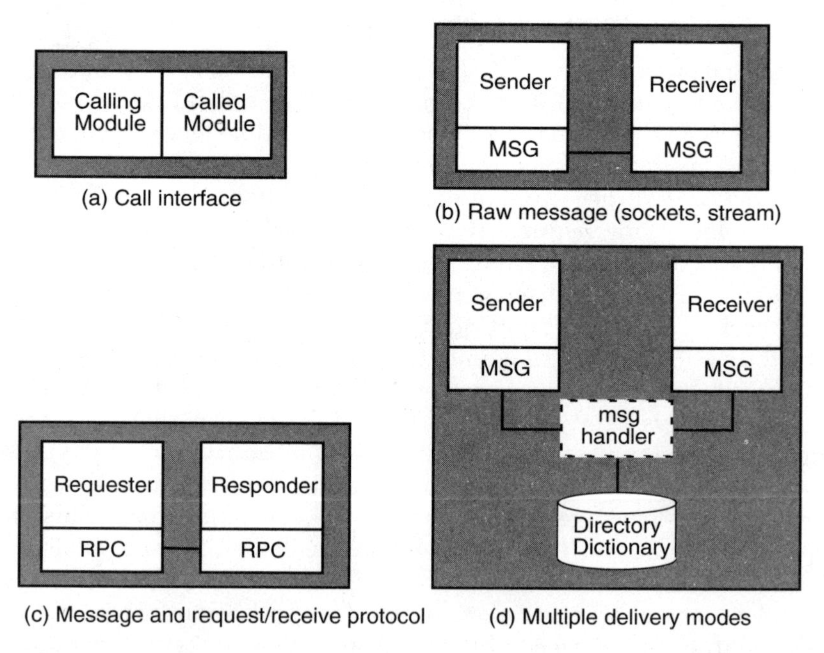

Figure 5.6   Forms of message passing.

tion act level has one mode—invocation. A function or procedure call invokes another procedure. The message content has few abstraction standards and therefore depends on the programmer's use.

Raw message communication.   The raw message form of communication does not hide much of the implementation detail. The message mechanics layer, however, is fairly standard. The programmer must manage many aspects of this layer, such as buffer management and naming services. The communication act and content layers are nonstandard, so the programmer must completely manage these layers. For example, the programmer might define the request/response interaction protocol. From an architectural point of view, use of this form of communication by application programmers is a court of last resort. It works well, but leaves a legacy of esoteric, custom code in its wake. UNIX sockets and SNA CPIC (or APPC) are examples. If there is no available commercial products, then the development should be performed as system level modules and there should be careful management of the reuseability and abstraction level. There are other forms of interprocess communication that are less "message"-oriented and use a metaphor of streams, pipes, or such, but the basic idea remains the same.

Remote procedure call communication.   The remote procedure call (RPC) form of communication is a well-studied approach that builds upon the raw message form. RPC provides standard abstractions for most of the messaging mechanics layer. RPC provides some standardization at the communication act or intention level, by providing a standard "request/response" protocol. Because RPC approaches are fairly standard, data representation is managed well. This allows the message content level to be a separate and distinct level. Without this standardization, applications must assist in the message mechanics by performing data representation operations at the implementation level. RPC provides this capability partly through the use of interface definition language tools which we will not discuss here.

Nearly transparent distributed task management.   The next degree of sophistication is currently not wellstandardized. Two variations are important for business computing environments—transactional messaging and object request broker. In both cases, the message handling function provides fairly complete message handling transparency. The message handler has access to system data that allows the handler to completely hide implementation details. Participants register their name and other system information, such as their interface information and services offered. To communicate, the participants need only identify the type or name of the other participants and the delivery characteristics required.

The handler manages the relationship of the interacting components. The handler component may be implemented any number of ways. Consequently, the diagram does not depict the handler as a part of any specific component, but that it transparently performs the logical function.

This explanatory framework identifies an encapsulated behavioral layer that accounts for message exchange between components. Location, naming, reliability, and other design issues are handled transparently. Any particular implementation may achieve any of several levels of sophistication due to richness of abstraction and transparency of operation. Regardless of the level that we implement, we can assume that the communication is message-based, representation issues are managed, there is some degree of location transparency, and that delivery characteristics can be specified with some degree of transparency.

5.6.3   Distribution Substructure—Management of Communication Act and Content

Communication is more than just message passing. This section discusses several uses of messages that require specialized frameworks to manage the intent and content of messages.

Transparent access to relational databases.   One of the most common forms of Client/Server architecture is remote data access involving a relational database as shown in Figure 5.7. In this form most of the mechanics of messaging are handled transparently, typically by ordinary RPC mechanisms. This is shown as the message layer in Figure 5.7.

The other communication levels, however, have some fixed patterns that are handled at the remote data access (RDA) level and above. For example, to access data from a relational database, the requester may issue any of the commands in Table 5.1. The interaction between the requester and the database will involve exchanging information and re-

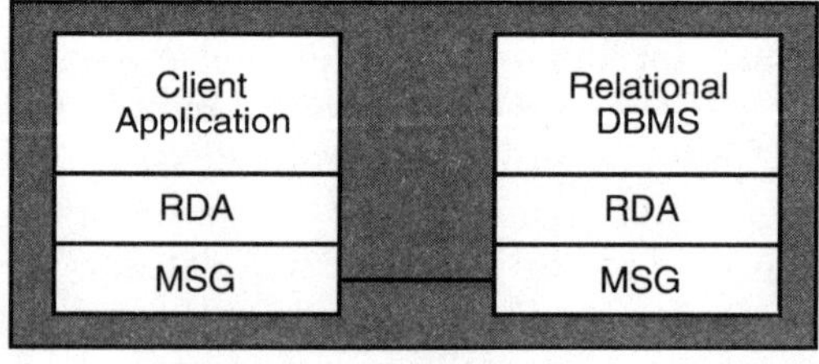

Figure 5.7   Access to a remote relational database.

Table 5.1   Some Typical Commands to Request Services from a Remote Database

Command	*Description*
connect	create a session
describe columns	query catalog about specified columns
execute SQL	prepare and execute an SQL statement
submit parameter	modify SQL-prepared statement
get next row	get values in next row
position at next row	reposition cursor to next row
execute RPC	invoke a remote procedure
commit	complete transaction by saving results
rollback	complete transaction by restoring original state
disconnect	terminate a session

acting in standard ways. For example, a major protocol that must be handled is passing tables of data. If a database contains millions of rows of data, the requesting application may not be able to manage the storage of all of those rows at once and not have the time to wait for such an operation. Therefore, there is a protocol to fetch rows in a systematic manner.

The SQL access group and others have established a basic process for SQL-oriented interfaces. The process can be quite complicated in some cases. For example, with dynamic SQL, the software does not know what data sources, tables, or attributes it must handle until run time. For example, until run time, the query may be in the form

SELECT X FROM Y WHERE W

Until run time, X may be any set of column names, Y is any set of table names, and W is any condition statement. Therefore, the software must set up a working environment at run time and query the data source to determine the size and type of data that the query refers to.

The remote data access (RDA) layer provides the capabilities to handle this aspect of the communication. The messaging layer, supporting the RDA layer, makes sure the messages are delivered. From an architecture point of view, we know that if these standard layers are provided, access to remote relational databases is relatively transparent. That is, applications can use remote and local databases in exactly the same way without having to cope with distribution issues.

There are a number of other common distributed processing forms for other types of communication acts and types of message content. For example, one form of services, distributed transaction management, specializes in managing the communication act or intention level of communication. It is shown in Figure 5.8(a). In this form of communication, the client signals his intention to conduct a series of actions that must be committed in whole or not at all. The transaction manager coordinates the actions of the multiple resource manager to guarantee basic syntactical integrity. We have more to say about distributed transaction management in section 5.6.10.

Another form of services, variously termed gateways, mediators, or information servers, shown in Figure 5.8(b), specializes in managing the message content layer of communication. This mediation component contains enough intelligence to translate raw forms of data into a

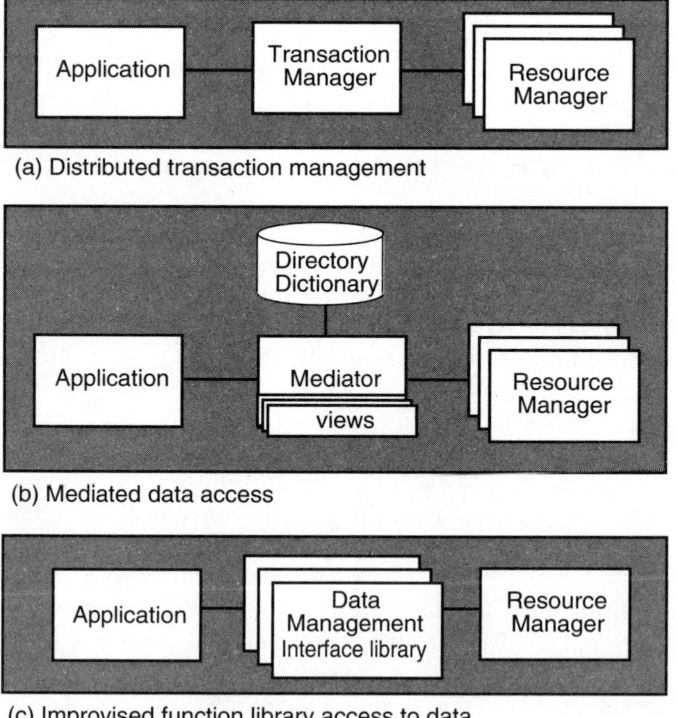

Figure 5.8   More distributed data services.

more abstract model. Refer to subsequent sections for more detail on this form of services.

Data management interface libraries, shown in Figure 5.8(c) are the needles, thread, scissors, and cloth level. Any of the forms of communication just discussed can be achieved with a library of functions. However, because of the custom fabrication, there is a high risk that the programmer will produce a legacy of poorly abstracted code.

5.6.4 Extended DBMSs

One direction to go to improve information management is to extend database management systems (DBMS). Recent advances along these lines are:

- DBMSs with stored procedures (constraints, triggers)
- Object-oriented DBMSs
- Distributed DBMSs

Databases are a means to centralize the definition and maintenance of data and to establish independence between applications and data. A distributed environment introduces a number of factors that exceed the capabilities of standard database to achieve centralization and independence. Several approaches have been offered to address these problems.

Stored procedures, shown in Figure 5.9, are a technique used by some databases (and are being addressed by ANSI standardization efforts) to relieve applications from some of the basic data operations, such as constraint management and triggered actions. Other DBMS extensions add other capabilities such as object management and distributed transaction management.

Distributed DBMSs. Highly specialized mechanisms can be used to provide high performance operation of distributed databases or file systems. However, there are no wide standards for such optimized mecha-

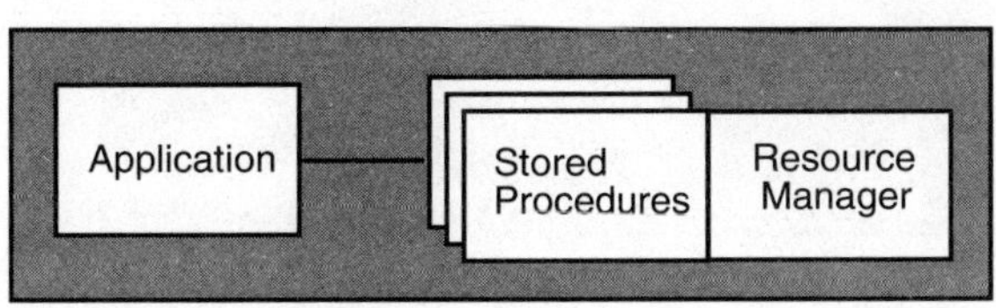

Figure 5.9   Stored procedures.

nisms. Consequently, if heterogeneous resource managers are a requirement, the architect cannot assume it is feasible to achieve transparent data distribution among diverse products. Electronic mail is a good example. There is more than enough motivation to interconnect various types of electronic mail managers. However, it has taken a very long time to establish standard interfaces. In the face of heterogeneity, gateway technology can be used.

Distributed DBMSs, shown in Figure 5.10, extend basic DBMSs specifically to accomplish integration where data operations are dispersed geographically. One critical function of a DBMS is to manage concurrent transactions (updates). However, transaction processing in a heterogeneous environment is an exceptionally difficult technical challenge. To compensate for that, distributed DBMSs require homogeneous system elements. Since the transition from legacy systems requires using preexisting data systems, we are faced with integration of mixed systems.

5.6.5   Data Gateways

Data gateways are a form of mediator, as shown in Figure 5.11. The term is adopted from data communications technology which distinguishes bridges and gateways. A bridge simply provides a connection between

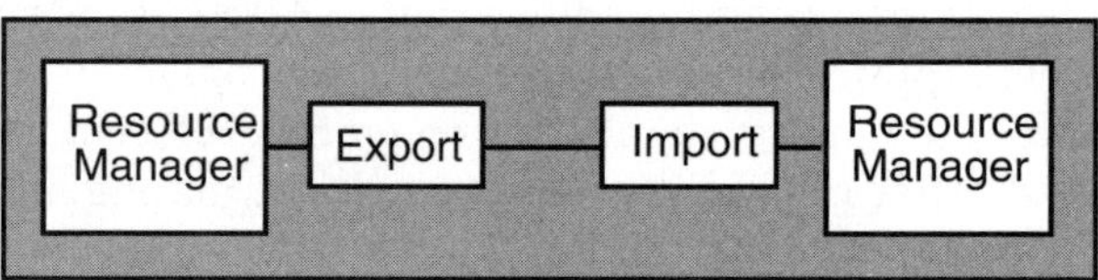

(a) Extract-oriented replication management

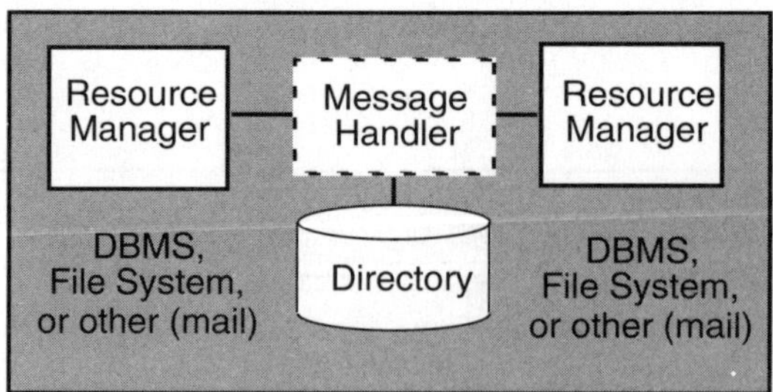

(b) Real-time, cache-oriented distributed data

Figure 5.10   Transparent data distribution among resource managers.

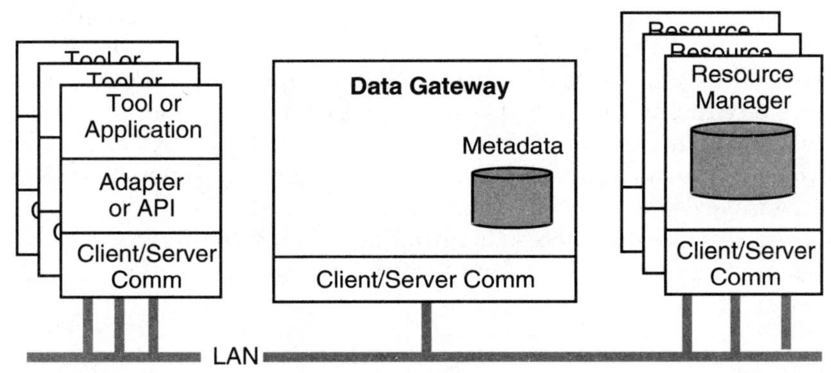

Figure 5.11   The data gateway.

networks supporting compatible communication protocols. Gateways, in data communications terminology, translate between incompatible protocols, such as between SNA and TCP/IP. Data gateways, then, are devices to adapt heterogeneous clients to servers. In their simple form, they are translators or they may simply absorb diversity in implementation details. In a more complex form, they may translate from one paradigm or data model to another. They can be viewed as "wrappers" that encapsulate either an incompatible data model or implementation approach. Simple data gateways perform the following services:

- Translate SQL dialect and data representations
- Standardize remote data access protocol (buffers, cursor management, dynamic SQL management, and variable bindings)
- Standardize Client/Server communication protocols
- Hide data source platform differences
- Use a directory to provide location transparency
- Provide access control and authentication mechanisms

Data gateways have the following characteristics:

- Normally limited to relational database paradigm (first normal form, unitary data values with no repeating groups)
- Provides a single database model to applications
- Provides static data abstraction and integration
- Provide relational/table view of nonrelational data
- Use SQL translators and storage system drivers

If the client is a commercial tool, then the interface must be standardized at the outset. If the client is a custom tool, then the programmer can accommodate various data source implementations. Standardization must take place along several fronts: SQL expression contents, data exchange environment and process, and data representation. ANSI SQL provides standardization for message content. SAG, ODBC, and ODAPI approaches provide standards for data exchange environment and process. Standards for data representation are mixed.

Other remote data access facilities are similar to this category such as remote file services including file transfer services and information retrieval.

5.6.6   Mediation

If applications are responsible for solving distribution design issues, then applications become excessively encumbered. In this section, we discuss the use of a mediating element of the architecture to uncouple applications from resources. Mediation, in this sense, is a further generalization of the concept of a gateway. In heterogeneous or distributed processing situations neither the data storage component nor the application can easily handle the encumbrances placed on them due to distribution design issues. The mediating element addresses three broad cases. First, whenever there is a source of diversity, a mediating element is needed to unify it. Second, to take advantage of the benefits of reuseability, a mediating element provides a source of common functionality. Third, a mediating element is required wherever a global view of the context is needed.

Unifying differences.   In a large-scale computing environment there are multiple application domains, storage systems, processor environments, software architectures, implementation details, data definitions, data models, and so on. Solutions used to match these sources of diversity can be interwoven within applications, thereby creating increased coupling between data and application. The mediating component of the architecture provides a mechanism to avoid this and thereby decouple application and data environment. Definition knowledge (that might reside in an online dictionary) can be used to rectify or ameliorate differences between related storage representations, whether between applications, applications and resources, or between resources.

Generic functions.   Functional information cannot always be represented declaratively in an effective way, but rather often must be captured in a procedure. Procedural components of data evolve into generic forms and should not be interwoven with application code. The mediation component of the architecture is the mechanism to implement generic procedures outside applications and resource managers.

Global visibility.   Neither applications nor resource managers have a broad view of the computing context. The mediation component can have global visibility and thus can perform a number of functions that require broad context knowledge.

A number of important functions can be performed depending on the available information. A mediation element is needed in many cases to achieve distribution transparency. Ideally, applications should not have to manage network communication and remote process invocation. The mediation component can use directory services and global data definitions to present an image of location transparency; that is, it shields applications from location dependencies. Similarly, where the mediation component has access to data view definitions, mediation can provide multiple views of data. The mediation service formulates views by aggregating and transforming data according to a generic data model. The mediation component can provide global optimization based on available performance objectives, constraints, and known variables. In general, the mediation component can use available policy definition to perform policy execution.

5.6.7   Co-Processing Using Gateway Technology

For most large-scale information systems the transition strategy requires an approach that allows incremental development and cut over. Also, in virtually any large business there will be a mix of information technologies used to manage company information. Sharing information in a changing and heterogeneous environment is always a challenge. Sharing information between centralized mainframe systems and distributed systems adds to the challenge for two reasons. First, the stored information in centralized mainframe systems is critical to the company, but is also buried behind a complex or an awkwardly built system. Second, distributed systems represent an era of rapid technology change that permanently keeps a company just a little behind the power curve.

In this section we describe a general system software architecture for incrementally adapting and coordinating old and new information technologies. This architecture builds on the fundamental data independence mechanisms described in Chapter 6. Although the approach applies to any two autonomous systems, we focus on bridging the gap between the typical mainframe legacy system and a distributed server-based system.

System access points versus service interfaces.   Legacy systems are composed of systems that are, to some extent, monolithic in structure; that is, they are poorly modularized. Whatever modularization exists tends to occur at a low level of abstraction. Definition of data is obscured in legacy applications rather than being available through service modules governed by metadata. Because well-defined service interfaces are not often available, access to legacy systems must often be achieved through several system-level access points as shown in Figure 5.13.

These access points also exist in a server-based system. However, by definition, access to a server occurs at a higher level of abstraction. Recall from our earlier discussion that access to a server is based on message exchange, supplemented by higher level services, such as standard remote data access or mediation. The quality of the mechanics of access and the definition of data are standard and well-defined in a server and, thus, are not at issue. By this definition, we say that access to a server occurs through a service interface. Certainly, a poorly designed or built distributed system is just as troublesome as a typical legacy system. In that case, we treat the server as if it were a mainframe legacy system.

Gateways. Sharing information between mismatched systems is accomplished through gateways. Gateways are service modules that mediate between other system components. Gateways not only insulate system components from changes, but also translate communications and thereby adapt components to one another. An important use of gateways is to lift the level of abstraction of a system access point to that of a service interface. Because of these properties, gateways provide a critical mechanism to change or upgrade the system one part at a time.

Brodie and Stonebraker identified two basic sorts of gateways—forward gateways and reverse gateways.[9] A forward gateway enables a legacy application to reach new data in a server environment. A reverse gateway enables a server to reach old data in a legacy system environment. Figure 5.12 shows both kinds of gateways.

Forward gateway.   A forward gateway is used for two main purposes. First, it can be used to propagate legacy system data updates to other systems. This can either be in (near) realtime or be in the form of batch extracts to be distributed to other systems. Batch extracts are commonly used in legacy systems, though they are not commonly called gateways.

A second purpose of a forward gateway is to redirect old applications to a new environment. This enables a legacy application to use the services of a new system to obtain or store data.

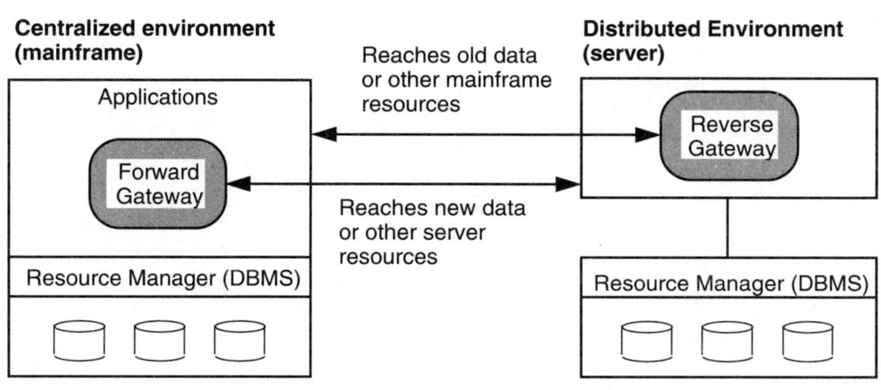

Figure 5.12   Forward and reverse gateways.

Reverse gateway. The reverse gateway enables server-based applications to gain access to legacy system data or applications. There are a number of possibilities. A data distributor process would use the reverse gateway to extract data from one or more legacy systems to be integrated and distributed to servers. This can be done in an online query or a batch mode. Batch mode allows important data integration efforts to be incorporated at build time. Refer to the section on metadata-driven integration for more detailed discussion of this approach.

Server applications can invoke legacy applications or procedures within function libraries on the mainframe for various purposes, such as using the possibly greater resource capacities on the mainframe or existing applications not available in the server environment.

Access points. Figure 5.13 shows the access points through which mainframes and servers can exchange information. These access points correspond to the following actions by a server:

- Submitting a query directly to a database
- Submitting a transaction through a transaction manager
- Submitting a batch job through the job control system
- Initiating an application procedure through a message-based service
- Initiating a system or utility procedure through a command interface

A mainframe accomplishes the same through a server's service interface. Mainframe technology is evolving to offer the kind of communication substructure available in a distributed server environment. Remote

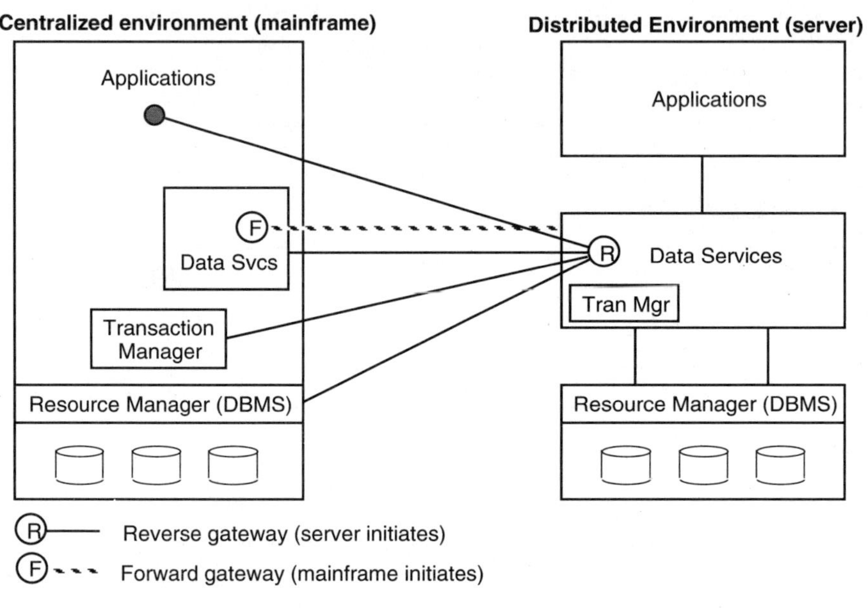

Figure 5.13   Access points for gateways.

procedure calls and other message-based communication are becoming available on the mainframe. Applications and data storage, however, remain in a more difficult form.

5.6.8   Replication Management

There are many reasons to reproduce data from one physical source and store it at another source. It improves availability, distributes the processor work load, and decreases dependence on centralized source operations, thereby providing increased autonomy. In order to share data among diverse data environments, data replication must combine with data conversion in order to make data compatible between or among the various environments. It is not unusual to extend the data conversion for the purpose of making data more useful. Chapter 6 discusses this form of replication as data regeneration. During regeneration, the underlying data model of the source data may undergo conversion. In the simplest case of data model conversion, the data structure is converted. For example, the hierarchical model of data in an IMS database may be converted from segments to relational tables of a relational database. In a more complicated case, transformations may be applied to convert low-level data records into more abstract data types that better resemble business objects.

The critical issue is guarantees of data consistency between copies. The data situation determines the requirements. Phone books, for example, are published at 6- or 12-month intervals. Users tolerate the lack of consistency because they can detect and tolerate occasions of invalid data and have recourse when necessary.

Theoretically, there are many approaches to manage replication, but only a few practical ways. Bulk copy is one approach, but not a very efficient one. Propagation, or store and forwarding, of changes as they occur is another more efficient way. Most approaches depend on the existence of a primary copy that is the authoritative version.

When managing against node failures, some approaches allow the primary copy to be reestablished at another node. Asynchronous replication is the case where updates are made to a primary version of data in a transaction manner and the updates are propagated to outlying resource managers. Queued transactions and possibly compensating transactions can be used to bring the remote data into synchronization. A distributed transaction manager could guarantee synchronous replication to guarantee full consistency, but that approach may be too severe since it essentially makes all participants dependent on the worst-case node.

Generally, replication management has the following process components:

- *Replica definition* provides the specifications that identify the mappings and transformations between the primary and secondary sources. The definition also specifies consistency requirements, often in the form of a schedule when to propagate updates or refresh the secondary source.
- *Replica creation* provides the initial loading of the secondary source or sources.
- *Replica currency* maintenance propagates updates to the secondary source to achieve consistency with the primary source.
- *Replication operations management* schedules and initiates replication processes. It also handles exceptions and failure recovery.

Replication management can be done with varying degrees of transparency depending on the level of abstraction with which the replication management can be specified and managed.

Three levels of replication unit can be considered. Ideally, replication should be specified by a conceptual unit. A conceptual unit is defined in terms of a conceptual view of the data, by definitions of entities, attributes, and relationships, and by definitions of conceptual constraints that form business rules. Commonly, however, replication is specified at a slightly lower level of abstraction. If the data is in a relational database environment, replicas can be specified in terms of tables, columns, or SQL queries. Table dependencies, key consistencies, and referential integrity may be specified. An SQL view may be specified. If the data is in an object-oriented environment, replicas may be specified in terms of data types. At the lowest level of abstraction, replicas may be specified in physical units such as records, record fields, or even bytes. Whole files or databases may be the unit of replication. Stored procedures may be specified as the unit of replication, though there is no general approach to manage this form of unit. Performance oriented units may be specified such as indexes or cluster definitions. Generally, the more procedural components there are in a replica specification, the less transparent the process, because of the lack of abstraction in procedural specifications.

Along with specifying data units to replicate, some consideration must be given to replicating administrative elements such as authorizations, accounts, and roles.

Recurrent replication is used to maintain consistency at the secondary data store. That is, according to a schedule or event, primary source data is recurrently propagated to refresh the replicated data. In small-scale situations where there is only megabytes of data to be propagated, it may be feasible to completely reload the secondary store. But, as the requirements scale up it becomes necessary to merely propagate changes. There are two main approaches to change propagation. If primary data store updates can be logged, then the log can be used to identify what must be propagated. If there is no log available, it may be necessary to use file-compare techniques to identify changes that need to be propagated.

Change propagation raises complex issues concerning maintaining data integrity. For example, a change to a customer database that deletes a customer when propagated can create referential integrity problems at the target data store.

Generally, replication of data across heterogeneous data environments is technically challenging.

When updates are being made from the remote site, there may be severe performance issues due to network communication bottlenecks. Ownership of the primary copy may need to be shifted dynamically to accommodate performance requirements. However, the management of shifting ownership is a technical challenge.

Other approaches to replication management must be considered.

For example, one approach is to fragment or partition the data source so that updates are less likely to affect multiple sites. Update conflicts and automatic resolution mechanisms may be an effective approach to balance performance trade-offs.

Since there are so many combinations of requirements, commercial technology is still a long way from providing many of the needed solutions. For basic situations, though, resource managers are developing more effective replication management mechanisms. Network file systems (NFS and AFS) have highly sophisticated built-in replication management. They are able to do so because they control the homogeneity of the environment or the narrowness of the requirements.

Replication management and transaction management have some overlap. Both guarantee consistency and integrity. Transaction management is more specifically aimed at consistency guarantees rather than providing increased availability through redundancy. Version management also is related to replication as consistency guarantees are relaxed.

5.6.9 Objects and Object Brokers

In the object-oriented programming framework, objects have two sides—interface and implementation. An object's interface is its public side. Objects use their private, implementation side to send messages to another object's interface. The object implementation is its behavior. Part of its behavior is to send messages to other objects that have publicly declared their interface.

Object programming standards[10] focus on two key aspects of object technology. Application-defined interfaces are written in a declarative interface definition language (IDL) that shields the intricacies of implementation. A compiler uses these interface definitions to generate interface stubs that perform such services as type checking and parameter handling. The second key aspect of standardized object technology is a set of system services that simplify programming tasks. A naming service provides a directory to convert object names to system addresses. The event notification service pushes and pulls events between objects who perform various roles, such as consumer, supplier, channel, or factory. The life cycle service creates, copies, removes, and otherwise manages the life of objects.

An object broker's job is to implement this interaction of objects (see Figure 5.14). The broker locates objects and dispatches requests to them. Whereas object-oriented programming has introduced important abstractions for information representation and behavior, the object broker concept introduces important concepts for certain forms of process management.

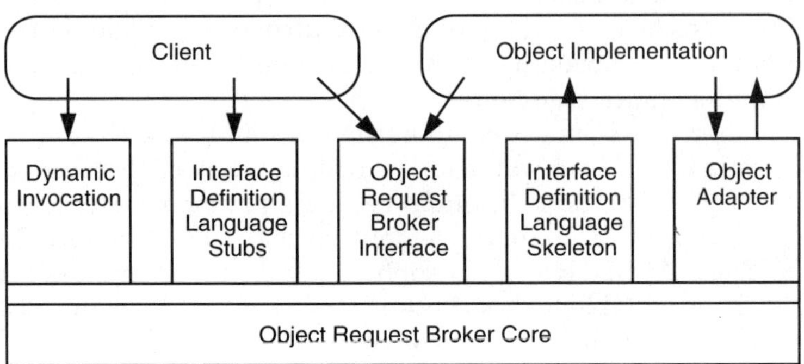

Figure 5.14   Object management is one example of general message handling.

5.6.10 Distributed Transaction Managers

If we step back and think of the purpose of databases and other stateful devices, they simply collect and share facts or states. When it becomes necessary to change the content of facts, there are a few basic phenomena that we intuitively expect to be managed. A completed change should persist. If multiple agents make changes, they should not inadvertently undo one another's changes. If multiple granules of a fact are changed, such as rows of multiple tables, they should not inadvertently become inconsistent because only part of the changes were made. Services that guarantee these characteristics of changes are called transaction managers.

Transaction management services are invoked by handing a transaction manager a bracketed "unit of work." The unit of work is bracketed by a "begin" indication to start the work and one of two indications to close the work. If invoker is satisfied that all work is satisfactory, the invoker tells the transaction manager to "commit" the work. If the invoker is not satisfied with the work, he tells the transaction manager to "abort" the unit of work. Then the transaction manager either makes the work permanent or undoes all interim changes. With a distributed transaction manager, the complexities of remote location and independent agents are transparent to the invoker.

To guarantee these characteristics of transactions, transaction managers must be able to recover from failures in the transaction, the server process, the processor node, or the storage media. When facts are distributed among multiple resource managers, additional sources of failure emerge. One of several resource managers can fail. The processor node hosting one resource manager can fail independently of other resource manager nodes. Communications between nodes can fail. Transaction management is the ability to manage the overall state of the various components involved. Distributed transaction management adds significant new complexity because there are more and different kinds of components to manage and types of failure from which to recover.

In a complex system it is natural to adopt a strategy in which simpler parts of the system are modernized and distributed first, before dealing with the more complex parts of the system. Query and report functions are simpler than transaction functions and, thus, are usually scheduled for transition first. However, one of the first "gotchas" in the transition is the attempt to transition query components without creating a negative impact on the transaction components. Thus, one of the most critical success factors in making the transition from legacy systems to a distributed architecture is graceful, incremental transition to distributed transaction processing.

In a distributed transaction processing environment, the distributed processing factors that are introduced, such as loose coupling, heterogeneity, and partial autonomy, have profound effects. These factors drastically increase the complexity of making changes. Because transaction processing is subtle and complex for all participants in the transition, we will introduce some of the key theoretical issues.

During the development of legacy systems, transaction functions were not only highly esoteric—known only to highly skilled developers—but also always tightly packaged and therefore quite invisible to users. In distributed systems, these functions should also be packaged and operate unobtrusively. However, loose coupling and heterogeneous vendor implementations introduce the additional degrees of freedom previously mentioned.

The resource manager is the basic system abstraction used to manage data in storage systems. The most common forms of a resource manager include file systems, database management systems (DBMSs), and other server applications, such as electronic mail or calendaring. A transaction manager is much like a resource manger except it manages resource managers instead of data storage systems.

Figure 5.15 shows a transaction manager managing a distributed transaction. For example, the application may be an office utility such as a calendaring or electronic mail. When a user schedules a group meeting, that person wants to be sure that any personal calendar update is consistent with an update to calendars on other workstations. Similarly, if a medical professional orders supplies from a pharmacy, the same information should be recorded on the patient's folder.

Let us look at a transaction processing system from several viewpoints.[11]

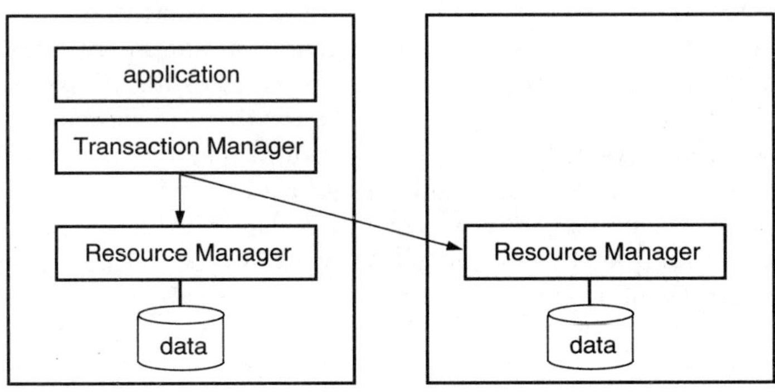

Figure 5.15   Transaction manager.

User's view. The user uses a set of menus and forms to select a transaction, then fills out the form, and finally submits the filled-out form. The user is unaware of the underlying actions occurring and unaware of others using the processing resources, except that waiting time may differ at different times. The user does not experience any unintended side effects due to system failures or other system behaviors.

Programmer's view. The programmer acts as if that program will be the only one executing during the transaction processing period. The programmer views the system as one logically centralized and local system. The data model is homogeneous. Locations appear local. System errors or exceptions are automatically handled. The programmer defines the scope of each transaction by bracketing a collection of actions with begin and commit or abort commands.

Designer's view. The designer of a transaction processing system views the system as many users concurrently operating on data resource managers. Transactions thread their way through specialized functions that lock resources, log events, control access, schedule resources, and so on. The designer views all data, processes, and events as types so that he is not concerned with the meaning of the data or operations on the data. The designer is concerned with differences in the implementation or the approach used by component products.

Operator's view. The operator is concerned with a collection of computing resources that include network nodes, users, communication equipment and lines, applications, storage devices, and recovery procedures.

In a general sense, a transaction is a collection of actions that change a state of affairs. Participants in the transaction have expectations concerning certain dimensions of this process. For example, the change should persist and not inadvertently disappear or inadvertently be modified.

In a conventional database system, transactions are expected to exhibit three fundamental properties[12]—atomicity, serializability, and permanence. These properties help manage problems due to concurrent access to common data and to failures that occur during processing. The first property, permanence, required to manage data changes is to make changes permanent or persistent. This is shown in Figure 5.16, column 1.

> *Permanence* is the property of the successfully completed transaction that assures that results of the actions are not lost. The results persist in the database until the next transaction.

Of course, this is the basic capability all data professionals expect of a data management system.

The second property, atomicity, is required whenever data changes are made to multiple data stores. The desired property is that if a change affects multiple data elements, then if the change occurs, it must occur for all elements or not occur at all. If a change is made successfully to one element and an attempt is made to change the second, but fails, then the first change must be undone to avoid an anomaly. This function is shown in column 2 of Figure 5.16.

> *Atomicity* is the property that guarantees that a collection of actions must be successfully completed or any partial effects, caused by interruption or failure, are undone. When all actions are successfully completed, the transaction can be committed. If not, the transaction is aborted.

The third property, serializability, is required whenever there are multiple agents changing the same data. For example, if agent A reads data x and performs some calculation based on x, and then writes a new value for data x, it is possible that another agent changes x between agent A's read and write actions. When this happens, agent B's change is inadvertently undone. This is often called the lost update. To prevent such anomalies, a concurrency control function is required to prevent interleaving independent actions as shown in column 3 of Figure 5.16.

> *Serializability,* in the database system context, is the property that allows multiple, concurrent operations on common data to happen as if they were done as a set of serial actions. This prevents two transactions from undoing one another's interme-

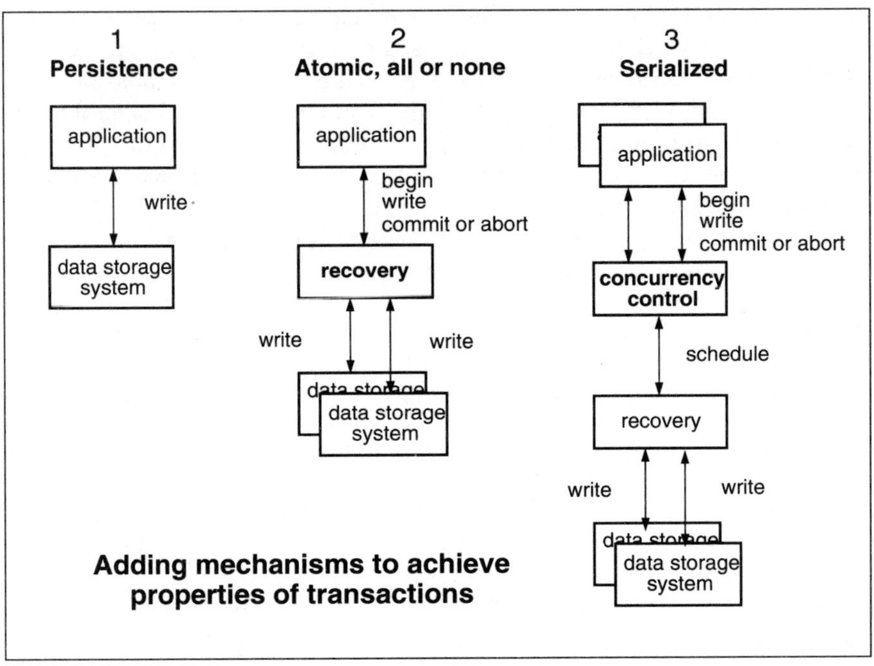

Figure 5.16   Mechanisms for transaction management.

diate results were they to interleave their actions. It also allows
a collection of actions to create a temporary inconsistent state
in the database. Serialization is a severe technique, but effectively provides isolation among concurrent transaction processes. In a distributed context, serializability is far too severe
for certain situations.

In a distributed processing environment, especially in a heterogeneous environment, these properties are extremely difficult to guarantee. Actions can be performed by processes executing on multiple
systems that use different approaches to guaranteeing transaction properties. For example, one system may use a locking protocol to assure
serializability, while another may use time stamps. The global transaction manager must be able to unify these differences to assure global
serializability. Or worse still, some of the component systems participating in a distributed transaction may not provide certain capabilities
to assure global properties. For example, some systems cannot partici-

pate in a two-phase commit because they cannot separate the prepare to commit and commit stages, or for that matter, if they can, they may not be able to communicate about the prepare stage.

Until recently, transaction management systems were said to exhibit four properties, often termed the ACID properties—atomicity, consistency, isolation, and durability. The previous model replaces consistency and isolation properties with a serializability property.

A data source is said to be consistent if the data contains no contradictions. Only some of the consistency can be controlled by a data resource manager—namely, where the data source manager has data descriptions that define the integrity constraints that the data must meet. The transaction manager contributes to consistency maintenance by controlling the effects of multiple concurrent operations on common data granules and the effects due to system failures.

Consistency is a complex issue. Assuring this property in a multidatabase environment often requires extreme restrictions on local database autonomy, including how and when operations are performed, what the design is, and how and when communications with other systems will occur. There are a number of dimensions along which a system may relax or alter requirements for consistency. Two such dimensions are:

> *Temporal consistency:* Two sources of data will eventually be made consistent. For example, a batch process may be used to bring a second data source up-to-date each morning. Design objects commonly require this form of consistency, whereby periodically two sources are merged and reconciled.
>
> *Partial data model consistency:* An object may be internally consistent, though multiple objects within the same overall model may not be.

The general distributed transaction manager model. The resource manager, as just described, needs a few additional capabilities to function in a distributed environment and a few more still to handle a wide variety of types of information, but it will remain the basic element. In order to function in a distributed environment, communications functions must be added.

We are in a position now to establish a general transaction model that identifies the basic functions required for all nodes on the network that will initiate transactions, as shown in Figure 5.17.

It is convenient to keep in mind two types of transaction management systems (see Figure 5.18). Type A is able to participate in a coordinated transaction that spans multiple environments. Type B operates very autonomously and simply executes basic commands with minimal coordination.

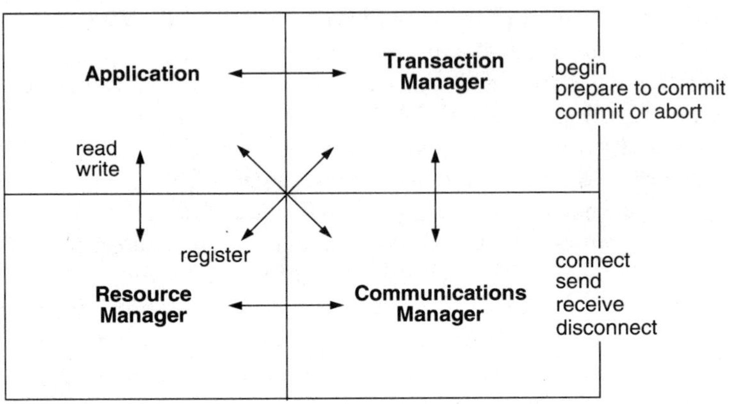

Figure 5.17   Basic distributed transaction functions.

Even with the limited built-in capabilities (or willingness) for global coordination, type B resource managers can still participate in global coordination. For example, compensating transactions can be used to reverse or correct a previous transaction.

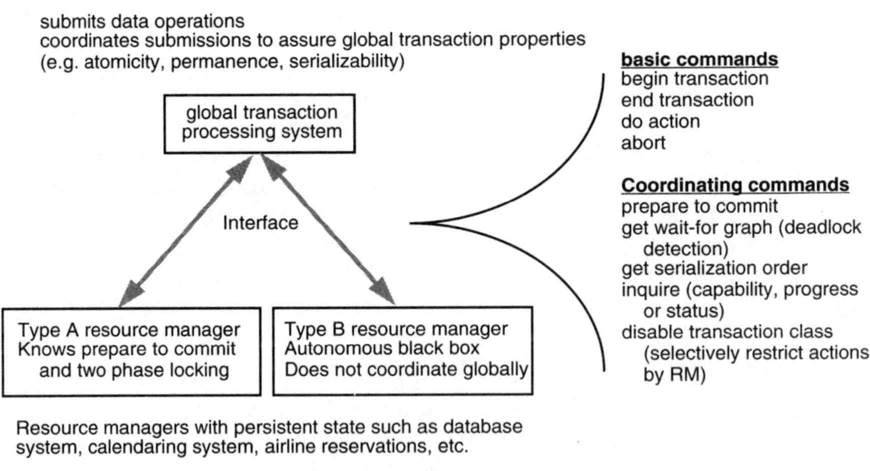

Figure 5.18   Coordinating resource managers.

5.6.11 Function Libraries

The evolution of computer science is keyed to the invention of abstractions. Software providers implement these abstractions. Over time, invented abstractions converge to standards. DBMSs, for example, package a collection of the more stable and standard abstractions for management of persistent data. The transition to distributed systems introduces additional requirements that DBMSs fail to cover.

It is easy for an end-user company to adapt the principle, "when all else fails, develop a software function." Legacy systems represent such a severe problem, partly because the abstraction development phase is undercut. When a standard abstraction is not available, the user company creates a custom function library to satisfy the requirement. Software procedures are developed that have limited abstract properties for various reasons such as lack of project funding, expertise, theoretical framework, or simply lack of time. However, in a distributed computing environment, new factors are introduced that make undisciplined function library development worse than the original legacy systems. For example, in distributed environments where processor environments are loosely coupled, there are many new sources of errors and failures, and the means to recover are much more complicated. There are many other factors to contend with including multiple name spaces, heterogeneous operating environments, mixed data definitions, and so on.

All software is ultimately a collection of function libraries. The issue is whether these functions implement a well-defined abstraction that satisfies a well-defined architecture. At any point in evolutionary time, this may be a tough question. For example, DBMS vendors currently recognize the need to provide mechanisms that ensure data integrity during updates. One approach for relational databases is to use stored procedures to define a set of actions to take to maintain data consistency whenever an update is made. The underlying abstraction is maintenance of conceptual objects. Yet stored procedures do not provide an object model. Consequently, development of stored procedures, as a vaguely defined function library, promises to become the next batch of legacy systems. Yet, without a well defined and implemented object model, the using company is faced either with doing without or with improvising a tailor-made function library.

5.6.12 Standards for Distribution Substructure

We have been describing services architectures primarily from an engineering perspective rather than a computational or programmer's perspective; that is, we have been describing major approaches and their key

Table 5.2   Prominent Standards Bodies for Distributed Computing

Acronym	Standards Group	Activity
COS	Corporation for Open Systems	Promotes OSI communications standards.
ECMA	European Computer Manufacturers Association	Promotes standards for interoperable computing systems.
IAB	Internet Activities Board	Internet standardization for TCP/IP and other standards.
OMG	Object Management Group	Develops and promotes standards and architectural framework for distributed object-based computing—Common Object Request Broker Architecture (CORBA).
OSF	Open Software Foundation	Promotes technology for distributing computing—Distributed Computing Environment (DCE) and Distributed Management Environment (DME).
SAG	SQL Access Group	Standards for SQL access to heterogeneous databases.
X Consortium	MIT X Consortium	Promotes X Window system.
X/OPEN	X/Open Company Ltd.	Coordinates development of a Common Applications Environment (CAE) for "practical implementation of open systems."

design parameters. From a computational perspective, there are many service functions and design issues not visible from the engineering perspective. Currently there are a number of operating system suppliers and computing standards bodies promoting several similar collections of service functions to achieve distributed computing.

Table 5.2 lists some of the prominent industrial standards groups. These sources provide and promote industry standards for such service functions as remote procedure calling (RPC), security, distributed file systems, directory services, and remote database access. The service architectures described in this section are based on these service functions.

CHAPTER NOTES

1. Schroeder, Michael D. "A State-of-the-Art Distributed System: Computing with BOB" in *Distributed Systems*. Sape Mullender, ed. New York: ACM Press, 1993.
2. Hughes, Keven. *Entering the World-Wide Web: A Guide to Cyberspace.* Unpublished White Paper. October 1993.
3. NFSnet statistics are available by FTP from nic.meeit.edu.
4. Hughes, Keven. *Entering the World-Wide Web: A Guide to Cyberspace.* Unpublished White Paper. October 1993.
5. McBride, James. "Before you ride the data highway, you'll need a set of wheels." *Inforworld* (July 25, 1994).
6. Hewitt, Carl, and Peter de Jong. *Open Systems*. Massachusetts Institute of Technology—Artificial Intelligence Lab AIM-691. 1982.
7. Law, Kincho H., et al. "Architecture for Managing Design Objects in a Sharable Relational Framework." *International Journal of Systems Automation: Research and Applications.* 1 (1991). Also see Smith, John Miles, and Diane C.P. Smith. "Database Abstractions: Aggregation and Generalization." *Readings in Artificial Intelligence and Databases.* John Mylopolous and Michael Brodie, eds. Morgan-Kaufmann, San Mateo, CA, 1989.
8. Sowa, John F. "Logic-Based Standards for the Conceptual Schema." *IBM CIM Colloquium on Standards and New Technologies.* February 1993.
9. Brodie, Michael L., and Michael Stonebraker. *DARWIN: On the Incremental Migration of Legacy Information Systems.* TR-0222-10-92-165.
10. Object Management Group. "Common Object Request Broker Architecture and Specifications." Document 91.12.1. Framingham, Mass. 1991.
11. Claybrook, Bill. *OLTP Online Transaction Processing Systems.* New York: John Wiley, 1992.
12. Spector, A. Z. "Distributed Transaction Processing Facilities" in Sape Mullender, ed. *Distributed Systems.* New York: ACM Press, 1989.

6

Cooperative Environment

"[most enterprises] . . . do not know how much they are spending on information, nor its business value. They have no metrics to help them understand what the value of integration may be."[1]

6.1 VISION

With the rapid proliferation of information technology resources and services, information technology is becoming commonplace. Individuals have computers at home that are more functional than the most expensive computer on the market was 20 years ago. Office, factory, and field workers are more and more likely to use a personal computer or workstation, which in turn is becoming functionally integrated into a suite of computing resources locally and even throughout the world. At restaurants, servers use hand-held devices to take orders. The device transmits the orders immediately to the kitchen and, at the same time, prepares the gathered information for other business purposes, including the meal payment, consumer statistics, and inventory. Express mail is managed from pick-up through delivery. Each item is given a serial number and can be tracked at any second, no matter where it is in its journey throughout the world. Manufacturing processes use information technology to configure a customer's product, design it, plan it, build it, deliver it, and so on.

As Chapter 3 pointed out, ironically there has been scant evidence that information technology, itself, has improved productivity. Thomas Davenport suggested the reason is related to the fact that information technology doesn't *implement a business process,* but that it *enables process innovation.* Thus, for information technology to make a difference, it is necessary to consider how information technology can help change the way business is done. The process orientation that is emerging in the business community changes the focus from narrow, local goals to business integration that achieves end-to-end goals. Therefore, in order for the transition to distributed information systems to enable process innovation, distributed information systems must be integrated to support a cooperative process. Consequently, the transition from legacy systems to a distributed environment means that cooperation must be built in to the conceptual framework. Several key concepts are critical for cooperative processing.

Federation is an approach in which computing systems can share information and information services despite heterogeneous and independent system elements. To support this arrangement, implementation details of information technology must not be embedded in the business process. That is, the workings of technology must be as transparent as possible to the business community. It should not be necessary to hold up the business community to reanalyze and recode software or reorganize stored data whenever users refine or modify their system of business obligations.

There is a range of objectives to strive for and methods to accomplish the objectives. For example, a fairly simple objective is to achieve location transparency to hide the complexities of finding and connecting to distributed resources. A good set of mechanisms that provide global naming capabilities goes a long way to achieving this objective. A much more complex and subtle objective is what we have called work-flow transparency. The concept is that in order to achieve broad integration across groups of business participants, information technology should work naturally within ordinary communication acts such as proposals, expectations, agreements, and work progress by individuals and groups assuming roles and responsibilities. Without this transparency, information must be treated like physical material to be manually transported and monitored to create a flow of work through a business process.

An objective that is examined in detail in this chapter concerns representational transparency. Information that is used to conduct business should be communicated and represented in a common framework. To achieve this objective, there are rather severe problems to overcome to achieve an integrated system.

6.2   THE SITUATION: MANY DEGREES OF FREEDOM

6.2.1   Autonomy

A fundamental property of a distributed system is that some or all of its components are separated physically; this separateness confers some amount of autonomy on the components. Autonomy manifests itself in any of several ways—design may be done independently, operations of the components may be managed independently, and components may independently determine the communications they engage in. Separated components form disjoint name spaces and naming issues become much more salient. Autonomous components may have heterogeneous implementations so that compatibility and interoperability issues become more important. Autonomous components can process in parallel which provides opportunities to design for increased availability, reliability, or throughput. Such benefits usually require trade-offs, however. For example, data can be replicated to improve its availability, but at the same time, it becomes more difficult to maintain consistency of distributed data.

6.2.2   Distribution

Various kinds of components can be physically separated: processor, application, data operation, and data mechanisms for data storage or data presentation. In a distributed architecture, at least some of the processors are separated and, thus, to some extent are autonomous. Application code, data manipulation code, and data mechanism code may or may not be separated from one another and, thus, to some extent is autonomous.

Wherever there are distributed components, there are general cases in which we either want to integrate separated components or divide integrated components. For example, data can be dispersed or collected by time, location, or form as shown in Figure 6.1.

With regard to data replication, there are several basic situations, each of which is analogous to well-known processes. For instance, in one situation where copies of centrally controlled data are distributed to remote sites, the process resembles a publishing process. Conversely, data from remote sites can be gathered into a central data store, such as forwarding point of sale transactions to a central repository.

For example, standardizing on relational databases in the business community has resulted in demand to perform ad hoc queries from desktop computers against production databases. Many users issuing queries

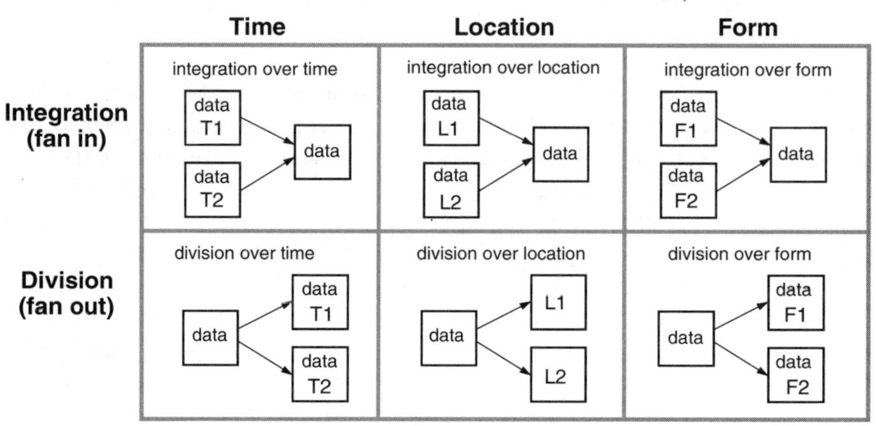

Figure 6.1   Various dispositions of data sources in the replication process.

against a relational database places high demands on processing resources. Commonly, production databases have to be shielded from un-
scheduled queries. This is not to mention the waste caused by similar
queries by different users that must be repeatedly processed. Because of
the relatively low cost of desktop or LAN server databases, a common
solution is to replicate the data from one or more production sources to
multiple remote sources. This corresponds to division over location as
shown in Figure 6.1. If multiple sources are provided, this would correspond to integration over location. In general, analysis processing will
often require all of these forms. The result is a data warehouse.

Data warehousing is a combination of these factors. Data is integrated over time, location, and form to create a database organized by
subject matter. Historical data may be appended to existing data (divided over time). Functionally grouped data may be divided over form
to create subject-oriented databases. The resulting data warehouse may
be divided among multiple sites for improved availability or autonomy.

Distribution of data may be replicated or copied along several dimensions. Data may be faithfully copied and distributed. Data may also be
partitioned so that the collection of molecular units (rows of a table) are
divided among multiple sites. Data may be fragmented so that molecular
units, themselves, are divided among multiple sites. These variations are
shown in Figure 6.2.

Component separation has a number of implications. First, of course,

Faithfully Replicated

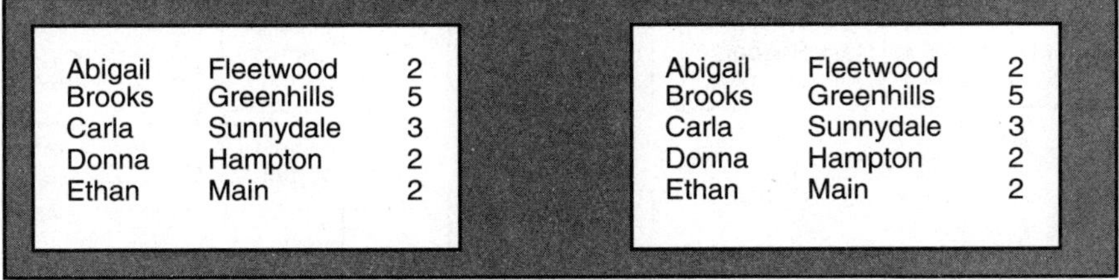

Partitioned - rows distributed

Fragmented - columns distributed

Figure 6.2   Ways to replicate data.

communications are affected because component coupling is loosened by the increased component autonomy and remoteness. Second, we must consider how to manage and integrate the various interactions among the autonomous components.

Data may be distributed by virtue of the separation of the service processor components distribution. Code components can be distributed among processors in various ways. Figure 6.3 illustrates some major variations regarding the kind of interaction among the service components. Separation and autonomy of the components are indicated by a jagged line in Figure 6.3.

In each case, one or more applications employ one or more resource managers (i.e., DBMS or file system). In the first case, the interaction is

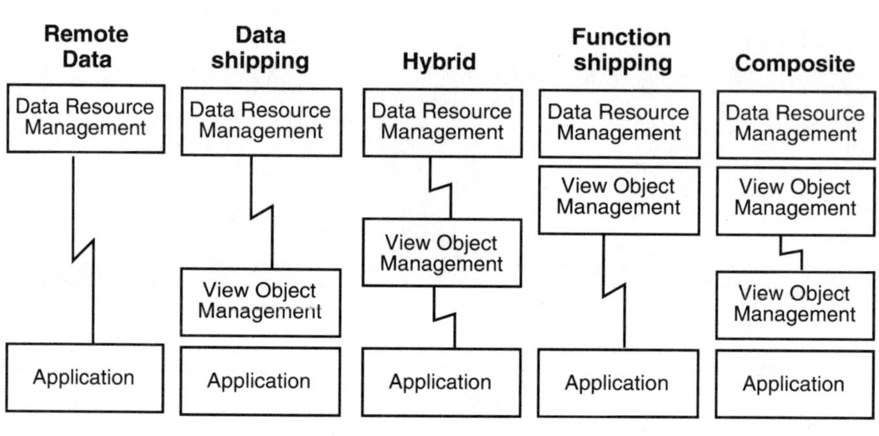

Figure 6.3   Varieties of data object distribution

direct. In the other cases, the interaction is mediated by a view object manager. A view object manager is a mediating service component that presents an image of data according to a particular perspective. In the case where operations are specific to the application, all relevant data must be shipped to the application site. In the case where operations are specific to the data, only result data is shipped to the application site; however, operations needed by the application must be made available to the data site.

The separation of application and view object modules is a relatively new approach. The original approach is illustrated in Figure 6.4. What is missing in Figure 6.4 is the mediating component that uncouples data resources from applications.

The difference between the architectures shown in Figures 6.3 and 6.4 is principally in the modular organization. In both cases data is physically separate from applications. Obviously, one wants to be able to share a data file without having to share all of the code that uses the file. However, code that interprets the data is reinvented in all of the applications in the module organization shown in Figure 6.4. That is a major characteristic of legacy system applications—simply reinventing data interpretation code. All the code that creates, interprets, reports, or otherwise operates on the data tends to be recreated in each monolithic application.

Of course, that means that the information is not only buried and obscure, but that it is redundant. Moreover, the more interpretation

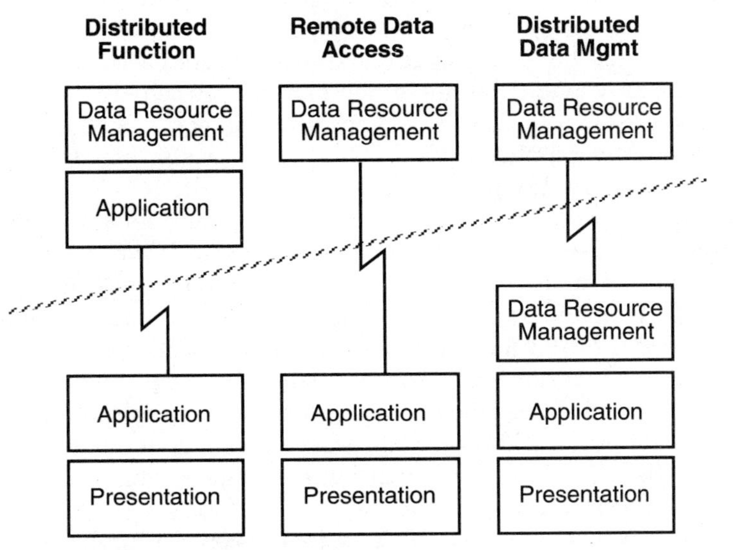

Figure 6.4   Variations of component distribution—more traditional view.

code the data requires, the more it is necessary to share the code that interprets the data. Commodity software does this, but with less worrisome consequences. A standardized version of the code can reside wherever the data is. Thus, for example, authors can electronically share text and graphics with the publisher because the author and the publisher have virtually identical text and graphics interpretation code that they share. Data and the code have different life cycles, but this works because of standardization.

The object-oriented programming community calls this phenomenon "encapsulation." The principle is that only the logical definition of data is exposed to the end user. The particulars of the implementation are hidden from view.

6.2.3   Babel

The rapid evolution of information technology has its downside in the form of not being able to share information because of the diversity in interoperation and information representation. Companies have acquired heterogeneous computing system components and have designed and configured the applications and databases with great diversity.

Because computers have become inexpensive, many new applications are on the market, and easy-to-use code development tools are available, companies have deployed computing systems throughout their operations. However, they have done so in a piecemeal fashion. Each functional area of a company has specialized needs. Consequently, each acquires computing platforms, applications, databases, and so on that are effective for that department or task.

A second source of heterogeneity that has become a problem is the definition and representation of the information that computing systems process. This diversity permeates information systems from the bottom up. At the heart of the issue is that there are weak standards for representing information. Standards are better defined at lower levels of system organization and progressively weaken at higher levels. At the lower levels there is a body of information representation standards based on primitives and basic concepts that all applications use. At the higher levels, the body of information concepts are more complex and more highly differentiated.

Computing technology and the sciences concerning linguistics, information, and cognition have less mature mechanisms and principles to apply at the higher levels of system organization.

Information representation issues can be classified according to levels of linguistic organization. In the following we list commonly encountered representational conflicts among diverse systems from a linguistic perspective. At the lowest level there is an encoding approach that provides a formal scheme to symbolize data. We will not address these issues here, except to say that computing platforms do have a few significant heterogeneity issues concerning such things as the representation of floating point numbers and multicharacter alphabets such as Japanese Kanji. *Lexical* and vocabulary information defines how to parse and identify individual data items. *Syntactic* information defines well-formed expressions or structures. *Semantic* information associates expressions or structures to a model of the world.

Lexical Diversity

- Domain or data type representation mismatch: dates and times—e.g., Jan 1 versus 1/1.
- Data type mismatch: padded fixed-length string versus token with maximum length. String delimited by a terminator versus string indicated by begin point plus length. Integer in one system versus character string in another.
- Encoding vocabulary: Blue = 1, Red = 2, etc.
- Lexical item delimiters—spaces, dashes, underscores, brackets.

- Field embedded in text: "Use model part number 2TX33Y for outside environments."

Syntactical Diversity

- Data model mismatch: The same data can be represented as a table structure or a tree structure. Unstructured versus structured—e.g., person name versus last, first, and middle names.
- Format mismatch—right- or left-justified field, year/day/month versus year/month/day.

Semantic Diversity

- Naming mismatch: synonyms and aliases—same object, multiple names. Homonyms and multiple contexts—multiple objects, same name. Qualified names versus qualification determined by context—e.g., Contract Tool Order versus Order. Abbreviations. Long descriptive names versus short names.
- Domain classification mismatch: employee (does it include retirees and/or consultants?).
- Domain scale mismatch: unit of measure differences—dollars versus francs; inches versus centimeters.
- Domain semantics mismatch: Postal code covers many places versus town name has multiple codes.
- Schema mismatch: husband and wife versus spouse and gender. One database may have one table with shares traded and date as columns. Another may have many tables, shares traded on each date.
- Aggregation mismatch: monthly versus annual salary, personal income versus family income.
- Dependency mismatch: Does date completed refer to an order or the part fabricated against the order?
- Identifier or key conflict: *Alan Turing: The Enigma* (for the reader) versus QA29.T8H63 (for the librarian) Is an order identified by an order number or by customer name and order date? In a larger context, order number may not be unique and have to be qualified by date or part number or such.
- Nulls: Does a null data value mean don't care or the data is not available? Null default ambiguity—binary, zero, blank.
- Timing dependency: e.g., before or after today's posting; proposed price, offered price, closing price.
- Authority mismatch: draft, formal release.
- Abstract data type mismatch: A date field must be a valid date to the database in one system, but is user controlled in another system.

There are a variety of ways to characterize information heterogeneity. For example, William Kent focused on what he called domain mismatch and schema mismatch.[2] He defines domain mismatch as treating some common conceptual territory, such as a unit of measure, in different ways. Here he seems to be referring to data values. Schema mismatch is treating some common conceptual territory in different ways when the mismatch concerns schema or structural components of definitions. He acknowledges other mismatch problems, such as naming.

These sorts of problems are encountered when integrating data from diverse systems because data definitions, or metadata (1) has a limited formal basis, (2) has few standards, and (3) is not openly available outside the original definition source.

6.3   FEDERATION

Federation is an architectural approach to information technology based on loosely coupled, autonomous systems that agree to share data and services. This approach is intended to enable cooperative relationships and processing among system components, while preserving local autonomy.

The effective interoperation of the components of a distributed system cannot be guaranteed by centralizing operational policy and standardizing technical and administrative elements. Distributed systems are not amenable to close central control. Besides, business trends are leaning away from centralized operational control, preferring instead to rely on centralized policies concerning business objectives.

Practically speaking, a collection of information systems cannot have a homogeneous design. Technology changes over time, yet only some elements of a distributed architecture incorporate a given change. Elements of the system will be administered in a variety of ways. There will be a variety of standards and products deployed. Business organizational structures that develop and manage distributed systems change over time. This means that authority and accountability relationships change. Consequently, policies that control funding, design, standards, and administration change. In short, distributed systems cannot be expected to be homogeneous in design, organization, or operations. "Instead there will be a vast number of potential resources and services, and an open heterogeneous community of service providers and users distributed over numerous components, belonging to a variety of interconnected subnets and organizational domains."[3]

The open distributed processing model defines a number of federation principles of accord to enable cooperation and sharing while not preventing some degree of local autonomy.[4] This model acknowledges the need to use elements in a found state, and promotes a means for ongoing efforts to unify elements of the system.

- *Voluntary Actions.* External authorities do not force a component to perform an action for another component.
- *Voluntary Sharing.* Each component determines what information or service it will share and what interface it provides to do so.
- *Autonomous Data Models.* No global information data model is imposed on individual components.
- *Contractual Arrangements.* Cooperation, interoperation, and integrity are established by contracts that establish agreed-upon obligations.
- *Freedom of Association.* As long as a component abides by its obligations, it is free to enter or leave a federation. Similarly, within bounds of its contracts, a component can modify its interface by adding or removing functions.

Experience has shown that the need for autonomy among the groups and systems within an organization is real; yet, the need to be able to interact and share information and resources is also real.

The primary method to establish a cooperative framework is the use of contracts. The concept of contracts has gained increasing importance in computing science. A contract is a specification applicable to a client of an operation and an implementation of that operation and entails benefits as well as obligations. A contract is specified in terms of conditions that hold independent of any operations (e.g., the semantic model describing the objects and context), preconditions that the client satisfies, and post-conditions that the supplier or implementer satisfies.

Federation elements can be described from various perspectives. From the enterprise perspective, contracts are ordinary business contracts. The policies that govern the release of product designs is an example of a contractual arrangement. Just-in-time inventory management is based on a contractual arrangement in which assembly parts are supplied when the assembly team runs out of parts.

From an information perspective, naming standards serves to enable parts of a system to cooperate with other system parts. Public metadata, in general, represents that information participants are willing to share and the contractual form in which it can be shared. Businesses sometimes classify information into private, shared, and release status to indicate the contractual basis for sharing information. Private information is restricted to an individual or closed working group and has no implications that it is meaningful, safe, or otherwise sharable. Shared information is information that is available to a set of working groups, but is not deemed formally released. Released information is formally approved for public use and meets some established standard of formality.

From a computational perspective, federation can be achieved by formally specifying and publishing software interface contracts. For example, interface contracts are specified in terms of their encoding type, signature, and semantics.

From an engineering perspective, federation is served by gateways or interceptor objects that encapsulate heterogeneous implementations. That is, gateways may translate between a standard interface and a proprietary interface.

From a technology perspective, standards may be specified for user interface or database products in order to enable cooperation among services.

6.4   DISTRIBUTION TRANSPARENCY

In 1987 the ANSA project defined the essential characteristics of distributed systems in terms of separation of components and transparency engineering objectives to achieve system management and integration. ANSA identified a number of forms of distribution transparencies as described in the following sections.

6.4.1   Location

Location transparency provides consistent appearance and behavior independent of the location of data storage, processor, and other mechanisms. For example, logical names are used to refer to services and objects rather than implementation-specific names. Naming Services uses a directory to provide such a level of indirection so that, for example, implementation specifics can be changed during maintenance or selection of an alternate resource instance without impact on the user. A more sophisticated model is necessary to select among alternate resources where performance parameters (size, speed, etc.) affect operations. In this case, the directory would need to contain the necessary information to make choices for each situation.

At the level of software design, location transparency is a relatively complex issue. Naming has to provide equivalent service handles for both local and remote identities across a potentially heterogeneous environment where domain, host, and network protocol standards differ.

At the user level, location transparency is a highly valued service. Even if the service must be cobbled together, it is likely worth the price.

Experience has shown that when users can be shown a data model and merely have to point and click at the data name to retrieve the information, they are quite pleased with the service. This holds true for other services such as print or World-Wide Web information retrieval.

6.4.2   Access

Access transparency enables local and remote objects and services to be accessed using identical access operations. This property is provided by such abstractions and mechanisms as a three-schema architecture, dictionary, mediators and gateways, data abstraction, Client/Server distribution model.

However, there are host of problems to overcome to provide this property. For example, it is not uncommon for a company to put a "fire wall" up at external interfaces. A fire wall is a host processor that blocks unauthorized external network traffic from accessing company resources. It also may have the effect of blocking internal users from gaining external access. Internal users may need to acquire an account on the fire wall host to be authorized and then may need to invoke additional operations when their access crosses that boundary.

Heterogeneous database systems also have a large potential to require diverse operations to retrieve data. Even though SQL is a standard relational database query language, each relational database supplier implements variations and extensions that may not be encapsulated by service layers.

6.4.3   Failure

Failure transparency enables the concealment of faults. Faults may be due to defects in the service or application software on the client or server, the operating system or hardware of the associated platforms, the network, or network interface. Failure can be caused by convergence of operational conditions such as when high contention for resources causes a time-out (where a system element quits waiting for a non-responding communication partner after a set period of time). To be failure transparent, distributed systems must have independent failures where the system keeps going despite a component failure.

Other characteristics of a failure transparent system include the following: the system provides self-corrective system actions; computing failures are undone or repaired without requiring user intervention; and all-or-none semantics are deployed where appropriate. For example, if a mail message is sent and there is an error during transmission, all-or-none semantics guarantees that the whole message is delivered intact or it is not delivered all. Mechanisms to achieve failure transparency include transaction protocols, reliable store and forward messaging, recovery procedures, and exception handling procedures.

Failure transparency in a distributed system is an intricate problem. Design issues from a computational perspective are out of scope here. However, assuming that a company's approach to deploying systems is to integrate off-the-shelf products, then one of the company's concerns is validating a system's ability to handle failure. From that point of view, the systems engineer should be aware of failure models commonly cited in the technical literature. Schneider identifies the following models with the assumption that "A reasonable abstraction for a processor in a distributed system is an object that sends and receives messages."[5]

Failstop	Processor fails by halting and remains in that state. Failure is detectable by other processors.
Crash	Processor fails by halting and remains in that state. Failure may not be detectable by other processors.
Crash+Link	Processor fails by halting and remains in that state. A communication link loses messages, but does not delay, duplicate, or corrupt them.
Receive Omission	Processor failure due to any previous conditions or to receiving only a subset of sent messages.
Send Omission	Processor failure due to any previous conditions or by sending only a subset of messages intended.
General Omission	Any of the preceding failures.
Byzantine Failure	Failure by performing arbitrary or malicious behavior.

One of the key questions that the systems integrator must ask is "how are partial (or independent) failures handled?" Partial failures are those where a system component fails while the rest of the system continues and the failed component later may recover to resume processing. Partial failures create indeterminacy so that it may be difficult to determine if the system is in a consistent state following a failure. The distributed system has no central resource allocator or monitor that is able to guarantee a correct interpretation of partial failures.

This and other immensely more complex issues that arise in distributed systems have led some individuals to be skeptical whether it is possible or even reasonable to achieve distribution transparency.*

6.4.4 Scaling

Scaling transparency allows performance characteristics to be maintained despite changing system load. With this transparency quality a system can be sized according to site requirements at proportional costs.

When processing power is a key factor, it may be possible to provide this characteristic with software that is portable to multiple processor platforms or with built-in parallelism to allow incremental processor sizing. In other cases, the services, data storage, or network may need to be structured for a variety of performance loads.

For example, data analysis processing places exceptionally large demands on data access and host processor power. To overcome this, decision-support systems perform a number of tactics. First, data is usually replicated from an operational host to a local analysis host to avoid draining the operational host processing cycles. Second, data is highly indexed to minimize sequential search. Third, copies of the data may be organized in several ways to keep it physically clustered. This minimizes the number of separate reads of the physical database.

6.4.5 Replication

Replication transparency ensures that the viewing and operating characteristics of copied data are consistent with original data within declared limits. This effectively improves availability of data and management of resource loads. Mechanisms to achieve this characteristic include propagation of updates and cache currency control. Currency is relative. Users are willing to live within stable and known limits of data staleness. Effectiveness of less than total transparency depends on the type of data and the user's inherent ability to recognize and compensate for errors and on the consequences of errors. Getting the wrong phone number is not too bad. Getting the wrong bank balance is more serious.

---

*For a pessimistic view of transparency see the unpublished white paper by Jim Waldo, Geoff Wyant, Ann Wollrath, and Sam Kendall, "A Note on Distributed Computing." For a sober and balanced comparison of the relative pros and cons of centralized versus distributed computing see Michael D. Schroeder, "A State-of-the-Art Distributed System: Computing with BOB," in Sape Mullender (ed.) *Distributed Systems*. Second Edition. New York: ACM Press, 1993.

Refer to Chapter 5 for a fuller discussion of replication issues. The end of this chapter also discusses replication management.

6.4.6 Migration

Migration transparency allows objects and services to change location without visibility to the user. Dynamic mechanisms such as late binding of names and parameters provide this capability.

6.4.7 Concurrency

Concurrency transparency allows multiple users to operate on the same granule of data without mutual interference. Transaction management protocols based on locks and time stamps provide this characteristic for simple and small transactions. Complex transactions that occur over a long period of time (e.g., authoring of design and planning documents) require more elaborate mechanisms. Long transactions that cover hours, days, or longer are often handled by a check-out/check-in process which uses multiple versions of objects to manage interfering effects of multiple authors. This procedure requires a conflict detection and resolution process to merge versions to complete the concurrent process.

6.4.8 Representation

This form of transparency is an addition to the commonly considered forms described previously. Representational transparency conceals differences in language use and information definitions. Several levels of representation are affected. Representation issues are so much at the heart of every interaction that standards are critical. Where there is a lack of standards, translation or conversion mechanism extracts a high processing price.

At the lowest level, encoding differences appear as different ways of representing characters and numbers. Standards such as ASCII character set, Abstract Syntax Notation, and other less broadly standard encoding standards are used. Special situations still cause common problems such as the representation of floating point numbers.

Syntactic standards are much less standardized. Low-level system services are usually fairly consistent within a given operating system. Higher level system services such as RPC mechanisms, user interface mechanisms, and database mechanisms have established certain syntactic standards within a given framework. The X-Window user interface and SQL relational database frameworks have a fairly standardized syntax. SGML is an example of a standardized syntactic framework for document markup language.

Semantic standards are practically nonexistent and will be discussed in a separate section below. Semantic issues, themselves, appear at multiple levels of system organization. X-Windows has a well-defined framework for window display object semantics. Spreadsheets or word processors, at a higher level of system organization, have a less standardized semantic framework. Electronic data interchange (EDI), at an even higher level of system organization, has some standardization of business object semantics pertaining to purchase orders, for example. Product definition standards are emerging from international standards organizations such as STEP. The Ontolingua project is developing ontologies for various subject domains. These ontologies are highly formalized definitions of the terms and concepts for a particular subject. Eventually, such ontologies may form a basis for semantic standards.

6.4.9   Work Flow

This form of transparency is an addition to the commonly considered forms just described and is somewhat futuristic. A recently emerging framework has begun to identify what might be called work-flow transparency. Research is beginning to show the need for information technology to work naturally within ordinary communication acts such as proposals, expectations, agreements, and work progress.[6] The concepts are taken from a branch of linguistics that identifies what are called speech acts. Speech acts are actions that are manifest by virtue of a social framework, not necessarily by virtue of mechanical movement. A classic example is the speech action of a judge pronouncing a sentence. By sentencing an offender, the judge performs an action. Any particular physical action accompanying the speech act is not at issue. Work flow should be supported along these lines. Information should not be treated like physical material that must be manually transported and monitored to create a flow of work through a business process. Instead of users manually managing the flow of work by routing and distributing documents, the various proposals, agreements, work progress, and so on should simply be part of the information fabric. Documents should be routed automatically depending on rules that define roles, responsibilities, and group membership. Documents not meeting expectations should appear in in-baskets of the originator for rework without manual intervention.

This form of transparency could be partially implemented by a paradigm invented by artificial intelligence researchers called blackboard architecture. In the blackboard architecture there are agents who attend to changing information in an information space shared by all agents. Each time information appears that an agent can use to combine with other information to form an inference, it does so and posts the new information to the shared space. This in turn makes it possible for another agent to continue the process, and so on. In addition to the blackboard architecture which provides certain information flow transparencies, additional mechanisms would need to be added to cover speech act concepts.

6.5 MAJOR AREAS OF INTEGRATION

The federation approach allows an adjustable balance between autonomy and interdependence. Distribution transparency objectives represent an engineering perspective aimed at hiding implementation complexities. Another architectural concern is to create integrated systems from multiple perspectives and to achieve integration at multiple levels of system organization. For each of the system viewpoints we have been using and at various levels, there are particular integration objectives and methods to be applied.

There is only a small body of literature and experience developing a comprehensive framework to achieve a broadly based set of information system architectural objectives.[7] There is, however, a rapidly growing body of information for parts of an overall framework. Table 6.1 suggests the scope and sorts of concepts that need to be organized into an overall framework. Any given major integration effort should attempt to formalize system architecture and design to cover the entire matrix. The rows of the matrix do not represent fixed partitions of the levels of system organization, so the formalization of the matrix, itself, should not be taken too seriously.

The examples are oriented by columns so that the examples are related at different levels of system organization (creating an example that is oriented by rows or both rows and columns and is left as a proverbial exercise for the reader). For example, from an enterprise point of view, a business objective may be to establish a general policy on the quality of service for which the collection of information systems must strive. A generic concept that applies to business policy concerning system management is the concept of a domain. Sloman defines a domain as "... an object which represents a collection of managed objects which have been explicitly grouped together for a purpose i.e., to which a common management policy applies."[8] For example, an access rule would specify a domain of managers, a domain of managed objects, and a set of opera-

Table 6.1   Suggestive Examples of Information Technology Integration Objectives

Level of System organization	Perspective				
	Enterprise	*Information*	*Computation*	*Engineering*	*Technology*
Business	Quality of Service Policy	Federated Data Definitions	Frameworks Patterned to Match Problem	Integrated Information Systems	Open Systems Standards
Generic Concepts	System Management Domain	Semantic Integration	Computing Frameworks	Data Independence	Relational Data Model
Basic Concepts	User Account for System Management	Conceptual Models and Database Organization	Object-oriented Discipline	Mediator as Independence Mechanism	SQL as Database Language Standard
Primitive Concepts	Access Control List	Database Schema and System Catalog	RPC as Communication Protocol	Modular Design	Database as Persistence Mechanism

tions that managers can perform on the objects. At the next level down, a system administrator for a department can set up accounts for users in that department. At the systems internal level, an access control list is used to authenticate users who log in to their accounts.

Since the transparencies discussion in a previous section covered the engineering perspective, the following sections explore integration objectives and approaches with more emphasis on the information and computational viewpoints and touch on several of the rows and columns in Table 6.1.

6.6   SEMANTIC INTEGRATION

The first principle of effective exchange of information is the use of a shared set of semantic and syntactic rules. This is the *Helsinki Principle* paraphrased as follows:

> A meaningful exchange of information depends on the existence of an agreed upon set of semantic and syntactic rules. Use of those rules to interpret exchanged information provides the basis for shared meaning.[9]

Because federation principles respect autonomy in its various forms, heterogeneity in the form and meaning of data presents one of the most severe challenges to information integration. In a previous section, a list of typical differences in the meaning and form of data in different information systems was presented.

We can distinguish between semantic reconciliation issues and semantic relativism issues. Semantic relativism acknowledges that users view and operate on data differently, depending on their context and problem-solving requirements. This is the "fit for purpose" dimension discussed in Chapter 4. To accommodate semantic relativism, it is necessary to provide services that present different views of the same information. Semantic reconciliation concerns the resolution of conflicts in the way that information is represented. This issue concerns the "function" dimension of information discussed in Chapter 4. For example, a representational conflict exists if two items of information that represent the same facts are based on two different representational models. A factual conflict may exist when two sources of information have different items of information about the same situation in that the information may be incompatible.

To achieve integration with respect to representational conflict, it is necessary to go through several steps. First, the form and meaning of the data in the systems to be integrated must be represented. That is, a model, expressed as metadata, must be created that describes the meaning and form of the data. Second, discrepancies in the representation must be detected. Third, discrepancies must be reconciled.

One increasingly common approach being used is enterprise data modeling in which the data for the entire enterprise is modeled. For large companies, this is an enormous task to perform. A large part of the understanding of the data exists either in the minds of domain experts or in application or report writer software. Formally modeling the enterprise data is time-consuming. Large organizations will often find that there are from 10,000 to 100,000 data elements stored in databases. One study reported ". . . an average of four hours per data element to extract and document data semantics when the task must be performed by someone other than the data owner."[10] That calculates to 20 to 200 person-years labor for medium- to large-sized businesses.

There are two key strategies to manage the scale of this task. The first is to apply data abstraction methods and tools. The second is to narrow the scope and focus on data that has been prioritized to meet some objective. Earlier, we recounted the story of one company whose business objective was to integrate a world-wide system of inventory operations. After many failed attempts, a solution was found when the company defined a subset of their data that needed to be shared for purposes of coordinating inventory operations. Another company narrowed the scope by focusing on key new commercial application packages being brought into the company to help reengineer the business processes. This company used the applications to "pull" the data by selecting only that data that the new applications needed.

Semantic integration issues occur whenever there is heterogeneity in representation or other information service dimensions. This can exist within a single application, a single database, a single host environment, or among a collection of environments. The transition to a distributed environment intensifies the problem since there is a greater opportunity for heterogeneity. In a later section an approach and an example are applied to this problem.

Architectural solutions to achieve representational transparency can range from tightly coupled to loosely coupled federations. A tightly coupled federation integrates data by providing a common definition framework, such as a database schema for most, if not all, available data. A loosely coupled federation integrates by defining a selected subset of data to be shared. Either approach may implement the definitions by structuring data in a common way or by using mediating services that reconstruct data view dynamically. The trade-offs weigh costs of dynamic transformation against structural rigidity. Both approaches are probably required to some degree.

6.6.1   Data Independence

The typical legacy information system is organized around departmental functions. Each function is supported by applications built specifically for those departments. However, important information and knowledge are shared across functional divisions, as shown in Figure 6.5, particularly as a company becomes more process-oriented. Organizational function and data are orthogonal. To exchange data among the functions, departments must have a shared basis in knowledge. The information systems must be designed accordingly.

William Smith provides a telling analogy. Grocery stores do not organize their goods according to the way the goods are to be used, that is by recipe. If they were to do so they would have sections for goods to make spaghetti, meatloaf, and barbecues. Each section would have its own hamburger, some a day old, some a week old. The spaghetti section would be managed by the Italian manager who has a pasta line manager reporting to him. Inventory control would be outrageous. Yet, this is the way that legacy information systems are organized.

Twenty years ago it seemed that database systems would provide this independence between function and data, as indicated in the presentation quoted below:

> A significant change in the computer field in the last five to eight years has been made in the way we treat and handle data. In the early days of our field, data was intimately tied to the application programs that used it. Now we see that we want to break that tie. We want data that is independent of the applica-

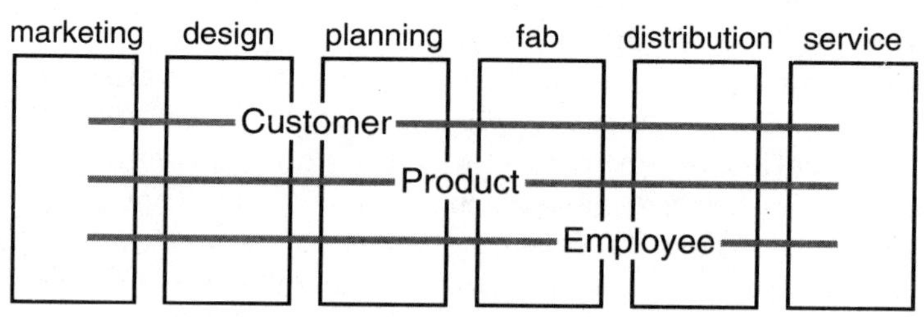

Figure 6.5   Process and data are orthogonal concepts

tion programs that use it—that is, data that is organized and structured to serve many applications and many users. What we seek is the data base.

Excerpt from Turing Award Citation
for C. W. Bachman, 1973

With twenty years of database experience, we find that data and applications are still tangled together. The database is an essential element, but not sufficient. A larger framework is needed for several reasons. First, to the extent databases provide an important mechanism, several factors must support their use, such as good data definitions. Secondly, factors are required to provide data independence when the scope of data goes beyond individual databases. What is needed to achieve substantially greater data independence is a combination of at least the following architectural factors:

- Multiple levels of data abstraction
- Encapsulation through public definitions, modularity, and mediation
- Language-based communication

The more completely each of these factors is implemented, the greater the degree of independence that is achieved.

Levels of independence.   Various levels of decoupling between application and data can be achieved depending on how completely the data independence factors are implemented. For instance, in Figure 6.6 two levels of independence would be expected. Application A that has direct access to data storage services will be much more susceptible to data design changes than application B which is isolated from low-level data storage services by a mediation component.

A closer look at just two of the factors—encapsulation and language mechanism—shows that there are four combinations as shown in Figure 6.7. Along one dimension applications may or may not be exposed to data implementation details. Along another dimension applications may or may not use an expressive, logic-based data language to achieve another form of independence.

The configuration in the lower right quadrant shows the maximum independence with these two factors. There is a possible performance trade-off between this configuration and the configuration in the upper left quadrant. The upper left configuration would be desirable where independence is less important than direct access (and the other factors that language and common functions provide are not needed).

The upper right and lower left quadrants are popular configurations.

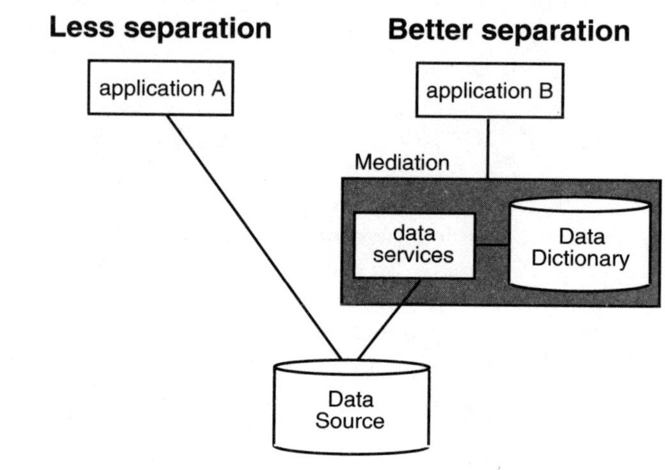

Figure 6.6   Levels of independence.

However, they can interfere with data independence. The upper right quadrant shows an approach that has limited encapsulation (SQL view mechanisms in the typical relational database). Consequently, data design changes potentially affect all applications using that data. The lower left quadrant shows an approach that, in a large scale or complex environment, requires a library containing many minor variations of similar functions. Lack of data abstraction is commonly a serious problem. The many variations present difficulties regarding appropriate use and configuration management. Design to achieve the maximum data independence must take into account all of these factors to balance conflicting requirements.

6.6.2   Database Organization

In this section we describe several architectural factors that must be controlled to provide transparent data integration:

- Database organization—business function oriented, information subject oriented, or design object based
- Transaction management versus decision support
- Warehouse approaches—most recent, version, and snapshot
- Build-time versus run-time processing

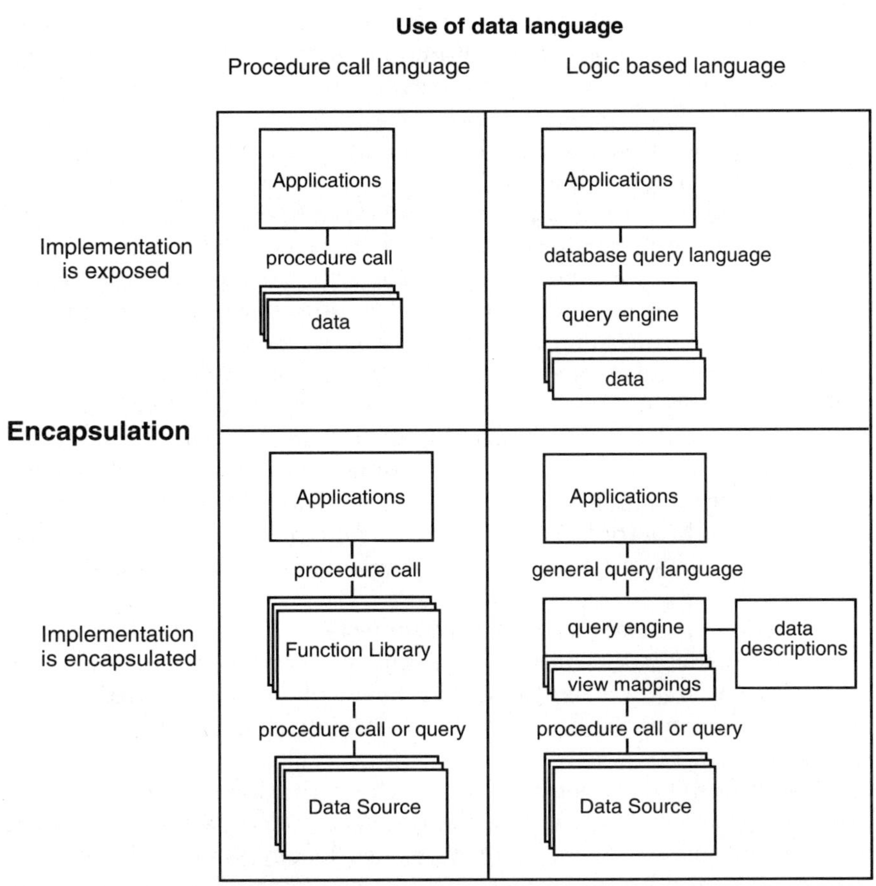

Figure 6.7   Analysis of independence factors.

The mechanics of the distribution of data and data processing resources are often hard to shield from the user. Diverse forms of service implementations often fail to operate in an integrated manner, and thus are hard to shield from the user. Data that is physically organized inappropriate for its use requires exceptional processing to reorganize dynamically.

Database organization.   There are three common organizations of data used for business databases—functional, subject, and object organizations.

Business Function oriented databases organize the data according to the tasks performed to carry out the business functions for an operational division or department. Function-oriented databases organize data definitions with respect to a local context and are concerned with performing cross-functional tasks serially. That is, data is provincial and is exchanged with other departments through hard-coded interfaces, usually in a batch mode.

Information Subject oriented databases are organized according to the categories of information subjects with which the company is concerned. Subject databases organize data definitions with respect to global context and are concerned with performing cross-functional tasks in parallel. Cross-functional tasks can be performed in parallel because data definitions are shared and information can be exchanged at any point in the process. However, subject-oriented databases are naturally record-oriented so that there are few crisply defined composite objects. For example, "employee" would be a subject, but there would be many data tables that make up employee data. There is no definition of a collection of tables that exactly make up an employee. There is no definition of versions of employee as in the object-based organization described next.

Multidimensional databases are subject-oriented. However, in these databases some of the data that would be data values (actually, primary key values) in a relational database is treated as metadata that defines orthogonal factors around which data can be summarized or grouped.

Object-based data is organized by the definition of integral objects types. Integral objects often require data services that implement part-whole relationships, something for which legacy systems have never developed general data services. Object basis introduces formally defined requirements for versioning, configuration control, and special transaction management (e.g., check-in/check-out). (Note that object basis is distinguished from object orientation to avoid implications of a programming style.)

Both subject and object organization are improvements to function organized data. Decision support tends to require subject orientation because problem-solving reaches across many predefined data objects. However, many business processes treat data in an object-based manner including bill of material, planning, and scheduling. As a general principle, when the emphasis is on authoring complex data, the object organization is preferred. When the emphasis is on problem-solving and data search, a subject organization is preferred. When the emphasis is on local process efficiency and standard, off-the-shelf solutions are not available, a functional organization may be preferred.

Transactions versus decision support.   Two major classes of business operational objectives govern database designs—transaction processing and decision support. The primary objective of *transaction-oriented* database designs is to allow many users to concurrently affect the data managed by a single resource manager. Therefore, transaction management design is geared for small transactions to accommodate many users concurrently. The primary objective of *decision support* oriented databases is to allow problem solvers to examine any portion of the whole collection of data. Therefore, *decision support* design interrelates the data items effectively and accommodates any query, even those requiring large proportions of the processing capacity.

Data warehouse approach.   The data warehouse approach emphasizes subject data organization with decision-support design objectives. To fully accommodate decision-support objectives, data organization is enhanced to provide aggregated and indexed data. Numeric data is stored in both detail and summary form. Data may be summarized by major business groupings such as by site, business organization, or other grouping. Data from transactional sources is captured with a time stamp. Data specifications capture these additional definition details.

From a data service design perspective, three kinds of data warehouses can be distinguished.

1. *The most recent.* This form of data warehouse contains an enhanced replica of source data from operational data stores. Enhancements include data abstraction and integration of multiple sources. The warehouse is periodically refreshed by replacing all warehouse records with source records. Either a total replace or incremental updates may be used for the refresh approach. Data is not versioned with this approach.

2. *The versioned.* This form of data warehouse contains a historical collection of object-organized data. Source data may need to be abstracted and integrated to form object-based collections of data and then versioning information added to maintain object identity. New data is entered into the warehouse such that it is appended or added to existing data rather than replacing existing data. Versioning is done in such a way that information object integrity is maintained. For example, if shop orders are archived, then rows from all tables that form a shop order are marked with the same version identifier (e.g., a date/time stamp) and all related data is processed as a whole. In other words, it is not sufficient to simply time stamp records as they are inserted into the database. Specifications that are established in the conceptual model define the versioning. In other words, versioning is not a system artifact determined by the programmer.

For example, an object that is archived may be closed orders. If so, the conceptual model must show the concept of a closed order including all order items belonging to the order.

3. *The snapshot.* This form of data warehouse contains date/time stamped records that serve as a log of changes to a source database. This form of a warehouse contains relatively raw data compared to the version archive warehouse.

Run-time integration versus precompiled integration. A decision-support view of data often requires data from multiple sources to be integrated and detail-level data to be aggregated into summary data. With the appropriate data definitions available, data services can provide a decision-support view of data no matter what the physical organization of the source databases is.

When using the *most recent* type of warehouse data or the *versioned* type of warehouse data, it is possible to apply data abstraction, integration, and replication services either on a scheduled basis or on demand at run time. If these services are scheduled, it may be most efficient to compile the procedure and run it in a batch mode. If the form of service to be applied is not known until run time, it may not be possible to precompile the results. However, processing time constraints often dictate whether integration and aggregation can reasonably be done at run time or compiled at development time. Data definitions should be general enough to satisfy both approaches since the approach may change depending on changes to the system configuration. In either case, the intent should be to minimize the negative impact on the end user or application.

6.6.3   Data Regeneration and Replication Management

In the basic *data regeneration model,* shown in Figure 6.8, we have several objectives. First, we have some source data that we want to make more available to a general user community. Second, since the source data may not be in the form that we want at the target location, we will want to perform data abstraction, integration, and clean-up. Third, we are required to perform this function in a repeatable, well-managed way.

To meet the first two objectives—data availability and improvement—it may be tempting to just throw programmers at the problem. However, there are commercial products that reduce the need for custom programming. Moreover, in a legacy system environment, there is probably a large degree of diversity of data and systems. To meet the third objective, process management, we must set up an overall pro-

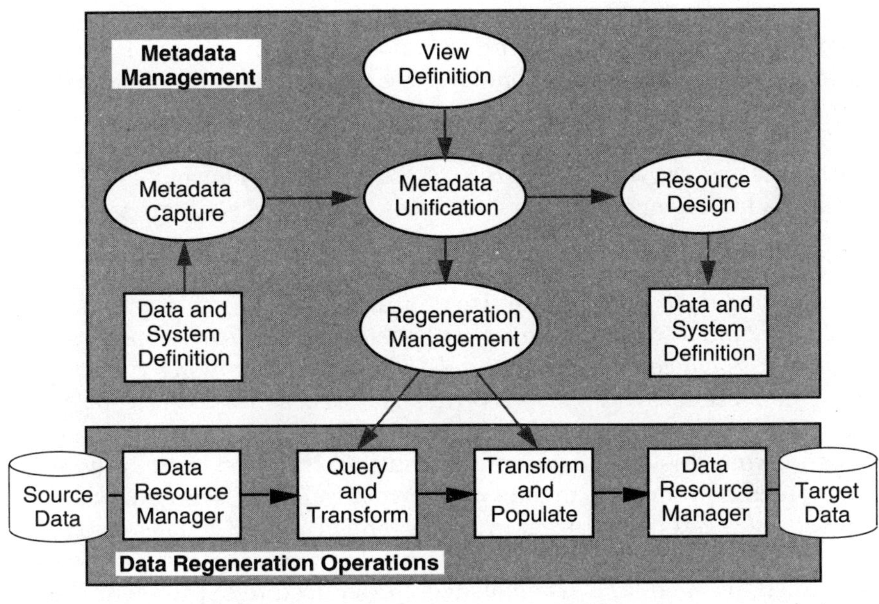

Figure 6.8   Data regeneration model.

cess. The process consists of well-defined mechanisms that are guided by policy, parameters, definitions, and other system information.

The data regeneration model defines infrastructure components for converting data from source systems (an operational or online transaction processing database) and reorganizing it suitable for new applications. For example, to satisfy needs of analysis processing, operational data is regenerated into a data store that is structured and managed in a way that facilitates decision-support operations, sometimes referred to as a data warehouse. For this purpose, the data may be reorganized from functional grouping to subject grouping. Detail data may be rolled up into accumulations. Data may be cleaned up or restructured to facilitate its use by end users. Since the operational and warehouse data stores are separate, there is no processor resource contention. Decision-support users are given more latitude to perform ad hoc queries or other processor-intensive operations without danger of impeding tightly scheduled operational processes.

The process described here concerns the process of publishing the data to a single destination without concern with managing updates or multiple targets. That is, the model just considers reloading a single target data store each time the data is published. In the more complex cases, we must consider incremental updates, appending new versions to form historical data, distributing concurrent copies to multiple destinations, and we must also consider the complexities of managing updated or evolving metadata.

The data regeneration process requires mechanisms in several general areas, as shown in Figure 6.8. The general concept is that the metadata management process produces configured software to migrate data from source data stores into target data stores.

The *view definition* process captures user view specifications. The *metadata capture* process acquires data definitions and system information about source data stores. The *metadata unification* process formulates the conceptual model and the mappings among the various forms of metadata. The *resource design* process uses the conceptual model and the environment description to generate a target data store design. From this specification information, the *regeneration management* process produces the code and scripts required to regenerate data from source systems to target systems. The produced code is shipped to the appropriate data resource managers and processors where the data is queried, merged, and transformed as required to obtain source data and to populate the target data store.

The regeneration process may be applied several times to stage a series of data reorganizations. For example, data in a awkwardly organized database may be first converted to simpler form and from there transformations, joins, and other operations may be applied.

The regeneration model highlights the critical elements to convert and migrate data from one environment to another. A second perspective is to highlight the elements needed to manage the process of regenerating data routinely. Figure 6.9 illustrates such a model. The replication model focuses on providing a management discipline for the process of replication in a complex context.

6.6.3.1 A Simple Example Let us walk through a simple example to illustrate the process. In our example we have an IMS database that contains information on parts used in a manufacturing process. Our objective for the example is to publish a very small part of the IMS database data and have it reside in a relational database.

User view definition. We begin by having the business user propose a scenario that defines his view of the data. Suppose that he says that if he knew where part suppliers were located he could use that information for some purpose.

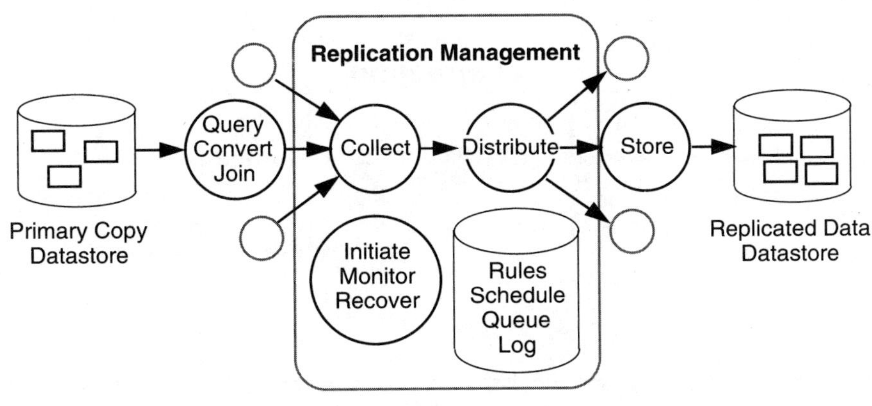

Figure 6.9   Data replication management model

Conceptual model definition. We define a conceptual model with two entities—Part and Supplier. We then determine the best existing source of that data and find that it is in an IMS database used by design engineers. We would then establish the metadata shown in Figure 6.10.

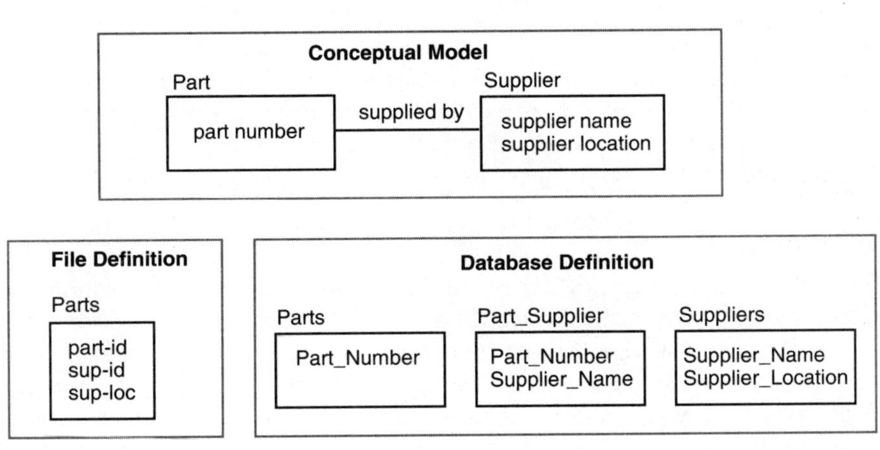

Figure 6.10   Example metadata gathered.

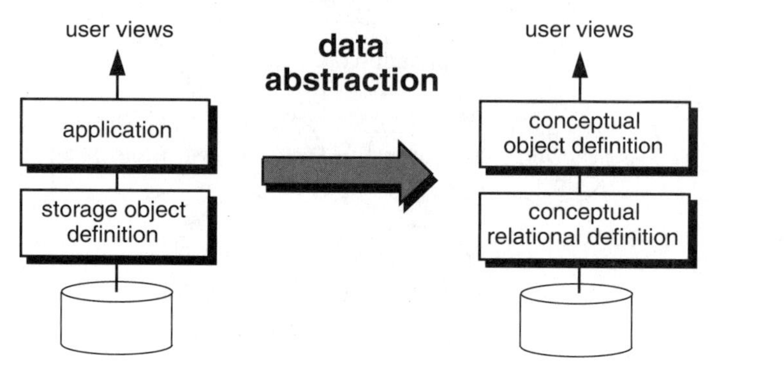

Figure 6.11   Data abstraction as a method of transparency engineering.

Whenever we design data systems, we should deal with data at the highest level of abstraction commensurate with its end use. If the end users are dealing with purchase orders, part drawings, or mail messages, then the data system should have definitions of the data in terms of orders, drawings, or mail. Older systems commonly underplay this principle in favor of optimized storage organization. Optimization is required, but that optimization should occur at the system level rather than at the user application level. The system should present data conceptual facts either as relations or as objects (refer to Figure 6.11).

Whether the data should be presented as relations or objects depends on its use—there is a fundamental computer science dualism at work here. As an analogy, consider shopping at a store. Sometimes you want ingredients, sometimes the finished product. If you want to make or analyze something, you want parts organized as parts. If you want to use something, you want parts assembled into the usable object.[11]

Source system metadata capture. Capture source metadata from application program declarations or database DDL. In our example, we have COBOL file definitions and IMS control block information that defines the source data. We would also gather system information concerning the use of the IMS database on its mainframe processor. For example, we would determine the type of IMS database, existence of indexes, the network node, and so on. Frequently, data definitions are in multiple libraries corresponding to the development, test, implementation cycle. It is critical that the correct libraries are identified.

Target database definition. The metadata for the target data store can be manually or automatically generated from a CASE tool where we have entered the conceptual data model and used to define the target data store tables with their respective data elements. This may include extra design processes to denormalize the conceptual model for performance purposes. For example, the Part and Supplier tables may be prejoined into a single table by moving all of the columns from one table into the other.

Define mappings. Through the metadata definition process, mappings must be defined as they are determined. This is required for coordination of the various team members as they develop their part of the metadata. For example, we would define the mappings between source and target elements. Here we associate source and target table and element names such as "part-id" which is mapped to "part_number".

Configure regeneration tools. Having gathered metadata and system data into dictionary, directory, and catalog form, the next step is to configure software and other system elements to perform the replication. We could build the mechanism on the spot—for example, design and build data conversion software. Preferably, we would use data conversion tools that we can just configure to generate the software. We configure these products by entering the following information:

1. Define the query, transformation, join, sort, and other conditions for each mapping. Our example does not show any of these additional requirements. However, we could specify that the Part and Supplier source tables are to be joined, or we could restrict our data to only those suppliers whose location meets some criteria.
2. Define the processing plan that determines the steps and locations for executing the queries, transformations, sorts, merges, and joins. We must anticipate many conditions that would cause performance problems. For example, if part and supplier data are in separate data stores, and we were to do a full sequential search on the supplier data store for each part, the processing time may be extremely costly. The processing plan would have to take into account the availability of indexes, moving data onto a common processor, performing sorts before processing, and so on.
3. Define the system information to access the data resource managers, to execute jobs and processes on the respective processors, and to perform file transfer. For example, JCL to execute batch message processing programs (BMP) must be defined. Load utilities for the target database must be identified and configured. The file exchange protocol, such as FTP, and network parameters must be identified.

The configured replication generator can now generate the replication mechanisms. The generated replication components must be shipped to their processor. Invocation of the replication can be manual or automatic. Jobs that have been generated must be scheduled as appropriate for the processors involved. Many mainframe installations have job scheduling systems that must be used.

CHAPTER NOTES

1. Goranson, H. T. "Dimensions of Enterprise Integration. Enterprise Integration Modeling." *Proceedings of the First International Conference.* Charles J. Petrie, Jr., ed. 1992.
2. Kent, William. "Solving Domain Mismatch and Schema Mismatch Problems with an Object-Oriented Database Programming Language." *Proceedings of the 17th International Conference on Very Large Data Bases.* Barcelona (September 1991).
3. Tschammer, V., and D. Strick. *Principles and Models for Integrating Distributed Systems from Existing Components.* Tokyo, Japan: IFAC Distributed Computer Control Systems, 1989.
4. Brenner, John, ed. *OPENFramework: Distributed Application Services.* International Computers Limited, 1993. Prentice-Hall International (UK) Ltd.
5. Schneider, Fred B. *What Good are Models and What Models are Good?* in Sape Mullender (ed.) *Distributed Systems.* Second Edition. New York: ACM Press,1993.
6. Medina-Mora, Raul, Terry Winograd, Rodrigo Flores, and Fernando Flores. *The Action Workflow Approach to Workflow Management Technology.* CSCW 92 Proceedings (November 1992).
7. A classic treatment of an overall information systems architecture was proposed by John Zachman in the *IBM Systems Journal,* vol 26, no.3 (1987). In many ways Zachman's idea was important because it stimulated the information technology community to think architecturally. The framework was developed before reuseability, data abstraction, object-orientation, application frameworks and patterning concepts were popularized. Consequently, Zachman's framework has a strong flavor of the waterfall method of engineering data systems from scratch on each project.
8. Sloman, Morris. *Management for Open Distributed Processing.* IEEE. 1990.
9. ISO TC97/SC5/WG3, Helsinki, 1978.
10. Ventrone, Vincent, and Sandra Heiler. *Some Practical Advice for Dealing with Semantic Heterogeneity in Federated Database Systems.* Unpublished White Paper.
11. Barsalou, T., N. Siambela, A.M. Keller, and G. Wiederhold. *Updating Relational Databases through Object-based Views.* ACM-SIGMOD 91, Boulder, Col (May 1991): 248–257.

7

Application Systems

Legacy systems in an enterprise consist of various applications programs. An application system typically includes business logic encoding, data manipulation (flat files, databases) routines, and user interaction screens as a minimum. Depending upon the location of users, the applications will also include detailed communication protocols embedded in them. Modularization of these components is typically done in an ad hoc manner. Therefore, legacy application system is a complicated monolith that has evolved over a period of time.

Application systems are essential to run the business processes of an enterprise. Automation of the business processes will require that the data operations (i.e., update, delete, insert procedures as dictated by the business process rules) be encoded within and between application systems. The data management function, therefore, is solely dependent on the process definition and is encoded into the application systems. Figure 7.1 shows the various components of an application.

The design philosophy of monolithic applications results in a legacy systems web as shown in Figure 7.2. This is a typical legacy system design philosophy in most enterprises. The result is a spider web of application conglomerates managed by an army of Information Systems personnel. This result (business problem) was also described in Chapter 1. To understand the legacy systems transition process we should be able to parse an application into these various components as shown in Figure 7.1. Bill Inmon[1] discusses the legacy phenomena and evolution of systems in detail.

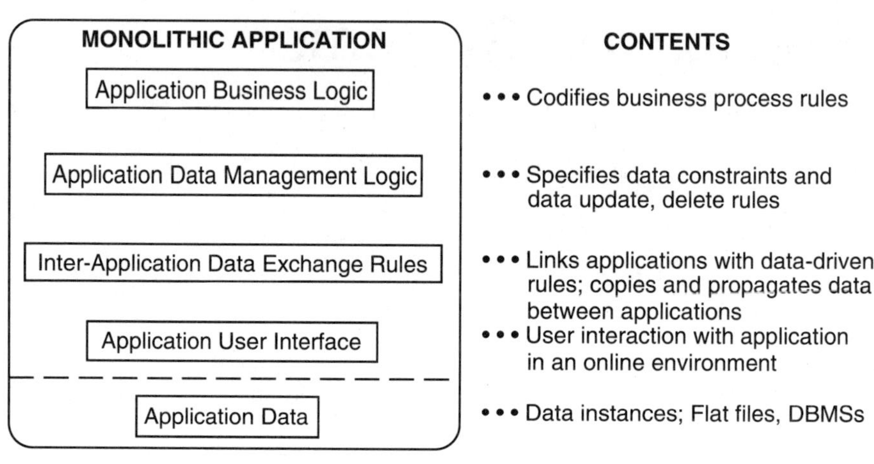

Figure 7.1   Application architecture of legacy systems.

Some observations for legacy systems in the context of transition to a distributed environment based on the previous discussion are as follows:

Data considerations.   Data is pushed as dictated by functional requirements in a stovepipe manner in legacy systems. Data is pulled not pushed in an architected environment; for this to happen we should provide the most flexible data-access environment, not premeasured, prepackaged data through canned reports and such. The user, not the application programmer, decides what data is needed and how it should be presented.

An often-mentioned data resource management objective is to deliver the right data at the right time in the right amount to the right people. An application developer alone cannot accomplish this without a knowledge of the business process; to attempt to do this will require second guessing the business processes and the user needs.

The process relevance in the mainframe environment.   The web of legacy systems on mainframes executes the business processes. It is the only place where the enterprise process knowledge is codified incrementally. This has happened over an extended period of time. The coding details are not documented in most cases. Lack of time and incomplete enterprise business process knowledge is the prime culprit. Inadequate computing systems architecture of the past exacerbates the situation.

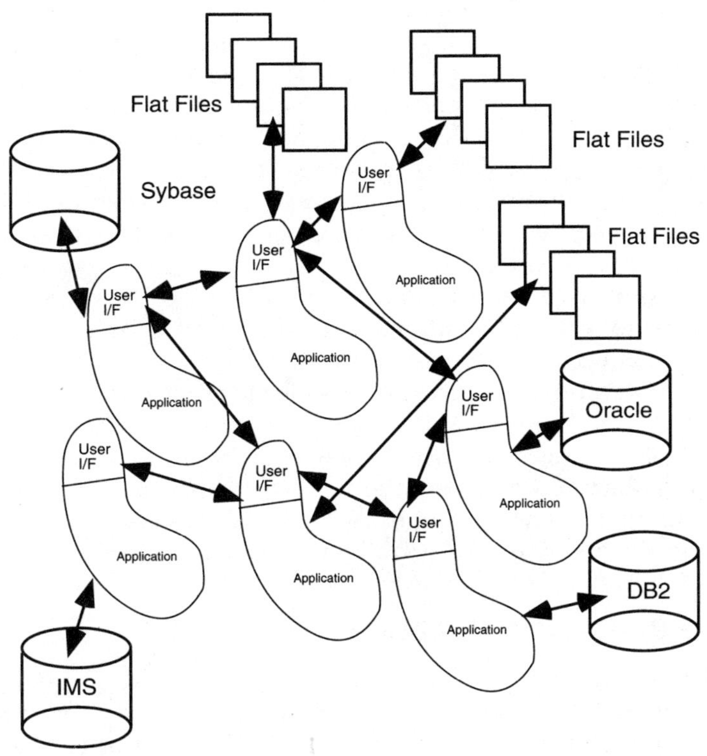

Figure 7.2   Legacy systems web.

Moving data to server platform in the mainframe environment.   When we want to move data from mainframes to a server environment, we have to untangle the complex web of process knowledge codified in the applications, among other things. "Data regeneration" as described in Chapter 4 partially captures the metadata along with semantic information, and data instances. It leaves behind the process knowledge—the crown jewels of the enterprise. The legacy application code cannot be reengineered to isolate and deliver the entangled process encoding in any reusable computer-sensitive format. The reason is that isolated process knowledge obtained from individual applications loses the semantic dependencies and definitions when the process is considered as a whole. A number of questions need to be answered such as: What are the processes of interest? How do these relate to the enterprise-wide processes? How are we going to convey these in a computer-sensible format? What should be the repository concepts to store these for reuse instead of codifying these into application logic as in the past? In short, what are the processes to applications mapping when data is available as a "regenerated" resource as extracted from the legacy applications? Do we have an idea of the new reengineered processes and have the "new process owners" figured out the "new data" world order? Such probing questions force a process-oriented thinking, not centralized data-driven and application-controlled (stovepipe systems) paradigms of integration that resulted in legacy webs. Data-driven thinking without cross-functional integrated business process linkage is behind the conventional and rigid centralized information resource management strategies of the past.

To understand the transition process for legacy systems, it is essential to classify the applications in a consistent manner based on their use in running the business operations. The following sections describe how to classify applications and the essential integration considerations.

The examples shown in Figure 7.2 are a worst-case situation. The actual conditions may be much simpler than those described here.

7.1   APPLICATION CATEGORIES

The legacy transition process is usually performed in stages. A complicated engineered set of applications—as will be the case in many instances if staged—using a systematic classification criteria, will result in rapid benefits. A criterion can be to classify computing applications around business processes. Process-based categorization of applications will ensure a staging (incremental) strategy for legacy transition. A staging strategy essentially consists of selecting those systems that will provide rapid benefits and stabilize the transition process. A level of disruption to continuing operations can also be mitigated in a staged deployment. The application categories will ease in selecting the right systems for implementing reengineered processes.

The following discussion will make it clear that legacy systems do not always have clearly circumscribed business process control points. Control points are process boundaries (of a business unit) across which cost, schedule, delivery, and product status data is exchanged per a business protocol. This is so because the legacy systems were designed to meet functional organizational needs in a hierarchical management model. In such a model, key business processes are vertically integrated along functions such as contracts, legal, material, engineering, and so on, to name a few. The legacy systems are logical collections of application systems that appear as functionally integrated monolithic assemblies using hard-coded, point-to-point interfaces. When cross-functional integration is required, the same interfaces replicated data instead of sharing common data. The replicated data often causes data synchronization problems.

Applications can be broadly classified as strategic, tactical, and decision support systems based on their functional use and business process support as described in the following sections.

7.1.1 Strategic Systems

Strategic systems support an organization's critical success factors. Critical success factors can be rapid implementation of product features, introduction of marketing promotion plans, and so on, not all applications are strategic to all functions. Strategic systems help an organization to penetrate new markets or mitigate competition to stay in business. Sometimes strategic systems become tactical systems over time.

7.1.2 Tactical Systems

Tactical systems are the basic bread-and-butter applications of an enterprise. They are stable and intimately integrated with the processes and business culture of a functional department in a large organization. The stability and the performance of the applications are the very essence of the legacy systems web phenomena. Almost all tactical systems have levels of data integration accomplished by virtue of hard-coded interfaces and data manipulation routines among legacy systems. This situation results from the mainframe-centric, resource contention-based design of the past. While that kind of legacy system design may be acceptable in the past, the processes described in this book are opposed to perpetuating the legacy design philosophy.

7.1.3 Decision-Support Systems

Decision-support applications access data from a number of sources and aggregate these for decision-making. Generally, these applications fall into three subcategories: executive information systems (EIS), advanced decision-support applications, and query and reporting applications. EIS is usually associated with applications that employ an easy to use interface with graphical displays of the data. Advanced decision-support applications include a broad array of tools such as spreadsheets, statistical modeling programs, and custom written algorithms specific to the business intelligence (strategic) of the enterprise. Finally, query and reporting applications are typically used by those needing access to data, often through predefined reports and query generation tools.

7.2   GENERAL OBSERVATIONS

When we try to classify applications based on the aforementioned considerations and how these have evolved, we observe the following in a legacy environment.

- Applications tend to be tactical, strategic, or decision-oriented based on their implementation date. Old applications are tactical, new applications are strategic, and the most recent applications are decision support-oriented.
- The data management and processing characteristics are driven by the complex legacy web as described in Figure 7.2. It is difficult to isolate an application for replacement without upstream or downstream impact. This situation was referred to as the "Gordian" knot in Chapter 1.
- The most recent changes to legacy applications are driven by strategic and decision-support requirements; very few, if any, are for process improvement reasons.
- Data is managed and controlled by individual applications. The applications are inseparable from business processes. The business processes are distributed across applications and are embedded in interface routines.
- The monolithic characteristics of the mainframe environment will make reverse engineering of legacy applications very difficult, if not impossible.

7.3   APPLICATIONS REENGINEERING

The basic description of the legacy systems, their evolution and business impact on current requirements was described in the previous sections. We now explain some new approaches to reengineering computer applications. All the concepts of data architecture described in earlier chapters should be applied to the application reengineering process.

7.3.1   Why Reengineer?

The dynamic business environment of today demands fast solutions. The application backlog situation of the past is not acceptable. A new paradigm should be used to meet the customers' requirements. The essential need to reengineer is driven by the high maintenance costs of the legacy systems. To the most experienced programming staff (a euphemism for MVS COBOL and Mark-IV report-writer programmers) it may appear that nothing is broken—why are we engaged in considering reengineering at all. The answer to this question is obtained by analyzing facts and data. Common experience shows that the total computing budget spent for maintenance is approximately 80 percent. The balance of 20 percent is for new developments. If we were to stabilize our budgets at some past expenditure level, then, the only recourse is to cut the maintenance costs in half and free up 40 percent of the budget for new development. We assume that as newly architected systems come online the expensive legacy systems will be retired. The cost of developing new applications will be dramatically reduced by using rapid applications development techniques and technologies.

We reengineer applications to improve the overall quality both in functional and technical areas. The improvement in functional quality is accomplished by modularizing applications into functionally reusable chunks of application code. For instance, we can develop a financial application by just coding (in-house) the business-specific rules and employing a commercial spreadsheet to provide analysis capabilities and graphics. Similarly, a reporting tool can be integrated into the application transparently. In such a scenario we are breaking up the application into manageable chunks and coding only value-added applications unique to our business processes. Figure 7.3 shows certain service components to illustrate the point, but these are not the only available choices. The in-house constructed code is limited to only unique functionality that is not available in commercially produced components or has not been previ-

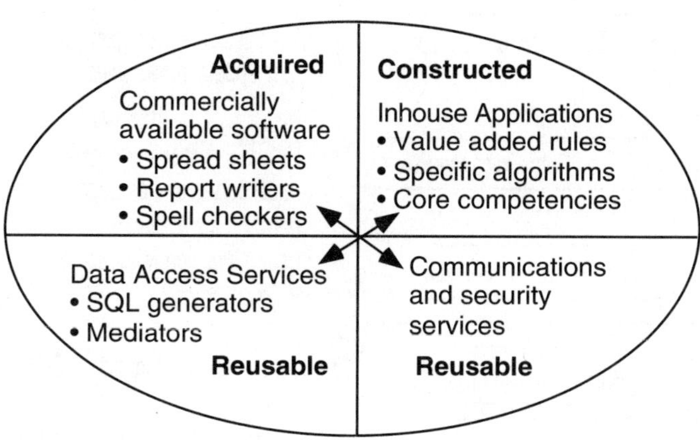

Figure 7.3   Applications are modularized to transparently integrate commercially available programs and enhance reusability.

ously defined. This method of segmentation of developing the application recognizes three different business streams, that are discussed later in this chapter.

The distributed architecture is very effective in such a development scenario. The technical quality enhancement is resonated by the properties of flexibility, reliability, and cost effectiveness. New technologies, as shown in Figure 7.4, can be exploited. These, for instance, can be the implementation of object-oriented programming techniques, using object classes for presenting user views of data, graphical user interfaces, and intelligent agents[2] in a distributed Client/Server environment to name a few.

7.3.2   Application Maintenance at a Specification Level

The application reengineering is based on the concept of maintaining application components at a specification level as opposed to maintaining a monolithic code. A specification describes a set of formal unam-

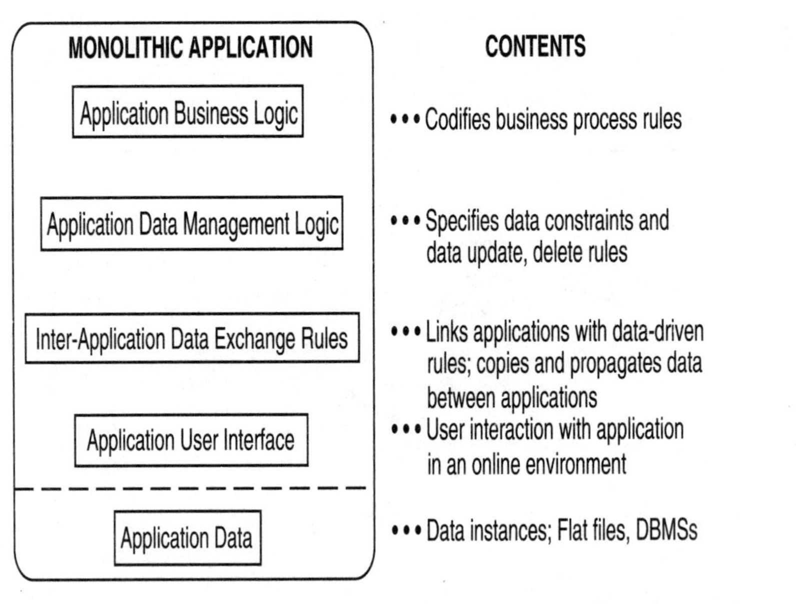

Figure 7.4   Applications take advantage of new and stable technologies to enhance technical quality.

biguous instructions that have to be encoded in a computing procedural language. A monolithic legacy code in practice does not have high fidelity traceable specifications to code relationship. Therefore, the processes of maintenance are prone to delays, guesswork, and high expenses. In a specification-driven environment the application code is produced using code generation tools, these tools employ specification panels. The programmer does not write low level code. When a function is to be deleted or added, we simply locate a previously defined panel or define an appropriate specification panel and alter it accordingly. The new code is automatically generated from the revised specifications. Figure 7.5 shows the process. The application reengineering means redeveloping existing applications with the goal of reducing costs, increasing quality, and positioning them to take advantage of new stable technologies. Implied in this process is a fundamental need to define an architecture and a new infrastructure to facilitate breakthrough productivity. However, it is not just rehosting an old application "as is" on a new platform or operating system. The new applications support and link the business process reengineering requirements.

While the business process reengineering is critical, it is tactically linked to the applications and information systems technology. Forrester Research maintains that to meet business process redesign needs, companies will need a "dynamic computing" strategy—a new computing style that fosters and facilitates change. Forrester Research states the impact

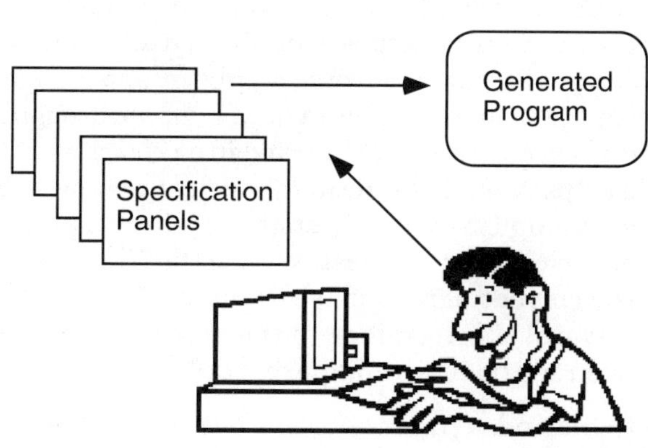

Figure 7.5   Applications are generated from specifications that feed into code generation tools.

Table 7.1   Impact of Business Process Redesign on Information Services

Impact on Information Service Providers	Response of Surveyed Persons in Percentage
1. BPR accelerates learning and acquiring new technologies.	36% of the sample responded positively to the question.
2. BPR focuses Information Services providers on business issues.	23% of the sample responded positively to the question.
3. BPR freezes old system development.	11% of the sample responded positively to the question.
4. BPR reduces Information Services providers staff.	11% of the sample responded positively to the question.
5. BPR has no impact on Information Services providers.	19% of the sample responded positively to the question.

of business process redesign (BPR) on information service providers, as shown in Table 7.1.

7.3.3   The Current Application Reengineering Paradigm

The current reengineering paradigm for most organizations considering applications transition from legacy mainframes to distributed computing is discussed by Pieter Mimno in *CASE Trends* (computer assisted software engineering). The starting point in this paradigm is the legacy applications suite. From these a code restructure is performed followed by a code stabilization step. The application is reverse engineered using a repository approach where the information is stored. We forward engineer the code reusing the chunks of code previously saved in a repository. All the conventional life-cycle steps of analysis, design, code generation, testing and enhancement are accomplished at this stage to rehost the application on a new platform of choice. In most cases, we use the Client/Server model for this purpose. The current paradigm is shown in Figure 7.6.

There are several shortcomings to the process shown in Figure 7.6, that are discussed in the following paragraphs.

Linkage to business process.   The old legacy applications evolved with technology and business needs as seen in a vertically integrated functional situation. The evolving requirements were added with nothing removed from the old application, because all upstream and downstream data exchange implications are not completely known assuredly. Therefore, we have thousands of lines of permanently residing obsolete

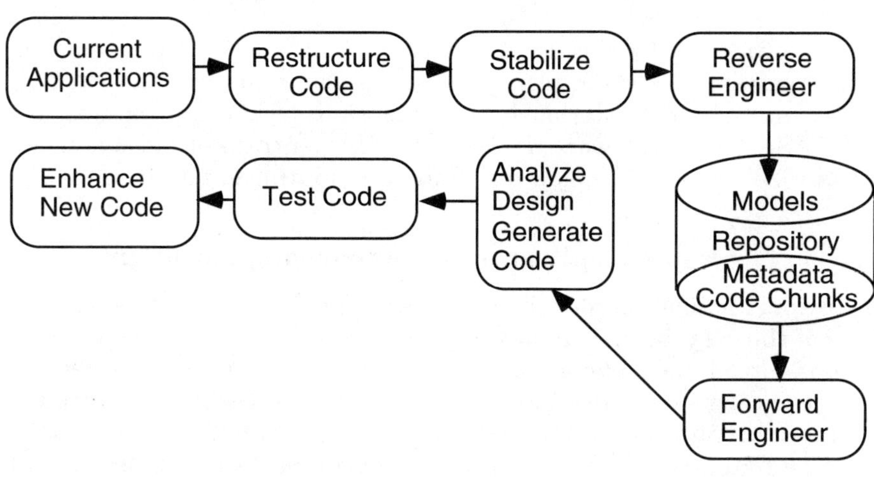

Figure 7.6   The current application reengineering paradigm.

code adding to the ever-increasing maintenance costs. The combined process encoding can therefore give flawed data and will cause non-value-added manual data cleanup steps. The applications generally perform a dual transaction and decision-support role, and may not be optimized for either function. An attempt to reverse engineer will retain the same legacy as before which may not be a reflection of the newly defined business processes. Concepts of portfolio management for applications are rudimentary or are not practiced at all.

Timely response.   The reverse engineering approach combined with the creation of a repository will bog down the process since the old data dictionary (if available) and allegedly current data models are highly suspect in terms of their currency. An integrated set of modeling tools did not exist when the legacy applications were originally coded. The resolution of these differences adds a lot of flow time to the reengineering project.

Tools and methodology.   In most cases, the reverse engineering tools cannot adequately extract the embedded business rules and rapidly express these as higher-level specifications that can be used by a CASE tool to forward engineer the application.

Computation model.   The mainframe-centric computation model is very tightly coupled and proprietary. It is optimized at the cost of flexibility. The Client/Server model of application design is loosely coupled and highly modularized. This facilitates rapid changes where they are needed, leaving large portions of the application untouched. Unit testing and system testing consume less resources and old bugs sometimes do not mysteriously reappear as in legacy applications. The old CASE tools that were designed for the centralized paradigm will prove insufficient in the new distributed computing environment.

7.3.4   The Rapid Application Reengineering Paradigm

The rapid application reengineering paradigm addresses the shortcomings of the current paradigm very effectively. First, the reengineering task is considered to be a business realignment activity as opposed to just rehosting old applications on a new platform. Technology introduction is on a "pull" basis. Figure 7.7 shows the process.

The fundamental difference is in determining what is exactly salvageable from the legacy applications. The actual code verbatim is of little use. The user-interaction screens and the embedded 3270 protocol-based data streams are irrelevant to a graphical user interface. The file-based data structures are also of no value. We are recognizing these characteristics in our processes. The most salvageable part is the metadata and user views that define the external schema of the data. The user views deal with the actual business objects the users employ in the performance of their job functions. Examples are: sales order, draw-

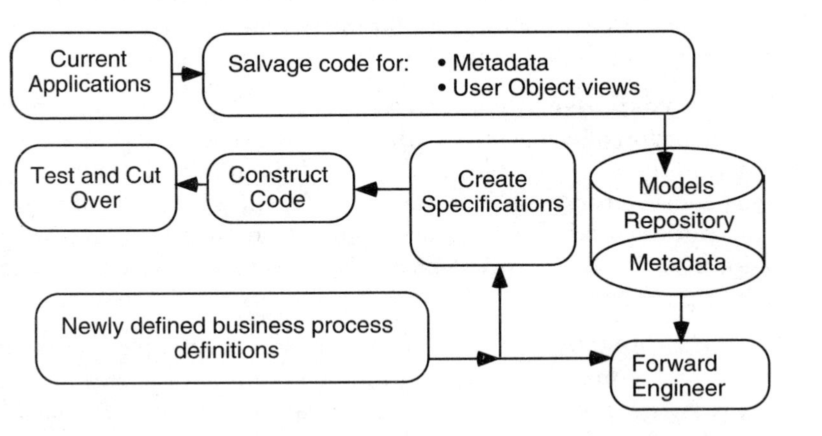

Figure 7.7   The new application reengineering paradigm.

ing, merchandise return authorization slip, and such. It is very important to retain these external or user views to a high degree of accuracy; otherwise we will have a system unacceptable to the users. The forward engineering process considers all appropriate automation requirements as applicable to the reengineered business processes in creating specifications. The specification panels drive the application code generator. The next step is to test and cut over to the new application. The data transition between the old and new applications requires a through process definition. In Chapter 6 several strategies to devise a workable process that may be different for specific situations were discussed.

7.3.5   Tools for Rapid Application Reengineering

The tools for rapid application reengineering generally fall into three categories:

- Application generators
- Flexible 4GL (fourth generation language)
- A single logical or online operational repository

Application generators. The application generators give the code designer graphical- and table-driven panels to input the specifications of the program to be developed. The driving impetus in defining the specifications is business processes. This particular impetus reduces maintenance costs as discussed earlier. There are different kinds of application generators. Some application generators are used to develop tactical and strategic applications, whereas others are used to generate applications that will map data schema from source legacy databases (or flat files) to the target relational database system automatically. Then, there are application generators that create a portable (platform-independent) windows environment for building a graphical user interface for the end-users. Figure 7.8 shows some commonly available application generator capabilities classified into three logical groupings. More such groups are evolving as more entrepreneurial computing companies sprout. The growth is dependent on the vendors' own published standards (e.g., Microsoft Windows) or open systems (OMG's CORBA, POSIX, etc.) standards.

Fourth generation language tools. The key characteristics of these tools are to provide portability across platforms. In a Client/Server model it is reasonable to expect several client platforms using desktops ranging from character-based MS-DOS (Microsoft DOS), MS-Windows, and X-Motif, to name just a few. The 4GL tool should be capable of

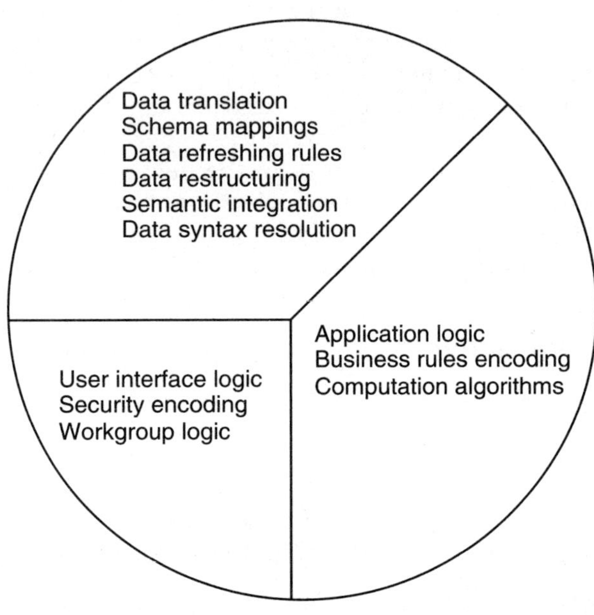

Figure 7.8   Different kinds of application generators.

generating the appropriate code for the target platform consistently. The 4GL tool is generally used to query databases from a client platform. There is no single dominant standard relational database management system. As such, many dialects of SQL must be supported to achieve the interoperability demanded by businesses. The same is true when accessing file-based or hierarchical database management systems. The old mainframe systems will not go away any sooner. Actually, when that happens is irrelevant to the legacy transition process, as we are business- and process-driven, not technology-driven. The purpose of the application redesign process is to tackle the transition problem in small meaningful chunks (incremental and staged, as discussed earlier). Good and thoughtful use of 4GL tools will help the transition process. An architectural framework is absolutely important for the redesign to occur. The centerpiece of this book is to present to the reader the approach that views business process redesign, rapid application development, transition from mainframe-centric model to Client/server, establishment of distributed data management environment, and finally implementation of an information architecture as a package in defining a holistic approach. Piecemeal hit-and-run technology implementations have seldom succeeded and many careers (of professionals who did not appreciate the holistic approach) have been ruined in this business.

Operational repository.   An operational repository is essential to systematically capture the legacy system's salvaged data for the reengineering task. It provides a central point of control and management of application development information. The repository can also be queried for information reporting purposes and self-documentation. In many cases the lack of up-to-date documentation makes the maintenance of legacy systems an expensive task. Perhaps, shortcomings of many commercially available repository products is the Achilles heel in the new application development paradigm.

7.3.6   The Rapid Application Reengineering Process

The rapid application reengineering process consists of four important and distinct processes:

1.   Salvage legacy applications for data and encoded business functions. (Figures 7.9 and 7.10).
2.   Conduct business oriented application design. (Figure 7.11).
3.   Construct and prototype new applications. (Figure 7.12).
4.   Cut over and deploy application. (Figure 7.13)

For each of the processes some critical activities are shown in Figures 7.9 through 7.13. The legacy applications are analyzed for data structure recapture. Several related concepts were discussed in Chapters 4 and 6.

In Figure 7.10 the various activities for capturing realistic business views as business objects are proposed. It is important to maintain this view. When we perform an empirical data element analysis we will find that a great many redundancies exist. A rapid way for data resolution or rationalization is to revert to a real-world view that the process owners have. The older legacy systems just evolved several data elements that were added to support a computing process, not a business process. Once the computing processes change and are redefined in our application development process, the artificial data elements of the past have no significance. This realization alone can result in significant resource savings. It is not uncommon to encounter thousands of data elements

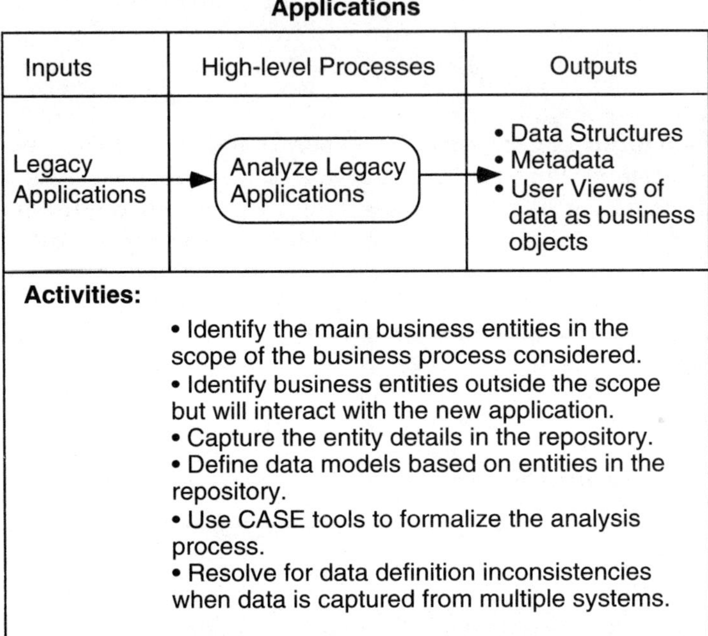

Figure 7.9   Salvaging legacy applications for data structure recapture.

for a handful of legacy applications. However, when we apply the real-world orientation, we may find an order of magnitude decrease in the number of data elements required to be carried forward in the new application environment.

Figure 7.11 shows the next step in a sequence; it concerns the application redesign process. Some general guidelines are suggested in the figure.

Figure 7.12 shows the construction and prototyping processes. In this new paradigm prototyping is an essential step to accomplish results that will be acceptable and meet the customer requirements. Most of the application generation tools and CASE tools are vitally important for rapid prototyping.

Figure 7.13 shows the final step of accomplishing the cut over to the new applications and the sunset of the legacy applications.

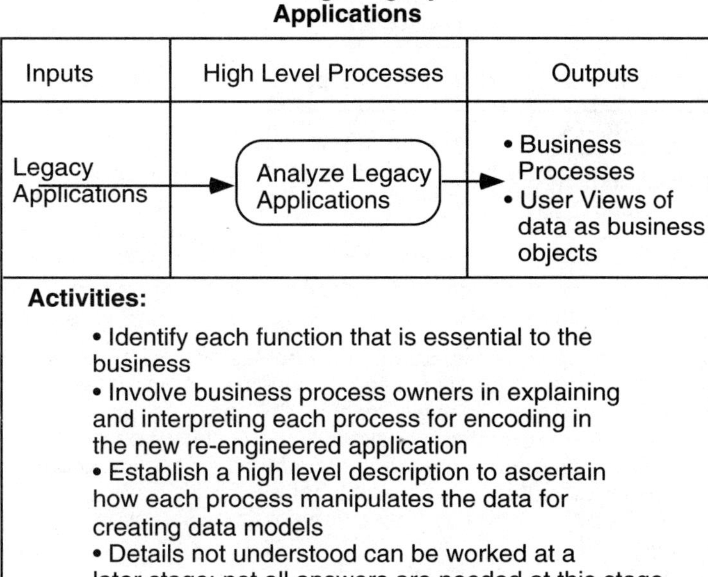

Figure 7.10   Salvaging legacy applications for business processes.

7.3.7   The Business Stream Concept for Applications

A business stream[3] is a set of defined activities that transpire repeatedly in a business enterprise. The concept of a business stream is simple. It merely aggregates activities that can be performed consistently in a stable environment producing the same results or deliverables predictably. The business stream concept works well in a manufacturing situation. If we regard the software application development process to be a manufacturing-like process, then we can develop the business stream concept in this regard as well. Figure 7.14 shows three distinct business streams relevant to software application development. The three business streams are described in the following paragraphs.

Basic features and configurations.   Commercial applications have many features that are common across an application domain. For

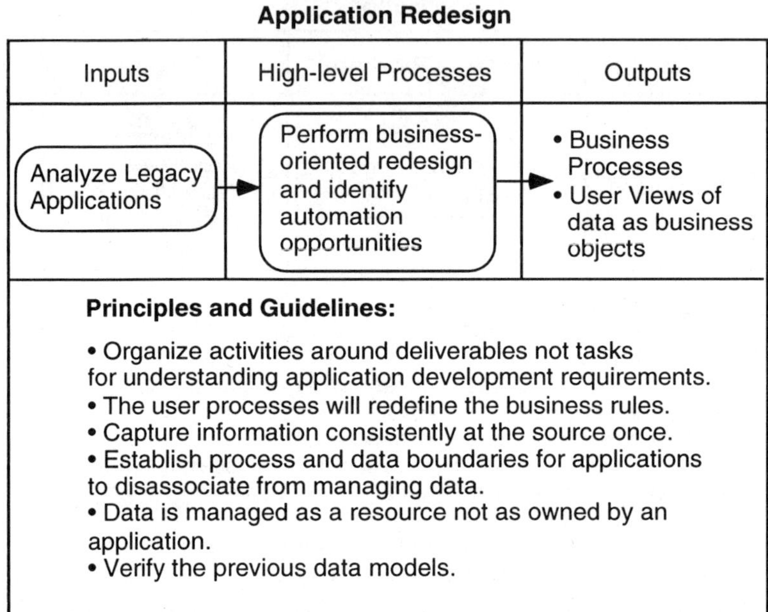

Figure 7.11   Conduct business-oriented application redesign.

instance personal productivity tools are generally considered as an application domain consisting of word processing, spreadsheets, graphics or presentation tools, and personal database products. These applications are packaged and contain many features that can be used out of the box. In the legacy environment such tools either did not exist or were too awkward to use. The key benefit of recognizing such a business stream is to refrain from the developing applications that are commercially available.

Reusable customized options. The second business stream concerns specific implementation of standard configurations available in applications used in the first business stream. However, options such as standardizing on application macros, network setup and so on are reusable though customized to a particular business process requirement.

Strategic and proprietary extensions. The third and last business stream includes new developments that are readily available com-

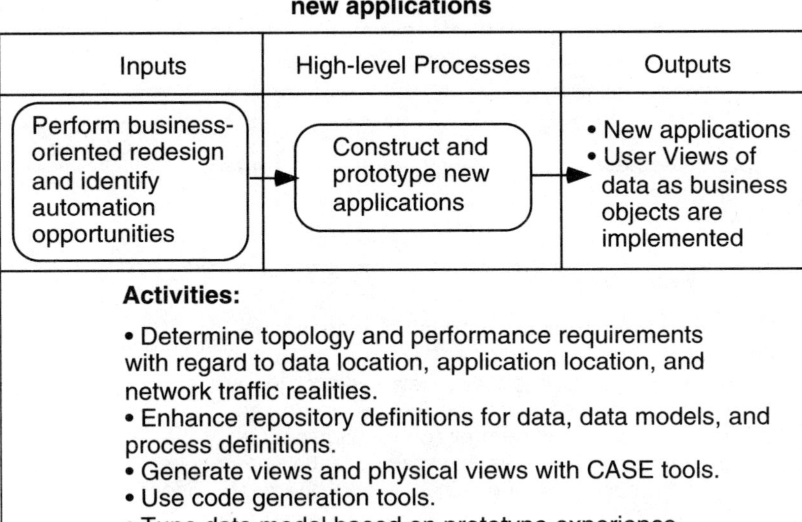

Figure 7.12   Construct and prototype new applications.

mercially. Additionally, certain processes and algorithms can be regarded as proprietary and unique to a business unit.

Classification of the entire application domain in three business streams will be beneficial in spending resources where and when needed as opposed to building stovepipe applications that satisfy a narrow functional needs as observed in legacy environment. Table 7.2 summarizes the software development business streams.

The purpose of this chapter was to understand application systems in the context of the legacy transition as a process that should be linked to the business process reengineering. Availability of new technologies should not be the only criteria to launch computing applications rehosting or redesign. We must have a solid business case to justify any major information systems development project. The next chapter discusses the alignment of business processes with information systems. Information systems are collections of application that use standard managed and disciplined data and construct information to support the execution of a business process step.

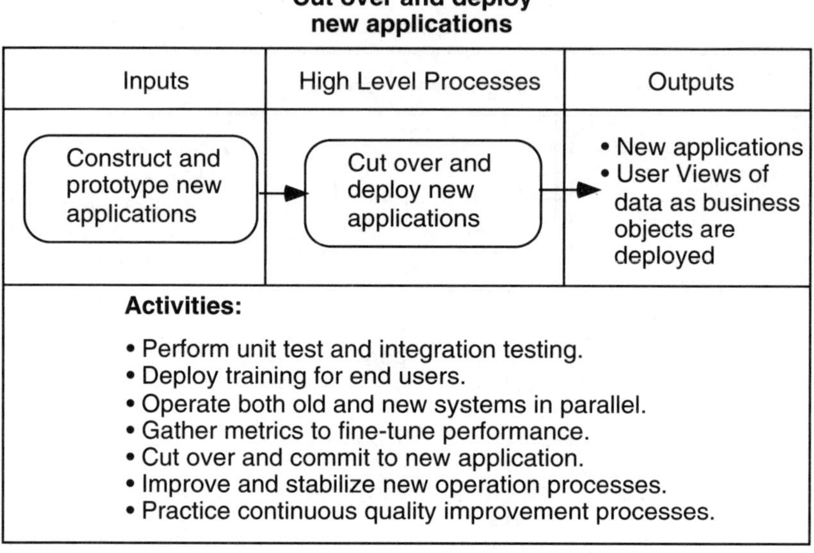

Figure 7.13   Cut over and deploy applications.

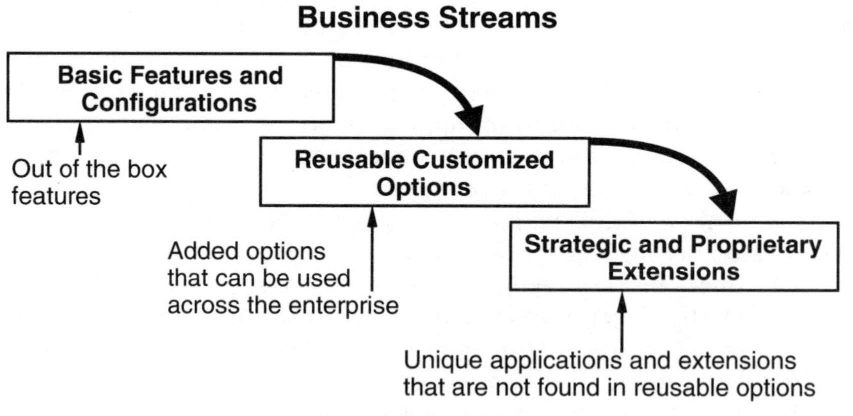

Figure 7.14   Business streams for computing applications.

Table 7.2   Business Stream Concepts for Applications

Business Stream Characteristics	Attributes and Description	Examples of Software
1. Basic and stable, independent of business process reengineering. Commercial Off the Shelf Software, COTS is an example.	Suitable to buy commercial off the shelf applications or modules that have defined standard open and published application program interfaces, APIs.	Spreadsheets, Grammar Checking Software, Report generators, graphics applications, shrink wrapped applications, work-groupware, operating systems, and desktops.
2. Basic and stable plus previously developed reuseable capabilities based on business process reengineering.	Adaptations on the basic and stable theme that can be reused. Code reuseability is the driver.	Spreadsheet macros. Point and click options for building SQL commands on the fly, Security profiles based on user processes.
3. Basic and stable plus custom defined capabilities to meet strategic requirements.	Unique situations to address specific business needs. Usually the applications deal with proprietary algorithms that are limited.	In-house code that may include modules available in the two other business streams.

CHAPTER NOTES

1. Inmon, W.H. *Building the Data Warehouse*. New York: John Wiley, 1993.
2. Intelligent agents are background applications that learn user behavior and execute the required processes of fetching information and launching computing processes transparently. Therefore, the computer programs are friendlier and interact effectively with the users.
3. Clausing, Don. *Total Quality Development*. New York: The ASME Press, 1994.

8

Alignment of Business with Information Systems

Today, business processes are changing faster to accommodate the delivery of a product that suits the customers' taste. The old competitive strategies of invention and mass production no longer work in an increasingly turbulent business environment. Successful firms are implementing the new competitive strategies of continuous improvement and mass customization. Continuous improvement means constant process improvement. Mass customization means a dynamic flow of goods and services via a stable set of processes.[1] Figure 8.1 shows the relationship of information systems to production processes.

While the mass production of most stable configurations may have served the customer well, the business reality of competition always perturbs a stable picture. The competition may be offering ever-increasing new features. An example of the video tape recorder is appropriate in this regard. Initially, very limited features were offered to the consumer on a video recorder. But competition stepped in; the only way to attract business was to offer more features. Now, if the old paradigm of mass production and stable product is not changed, extinction is almost certain. Therefore, a set of features should be designed as options to be melded with the standard basic part. Essentially, the manufacturing revolves around assembling new features around the basic stable configuration to attract more business. Such a mass customization process is shown in Figure 8.2.

When we want to align information systems with business, we have to consider such aspects. The information systems are now more distrib-

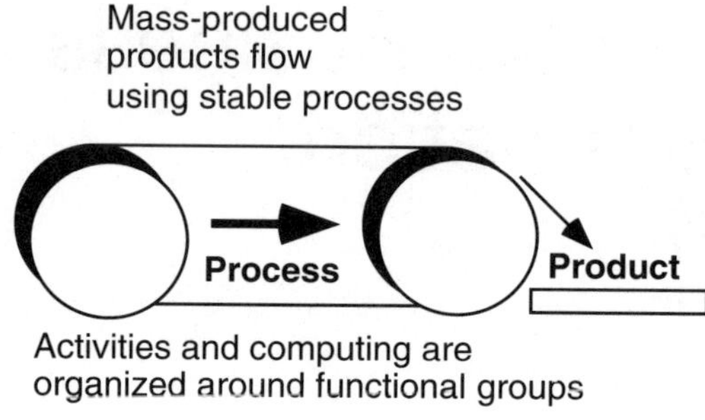

Figure 8.1   Mass production causes systems to be organized around functions.

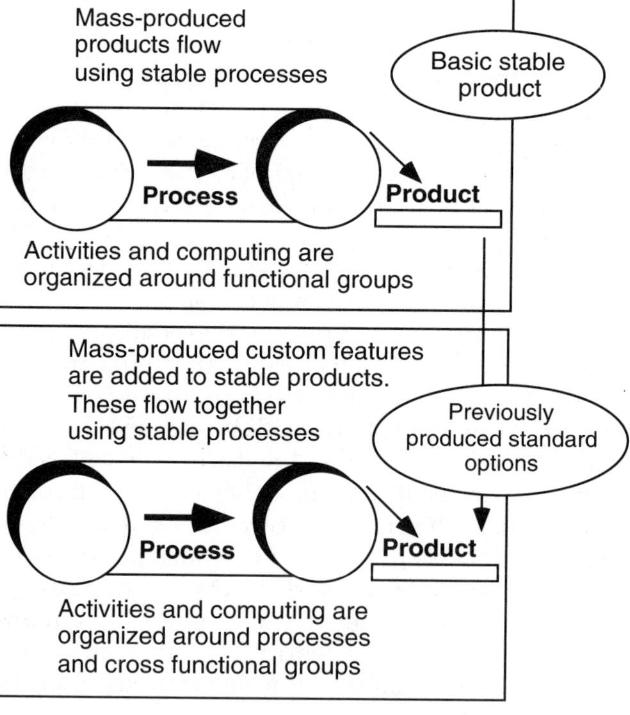

Figure 8.2   Mass customization causes systems to be organized around Processes.

uted to suit the mix-and-match nature of the business. Under such conditions we need to logically connect our systems to make them work cohesively. The flexibility of Client/Server-based systems is unsurpassed in this regard. However, because of the rigid coupling between data and applications in the legacy environment, we have to regenerate the data from legacy systems and then acquire or build new applications based on the regenerated data. The relationship between data and applications is now established through data services in a layered architecture.

Response to a dynamic business climate requires that the information delivery systems and services be adaptive and flexible. The evolution of information systems has thus far supported the mass-production paradigm. Response to the new business challenges will require a realignment of information systems with the business strategies. In a practical sense, we have to transition from current legacy systems to a more flexible architecture-driven environment. We observe that changes to current computing systems in a stable enterprise require long cycle times. The operation and maintenance of the legacy systems are costly. In a large, multibillion dollar enterprise nearly a third of the computing labor costs are directly related to data integration and independence. In the following sections we will examine the importance of linkages with business processes, integration with business process models, and the impact of total quality improvements; some technical and cultural issues from a legacy system transition perspective will also be discussed.

8.1   LINKAGES

Information systems should be aligned and linked with the business direction or strategies. It can be impractical to align legacy systems rapidly with the changing business and process conditions. We should transition legacy systems with a view to be responsive and remain linked to the business processes. Legacy systems transition is not a technology migration task from mainframes to distributed environment. It is a business realignment and process reengineering task.

Linkage of business direction with information systems implies that information is accessible and available. In reality, the accessibility to data to create information is not always possible. The data in legacy systems is enormous as revealed by the rate at which stored data in corporations is increasing annually. In the early 1980s, megabytes of data were considered to be large. In the mid-1990s, we are seeing data growing from terabytes to pedabytes in large high-technology firms. Does this mean that we have a lot of useful information, too? Not necessarily. Let us examine the business issue of information provisioning in the context of legacy systems transition in some detail.

In a less dynamic market environment, business executives could be driven with intuition, gut feelings, trial-and-error to make decisions. In general, past reputation and enjoying a stable market share have masked some real structural problems in many corporations. Today, the resources to invest in large technology projects that promise quantum leaps in information technologies are scarce. Therefore, we have to make the best from what we have. Figure 8.3 shows how the legacy systems data can be linked with business needs.

The data that has been accumulating in the legacy systems needs to be made accessible. The architectural principles of data services and data abstraction have been described in Chapters 4 and 5. The data is extracted and consolidated from the legacy systems based on the business process descriptions. In most cases, the extracted data is stored in a relational system. The data in such a database is also known as a data warehouse. What we call it is not important. However, the data content is of great value in analyzing and understanding the business situation. The interdependency between these two aspects—extracting needed data and the basis for determining what is needed data—makes the process of warehouse construction challenging. The purpose for extracting data is to facilitate analysis to support various information needs.

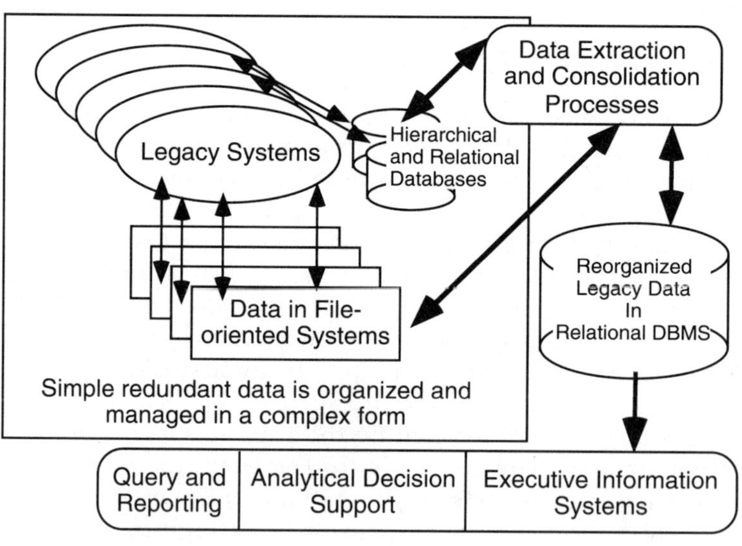

Figure 8.3   Linking legacy systems data to business requirements.

Essentially, the decision-support systems can be grouped into three broad classes: query and reporting, analytical decision support, and executive information systems. Figure 8.4 shows the essential features of each class. An important point to understand is that the legacy transition process should recognize the need to build this important data bridge by virtue of a data warehouse as the first step. The second step is to complete the data extraction process and build the decision-support application system. The decision-support capability will be provided by a number of vendor products. It will be important to architect the solution correctly so that data interchange and intercommunication between applications and data take place through well-defined service layers as described in earlier Chapters 5 and 6.

Simple reports are generated from relation tables in the lowest tier, generally by query tools. However, complex relations are not cost-effective or possible on simple two-dimensional tables. A frequent problem with

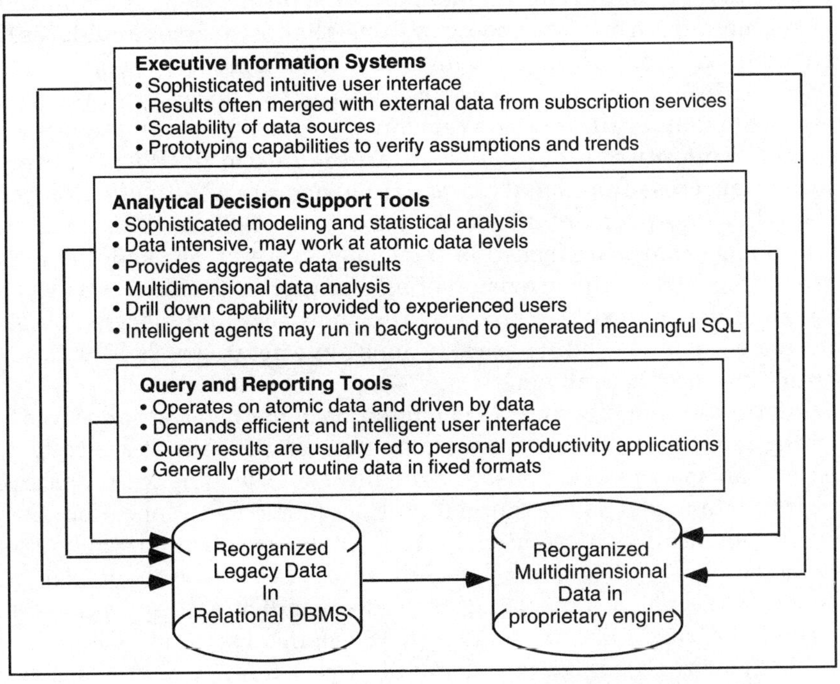

Figure 8.4   Decision-support applications and relationship with legacy data.

relational databases is that the user must have good knowledge of the underlying structures; otherwise, some illogical "joins" of tables may be requested inadvertently. Recently available query tools have some intelligent agents to verify a user's query. These intelligent agents are also called "wizards" in the industry jargon. Complex analysis and relationship among various tables are better addressed by multidimensional databases. These provide a more flexible structure for interactive discovery. The data is organized into a hierarchy of dimensions and measures known as a *hypercube*. When the hypercube is fully cross-indexed, it enables navigation along various directions. The multidatabase products usually run on proprietary engines. The data is downloaded from relation tables using special filters. The components shown in Figure 8.4 will be able to satisfy most known decision-support needs. If the legacy transition addresses this problem alone, then a lot of insight can be gained as to what processes need to be reengineered. Figure 8.5 shows examples of data organization.

8.1.1   Business Direction and Information Engineering

We need to understand the business direction in the context of information engineering in order to choose systems that are prime candidates for transition. Information engineering and business process reengineering present an interesting and necessary fusion of two disciplines. When we view this fusion intuitively, the relevance of cross-functional teams and continuous quality improvement comes into sharp focus. Without timely information, cross-functional teams cannot operate effectively. Continuous quality improvement efforts demand facts and data. The facts and data, in most cases, are locked in the legacy systems. We should have a method to facilitate the provision of information cost effectively. In the past, such needs were perceived by the end users and piecemeal solutions were implemented. These solutions have not unraveled the fundamental data access problem.

Information engineering is a combination of methodology and tools for creating reusable, common applications and components. It typically begins with an analysis of the business requirements, leading to the design of a logical data model as the foundation for a particular application. Once modeled, application information is stored in an organization-wide repository (accessible to developers). This lets the application be changed as the business rules change and enables the reuse of individual application components. The basic aim of model-driven development is to devise high-level specifications that transcend individual project implementations. Reuse cannot happen without planning. Model-driven development is the primary way to achieve that planning. These concepts were discussed in Chapter 7 from an application reengineering perspective.

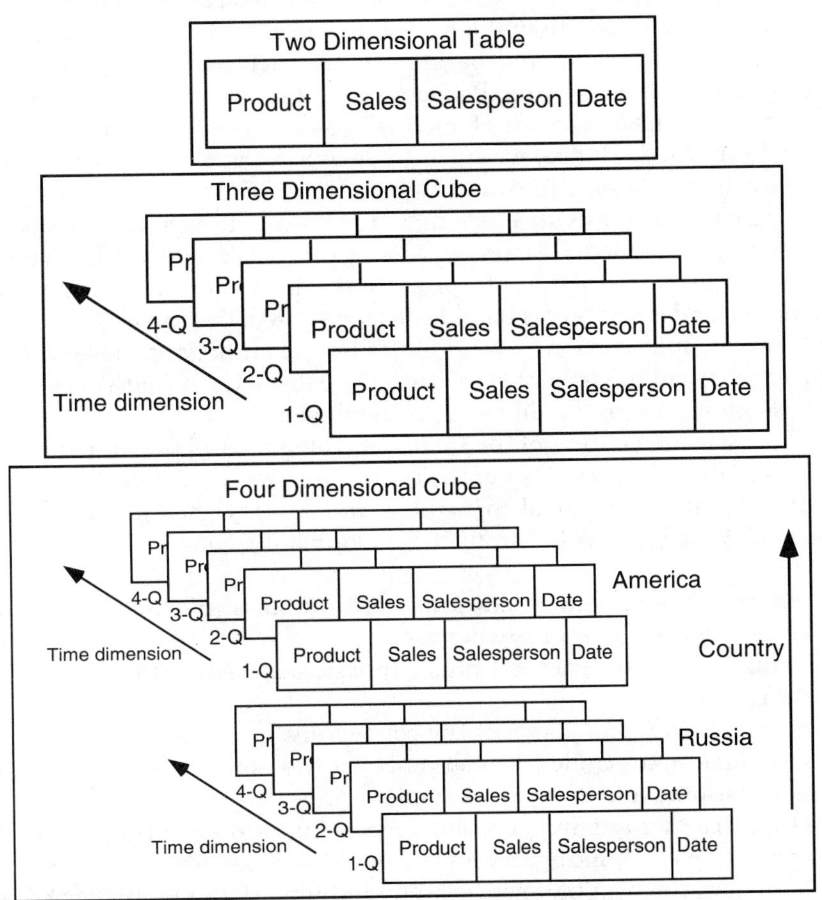

Figure 8.5   Multidimensional data organization for decision support.

A high-level enterprise model is an essential step in the legacy transition process. Both the process and application system owners have to agree on its content and detail. This should not become an elaborate task. In the past, several companies have not progressed beyond the modeling phase. That pitfall can be avoided if we set reasonable expectations for legacy transition tasks.

The business conditions will change while we are undergoing the transformation. These changes will require that the enterprise should strive for low-cost processes. New processes in the reengineered environment are defined by cross-functional teams. The cross-functional teams are empowered to make decisions based on facts and data. The information systems should be able to support cross-functional self-managed teams and provide the facts and data. The legacy systems still contain all the data necessary for a business reengineering process definition to proceed. Hence, we have to design a transition process that will allow new systems to run in conjunction with legacy systems.

Increasingly, companies are moving towards a horizontal corporation management model. Teams consisting of cross-functional skills manage the key processes of the enterprise. In this kind of model, hierarchical, functional, or departmental boundaries are erased. Customer focus is the key strategy. Information systems built along old functional lines will not support such a management structure. More directly, the data entrapped in these applications should be made available.

The combined efforts of the system developers and the process owners is essential at every stage of the transition process. Successful teams should operate on a set of principles. Ian Morley[2] has described the following 10 principles for product development teams.

- Select cohesive teams based on sentiments of mutual liking and respect for each other's expertise.
- Bring specialists from all major functional areas into the product design team.
- Ensure a common vision of the concurrent process.
- Organize a controlled convergence to the solution that everyone understands and everyone accepts.
- Organize vigilant information processing and encourage actively open-minded thinking. Avoid the facile, premature consensus.
- Maintain the best balance between individual and group work. Let individuals do the things that individuals do best—for example, the initial generation of new concepts.
- Use systematic methods.
- Use both formal and informal communication.
- Select at least some of the members according to how well-suited they are to the specific type of development work.
- Provide principled leadership.

8.1.2 Customer Satisfaction Dependencies

The success of the transition process depends on the involvement and commitment of the customer (the users of the system). Customer satisfaction depends on meeting cost, quality, and delivery expectations. Each of these can and should be measured by the project team. Improving the product quality is a necessary and relentless activity in keeping the customer satisfied. Continuous quality improvement is accomplished by introducing micro-process changes. The customer satisfaction has both an internal and external customer focus. Details are discussed in the following paragraphs.

8.1.2.1 Internal Customer Focus The internal customer is defined as the next person in the process who receives the work product of the previous worker. It is that simple. Therefore, if one does everything possible to delight the person next in the line, then we should have a very optimal and quality-oriented work force. Accountability is the key concept and measure. Figure 8.6 identifies four basic elements of the customer-supplier protocol: opening, negotiation, performance, and assessment. Using the customer-supplier protocol[3] to define processes allows a rich set of consistent measurements to be made of every customer-supplier relationship. These standard measurements contain three basic types of information:

1. Time (time for each phase, overall time, timelines of the supplier completion)
2. Overall outcome and the history of moves leading to it
3. Customer satisfaction

Figure 8.6 graphically depicts the various control points and outcomes using a pipeline flow representation and shows how a customer-supplier relationship can be established for maximum benefit.

8.1.2.2 External Customer Focus The external customer is somebody not directly involved with the organization, but is a consumer of the products and services produced by the supplying organization. In our context, the external customer will be the most important person for whom we are in business in the first place. Information is an indirect commodity that the external customer expects. Customer satisfaction principles are the same for all customers, both internal and external. An additional requirement of useability of the information product among internal customers becomes a consideration. The quality, cost, safety, and morale are key to satisfaction.

8.1.3   Business Process Articulation

The new business processes are articulated in a "to be" environment process model. Usually, a debate arises as to the importance of process models versus data models. In reality, both models are two sides of the same coin. Therefore, a degree of common sense needs to be exercised

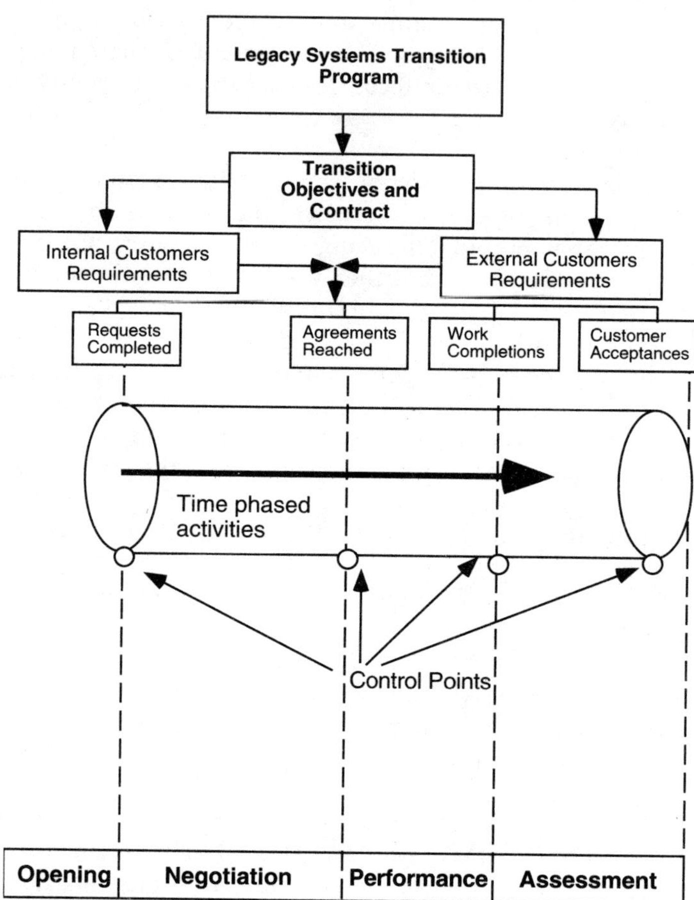

Figure 8.6   Customer focus.

when such debates become an impediment to progress. An example of a process description model is shown in Figure 8.7.

8.2   INTEGRATION

A key consideration is to continue to be able to co-process the residual legacy systems while we have partially transitioned some systems. The co-processing of legacy and new systems in a transactional environ-

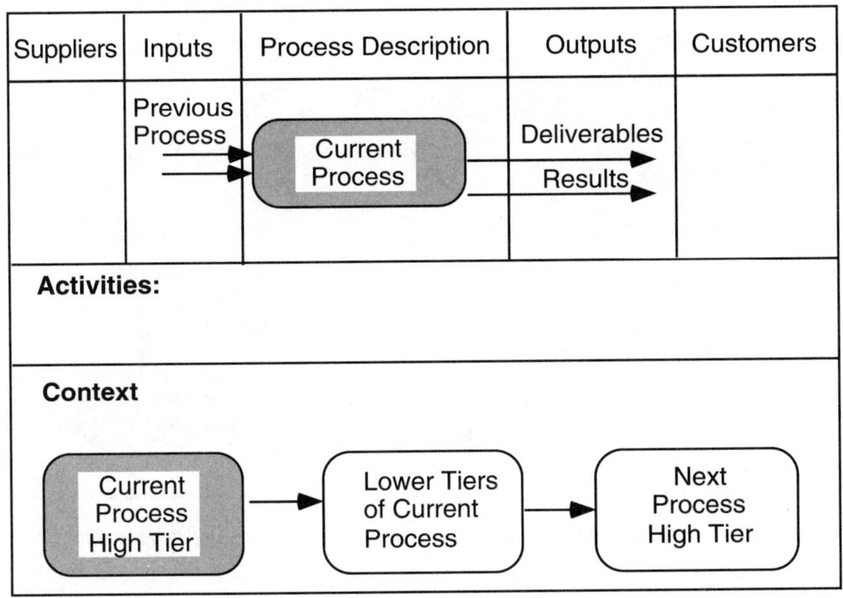

Figure 8.7   A process description model.

ment should not be accomplished with hard-coded interfaces. That is the old way of doing things. A new architecture for achieving transactional integration needs to be defined. We have to layer and isolate the changes by using data services (commonly called middleware). The data services layer mediates data transactions between residual legacy applications and the new transitioned applications. Through these architected data services, operational integration can be accomplished. Details of this technique were described in Chapters 5 and 6.

8.2.1   Operation Models

A concept of operations for the targeted legacy systems must be developed in the context of all enterprise-wide systems. This model defines a data management strategy in the new distributed environment and should address both the mainframe and server components along with the data they host. The model will also guide the staging of legacy applications in the transition process. An example of an operational model is shown in Figure 8.8.

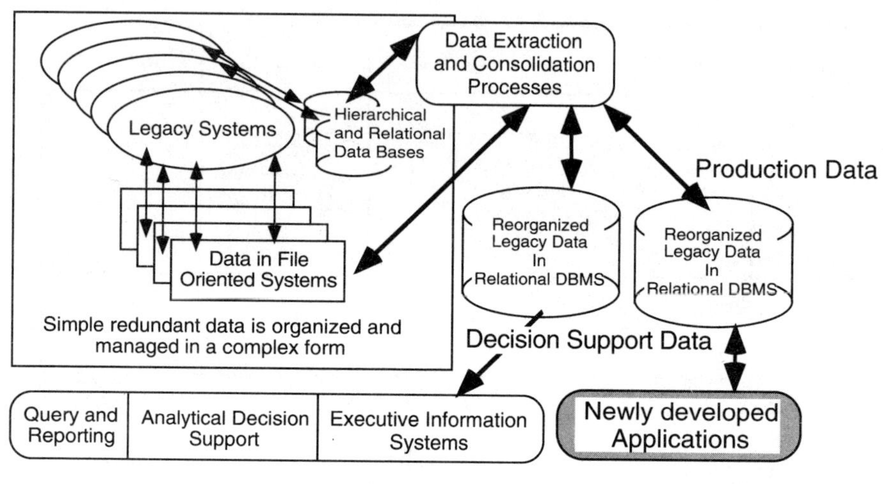

Figure 8.8   A concept of operations model for legacy systems transition.

8.2.2 Implementation Considerations

Implementation should be derived from the concept of the operations model. The implementation details are mostly centered around data management considerations. As observed earlier, we are not only

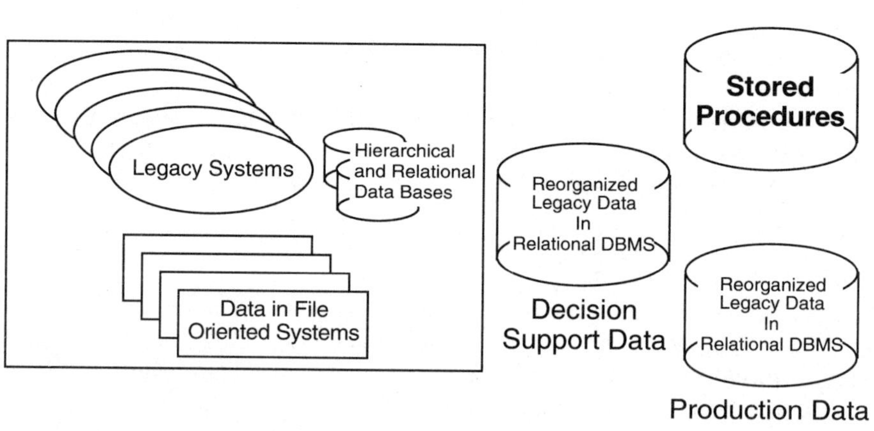

Figure 8.9   Scope of data management.

rehosting applications on a different platform, but also rehosting the process as well. The embedded processes in legacy applications are now rehosted as reusable procedures. The scope of data management is shown in Figure 8.9.

The data management in the distributed environment is different from the legacy environment. We are implementing application logic, data manipulation logic (process-based), and data with the associated metadata as separate resources logically connected by a distributed computing architecture. We are decomposing the monolithic code into manageable chunks of identifiable physical entities. Each entity is mapped to a relevant business process. In turn, the business processes support a macro or a micro process transformation. Thus, the quality improvements are manifested in computing applications as appropriate. This is a holistic approach that is necessary for the legacy transition process to be successful.

8.3   TOTAL QUALITY IMPROVEMENT

The transition process should be dependent on quality improvement initiatives. Normally, the process begins by questioning whether certain data is available to confirm an improvement proposal. This puts us in the domain of data access from legacy systems for decision support. In the traditional environment this entails a lengthy data restructuring and block point activity. The legacy transition project is to replace this lengthy process with a flexible data access and analysis capability. Therefore, it is essential that we keep the total quality improvement program in perspective while we perform the legacy transition process. A simple process to put the total quality improvement considerations in the context of the other applicable processes is shown in Figure 8.10.

8.3.1   Automation Dependencies

Total quality improvements are not limited to automation only. There will be situations where improvements do not depend on automation. However, for any process to be reliable, repeatable, and predictable we need facts and data. Hence, there is an indirect driver to the overall strategy of legacy systems transition—namely, information. The entire process of legacy systems transition should be driven with this consideration of providing information. The opportunities dependent on automation are the focus of this book.

8.3.2   Capturing Benefits and Costs

It is important to have a strategy and a process to capture benefits and costs of the transition project. The architecture should specify monitor-

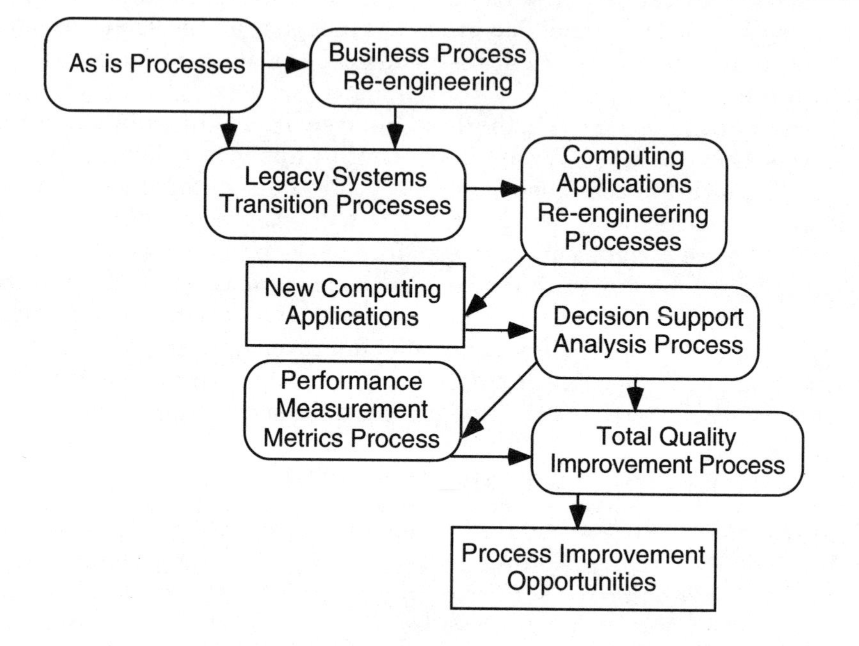

Figure 8.10   The context of the total quality improvement process.

ing applications that operate on data usage and storage costs. Rarely have information technologists measured the benefits that they have afforded the organization. In difficult economic times it is very important to justify and confirm the costs and benefits.

8.3.3   Macro Versus Micro Process Changes

The process changes dictated (total quality improvements) can be macro or micro changes. Typically, micro changes can be accommodated in the legacy transition process, where the application may not have changed substantially. In reality, the access to data and sophisticated decision-support capability given almost instantly during the transition will generate the required facts and data for specifying macro process changes. Macro changes are generally implemented in the new distributed environment and applications. The macro changes are considered at the highest level of authority, the process owners. These processes are described by global terms such as define, acquire, produce, support, and so on. Explanations of these terms are provided in subsequent sections. Changes are an inevitable occurrence of being in business in a dynamic environment. Information systems enable the new business dynamics.

8.4   TECHNOLOGY ISSUES

Technology issues should not concern the users overtly. Most of the implementation complexities should be hidden from the users. It is possible to do so by using sophisticated graphical user interfaces and data services as described in Chapters 4 through 6. The application designers need to be aware of separating user requirements that sound like technology specifications when providing a capability. Stated differently, user requirements should state what is needed, not how it should be implemented. There is a fine line between these considerations, but a skillful application developer can distinguish between a solution and a requirement.

8.4.1   Readiness of the Users

The legacy transition will certainly result in some procedural changes in how data is managed and owned. The user should be trained and prepared to accept changes. Involving the users from the beginning in the transition process will enhance the chances for the reengineering effort to succeed. The legacy transition plan should be coordinated with deployment plans in the user organizations.

8.4.2   Defining Policies and Procedures

The new infrastructure will consist of two distinct environments. The first is the mainframe-based systems and the second is the distributed Client/Server environment. A set of policies and procedures should be put in place before any implementation is started. The infrastructure includes:

- Data and application servers management
- Distributed data management infrastructure
- Network management and administration
- New application deployment plan
- Legacy systems sunset or retirement policy

The scope and depth of these policies vary with business enterprise.

8.5 PROGRAM DEPLOYMENT ISSUES

The deployment of the legacy systems transition program will be met with a number of issues, least of which have to do with technology. No matter how good the transition plan, it is a matter of fact that change will always be resisted. We should be prepared to deal with this reality right up front. The two primary categories of resistance are people and management, which are dealt with in the following sections. A general model will help in understanding the issues. Figure 8.11 is a model by its virtue commonly prevalent situations in large companies can be explained. Not all companies may fit the model. The scope may be different and all groups identified in Figure 8.11 may not physically exist in any single company. However, the model is logical and is designed to help the reader understand the following discussion. The legacy sys-

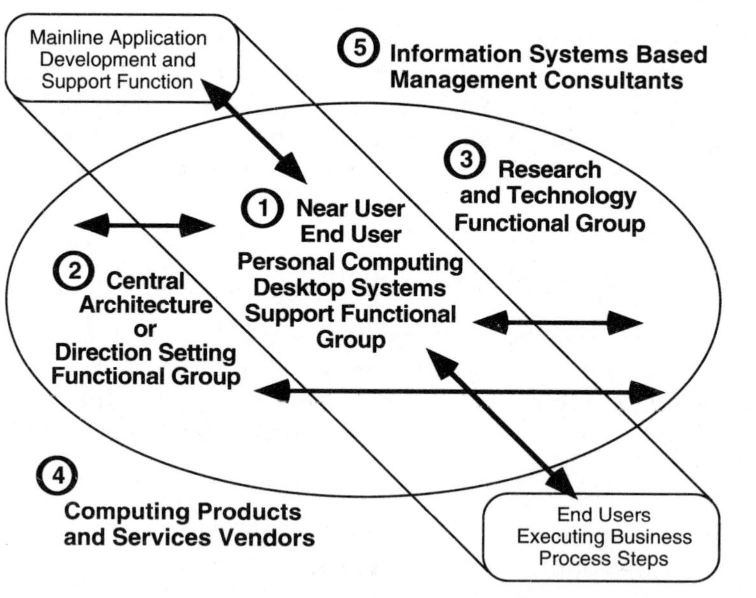

Figure 8.11 Legacy systems issues model and influence zones.

tems issues model shown in Figure 8.11 is interpreted as follows. The "influence rectangle" is the boundary of the information services and technology groups' influence scope on the enterprise chosen for discussion in this instance.

8.5.1 Influence Zones

Figure 8.11 has the following influence zones.

- Legacy systems are generally developed, maintained, and supported by a central information systems group shown in the top left-hand corner **"service provider rectangle."**
- At the bottom right-hand corner the ultimate user of the system is shown in the **"service receiver rectangle."**
- The set of two inclined parallel lines show the **"interaction zone"** between the developers and the users.
- The ellipse contains the various **"functional groups ellipse."**
- The space outside of the ellipse in the "influence rectangle" is occupied by vendors and consultants in the **"outside influence space."**
- The double-headed arrows indicate **"interaction and influence space"** between groups.

There are five distinct generic groups numbered in the figure that constitute the people areas where issues develop.

8.5.2 People Issues

People issues can be analyzed systematically using the general model shown in Figure 8.11. A detailed description is given by looking at each group in the overall context of the service provider rectangle.

8.5.2.1 Group 1—End-user Computing

The core area of the interaction zone is occupied by group 1. In this group the principal activities can be described as provision of all services that will help the users for whom the systems were developed in the first place. The arcane nature of mainframe technology is the primary reason for this group to be invented. As technology evolved, this group adopted several names to harness the power of personal computers, workstations, data download capabilities, local area network file-server systems, and such. This very visible group closest to the users also assumed the role of being the bridge between mainframe services and PC services. This group also has skills that are at various levels of maturation because of the instability of the personal computing's evolving picture.

8.5.2.2 Group 2—Central Architecture The central architecture group is a recent invention. This group is generally responsible for defining broad standards to bring uniformity in the products, techniques, and tools used throughout the enterprise. The function of the "Chief Information Officer" is generally responsible for creating this group. If the group is organized with skilled individuals and empowered to deploy and implement a cohesive computing architecture, then it can serve a key function in making legacy systems transition a success. However, we will observe later that the group can get mired in startup problems and lack of focus. The central architecture function was nonexistent in the mainframe world. The technology and architecture direction was set by marketing savvy individuals of large mainframe systems vendors. Their enormous influence and reach is indirectly responsible for the legacy systems' inadequacies. The legacy systems transition process can be expected to cure all the ills of past years in one magical step. At least that is sometimes the expectation of the executive management.

8.5.2.3 Group 3—Research and Technology The research and technology group is essentially charged with the responsibility in the information systems context to monitor, pilot, and transfer technology. It serves an important function in an environment where obsolescence is a constant. In the ideal situation this group acts as a primary supplier of information to group 2. In the past, the research and technology group also used to serve the role that is now served by group 2.

8.5.2.4 Group 4—Vendors and Suppliers Vendors and suppliers of computing products and services play a very important role in the overall legacy systems transition process. By virtue of their long-standing relationships with users, this group is influential in generating requirements to acquire tools and technologies by group 1. In a distributed environment, seemingly simple tools as SQL-Windows products and, 3270 screen scraping tools (mainframe data download products) can create enormous problems if improperly implemented. The validity of such products in the solution process is not questioned. However, such requests create interesting situations in the legacy systems transition program.

8.5.2.5 Group 5—External Consultants External consultants are very common in large companies. These consultants tend to influence chief information officers to an extent. They serve an important role in facilitating commercially available off-the-shelf-technology transfer and present useful information to management at various levels. The influence of external consultants in the context of all the other groups creates some situations that are hard to ignore in the transition environment.

8.5.3 Cause-and-Effect Analysis of People Issues

A cause-and-effect analysis of people issues is due mainly to perceptions of the legacy systems transition team. These can be classified and analyzed in the context of Figure 8.11 and the group descriptions. Tables 8.1 through 8.5 describe the perceptions of a group, change conditions, and suggestions for improvement. The discomfort zones or pathology are a result of some key symptoms. These are listed in the following tables. The contents only analyze negative perceptions. Many good things happen in all these groups; however, that is not the objective of the analysis.

People issues are mostly centered around either elimination of their current job function or a modification that may require acquiring new skills. Both situations are difficult to deal with. Benefits are predicated on reduction of direct labor and productivity enhancements. The management must be honest and up front as far as the reduction in labor is concerned. The second issue of training should be part of the project deliverable. The issue can be resolved by having a complete plan for skills redeployment and training. When the employees see that changes are handled honestly and positively, a gradual change in attitudes will occur.

8.5.4 Management Issues

The management issues stem primarily from negotiating the new data management and ownership situation. The data on servers will be a corporate resource as opposed to being owned by a particular organization. Also, applications no longer own and control data. Hence, we have to reengineer the entire change management and configuration control processes that were in operation for a long time in the mainframe environment. Replicating the mainframe situation in the new distributed environment will be a mistake. Perhaps this will be the most important management issue.

Table 8.1   Group 1 End-user Computing

Perceptions of the transition team	Pathology of the change conditions	Suggestions for improvement
1. Loss of control	Symptoms: Distributed data along with good decision-support applications renders information readily accessible and ubiquitous. Diagnosis: A loss of control.	Moving analysts into a consultant and requirements validation role as opposed to information filters. Control is a perception, not a real problem.
2. Fear of greater visibility	Symptoms: Acquisition of computing hardware located in the user area increases management visibility. Diagnosis: Fear of visibility.	Give tools to report cost/benefits and raise the knowledge level of management. Visibility is turned to positive success story reporting as opposed to being punitive and negative if expectations shortfalls occur.
3. Loss of job security	Symptoms: Mainframe reports tend to be terse and rigid. These needed a level of massaging with PC tools. Diagnosis: Loss of security.	Security is a measure of being perceived of value. Value enhancement occurs if benefits are reported and losses are cut rapidly with management participation.
4. Skill base inadequacy	Symptoms: Several new application generation tools are becoming available; management does not respond rapidly to provide just-in-time training. Diagnosis: A feeling of rejection.	Training is essential. A lot of personal commitment is required. It is unlikely that companies will remedy this situation. Face the reality, a lot of well-educated younger generation are knocking at our doors incessantly. Personal effort is the key.

Table 8.1 *Continued*

Perceptions of the transition team	*Pathology of the change conditions*	*Suggestions for improvement*
5. Unclear direction	Symptoms: Unclear mainframe to distributed computing transition plans. Lack of training budgets for transition. Diagnosis: Confusion, fear, uncertainty, and despair.	This is a startup issue. As more consultants and hype salesman pass through the doors, relevant questions will be asked. An informed analyst will not be confused, afraid, or in despair.
6. Business process reengineering impact	Symptoms: Savings projected on downsizing of support organizations. Elimination of management layers and associated staff. Diagnosis: Unclear direction of whom the group will support and how.	This is a business reality. No magic solutions exist in this regard. The informed and the flexible individual survives these impacts.
7. Paradigm shift jargon	Symptoms: The "paradigm shift" becomes an often-quoted term for communication. Diagnosis: Unfamiliar terms to establish communications. Doubt and fear become a growing behavior pattern.	Learn the jargon and use to your benefit. Skepticism is the first sign of self-rejection and refusing to be a team player. Doubt and fear are eliminated by educating ourselves in the technology and business direction of the company.
8. Change of the status quo	Symptoms: Downloading data from mainframes is fine. Nothing is broken; what are we trying to fix. Diagnosis: Perception to require a "stretch" from current mode of operation.	This is the biggest complacence issue. Smell the coffee; do something to get motivated.

Table 8.1   *Continued*

Perceptions of the transition team	*Pathology of the change conditions*	*Suggestions for improvement*
9. Outsource threat	Symptoms: Information services can be outsourced. Mainframes looked upon as a transition to be framed out for facility management services. Diagnosis: Dislocation, uncertainty, and despair.	As the inter-operability issue gets communicated and understood, companies will recognize that mainframe service disposition is an irrelevant issue. Asset use maximization should be demonstrated by rapidly bringing new applications online.
10. Mainframe mentality	Symptoms: Distributed computing will not succeed. How can we move mission critical application to any other environment? Diagnosis: Unwilling to accept reality. Stubborn and uncooperative behavior.	Once again, do demonstrate success in incremental steps. Do not risk the whole and do "big bang" projects. Prudence is the operative word. Skeptics will be on the exit list, behavior will change with time.
11. Communications	Symptoms: Transition plan not understood or communicated at all levels. Shotgun approach to implementation of critical projects. Diagnosis: Insecurity and feeling of being left out.	Transition plans have to be constantly reviewed against progress. Delayed communication will be lethal. Shotgun projects rarely succeed. Collect metrics to prove these claims.
12. Lack of team-building efforts	Symptoms: Team members not at same level of understanding project details. Communications happen outside of the project. Diagnosis: Exposure and vulnerability. Constant fire fighting to gain control over project.	Communication sessions, project visibility walls are some possible suggestions for team building. External facilitators for brainstorming improvements is another tool that produces good results.

Table 8.1   *Continued*

Perceptions of the transition team	*Pathology of the change conditions*	*Suggestions for improvement*
13. Someone else taking control of your domain	Symptoms: Reorganization of responsibilities for no apparent reason. New personnel taking over responsibilities. Diagnosis: Insecurity and instability of job function.	This mainly starts as a communications issue. Improper reporting will cause project redirection. Sometimes teams fail; that is a reality.
14. Turf issues	Symptoms: Duplication and violation of previously set ground rules. Diagnosis: Unclear roles in the new environment.	Distributed computing breaks barriers; turf issues will only settle with time. As organizations downsize, there will be little to fight for.
15. A reorganization mania	Symptoms: Lack of organizational stability with respect to reporting relationships. Diagnosis: Loyalty and threat to long-standing relationships.	This is a startup issue. As pilots and proof of concepts stabilize, an order will emerge in successful organizations. However, you cannot organize your way out of incompetence.
16. Rumor mill	Symptoms: Too much nonvalue-added activities. Loss of morale and a cohesive workgroup feeling. Diagnosis: Feeling of loss of control on events and dedication to job activities.	Communicate, communicate, and communicate.

Table 8.2   Group 2 Central Architecture

Perceptions of the transition team	Pathology of the change conditions	Suggestions for improvement
1. Lack of empowerment	Symptoms: Group 1 still controls most user communications and design decisions. Diagnosis: A loss of control.	Provide meaningful architecture direction in a useable form, eliminating ambiguous long-term visions. That way one can get control of decisions and feel empowered to act by virtue of persuasion not autonomy.
2. Vendor penetration with mainframe and end users. End-user meddling with nonstandard products introduction and proliferation. Distributed computing elements show up as low-value assets causing large-scale integration headaches.	Symptoms: Acquisition of computing hardware still driven by mainframe relationship of dominant vendors. Diagnosis: Frustration in implementing architecture direction. Fail to control hardware variation and costs.	Establish a vendor teaming policy at the highest level. Make vendors partners by negotiating very high discount levels for doing business. When commissions are hard to earn, the vendors do communicate with all concerned parties. The old carrot and stick is recast as partnership and cooperation. It is just a perception management ploy.
3. Lack of focus	Symptoms: Too many initiatives; network modernization, desktop systems revamping, legacy systems transition, and constant internal selling. Diagnosis: Missed goals and milestones.	Business case-driven approach, support large business process redesign efforts to get major benefits first. Out prioritize everything else. Do not indulge in technology pushing.

Table 8.3   Group 3 Research and Technology

Perceptions of the transition team	Pathology of the change conditions	Suggestions for improvement
1. Analysis paralysis	Symptoms: Pilots, proof of concepts, prototypes, and evaluations are conducted ad nauseam. Diagnosis: No useable technology gets to the users fast.	Have a time bound and negotiated technology transfer plan. Establish customer satisfaction criteria, such as quality, costs, schedule, and delivery. Clearly show the areas of uncertainty that demand a level of deliberation.
2. Technology push with no linkage to business processes.	Symptoms: Solutions looking for problems. Object-programming will cure all ills. There are silver bullets to solve business problems with computing technologies. Diagnosis: Efforts seen as irrelevant. Fundamental analysis versus technological analysis.	Produce operating plans based on business process redesign requirements. Support the key principles that drive information systems strategies. Analysis is for justifying goals and objectives, not for making a case for introducing a technology because it has some perceived benefits as opposed to real benefits.
3. Diffused business charter and responsibilities with respect to architecture group.	Symptoms: Crossed signals and confused architecture direction specification, especially in areas of standards setting and influencing external standards formulating bodies. Diagnosis: General confusion.	Value analysis of activities and understanding interference zones in job functions will greatly help the situation. Job rotation is another powerful means to establish relationships and technological bonding.

Table 8.4   Group 4 External Vendors

Perceptions of the transition team	*Pathology of the change conditions*	*Suggestions for improvement*
1. We will spend the money anyway, maybe not on mainframes	Symptoms: Increase on acquiring cheaper, larger computers in small increments but large volume. Proliferation in data storage and data server capacities with no perceptible increase in business data processing demands. Diagnosis: No decrease in capital costs.	Tighter control end-to end in a program environment. Distributed computing administration should not start with overnight financial transfer of budgets to the divisions. The producing divisions' budgets should be tied to profit measures. In other words, if there are no acceptable profits generated from the benefits accrued through computing, then do not embark on that procurement.
2. Vaporware	Symptoms: Our next version will do it. It is in beta test as we speak. Products perform on view foil platforms right now. We have the market dominance, we can deliver. Diagnosis: Reality gap.	Trust but always check your sources. Get procurement folks involved for pressing terms and conditions. No performance, no pay.
3. Endless demonstrations	Symptoms: Just saw a terrific product; how come we did not buy it? Diagnosis: Solutions chasing problems.	Balance education with knowledge. You must see the demonstrations, but do not get taken.

Table 8.5   Group 5 Management Consultants

Perceptions of the transition team	*Pathology of the change conditions*	*Suggestions for improvement*
1. New buzz words to deal with every day	Symptoms: Action items from executives to explain buzz words. Diagnosis: A loss of control.	Play this one carefully. Communications are important. Face it as a fact of life. No other suggestions are available.
2. If systems integration fails, the folks become management consultants	Symptoms: New proposals to provide just the silver bullet we are looking for. Diagnosis: Evaluations and more strategy meetings.	Identify value-added engagements and perform meaningful cost/benefits analysis.
3. Recruited to support corporate agendas	Symptoms: More program cancellations and redirections. Diagnosis: Loss of security.	Security is a measure of being perceived of value. Value enhancement occurs if benefits are reported and losses are cut rapidly with management participation.

CHAPTER NOTES

1. Boynton, A.C., B.Victor, and B.J. Pine II. "New Competitive Strategies: Challenges to Organizations and Information Technology." *IBM Systems Journal,* vol. 32, no. 1 (1993).
2. Ian Morley, "Building Cross-Functional Design Teams." In *Proceedings of the First International Conference on Integrated Design Management,* London (June 13-14, 1990).

The Transition Process

The legacy systems transition process is a delicate balancing act between the old and the new environments. An important consideration is to cause no disruption to the production environment and ongoing business functions during the transition. An understanding of these two environments is essential in determining the transition process. Therefore, carefully developed transition process is required. The starting point is the definition of business processes generally provided by the process owners. Business process definition is not a computing function. Certain business processes are suitable for automation; these automation opportunities are implemented in computing systems during the transition process. Some key steps for developing the transition process are as follows:

- From the business processes determine the metadata and data classification logic
- Classify data as released, shared, and private.
- Create classes of metadata based on business process rules.
- Create subjects for operational and decision-support data stores.
- Decouple "business rules or procedures" from applications and store these as metadata or reusable stored procedures, as appropriate.
- Create metadata stores satisfying each business process class; e.g., application development, end-user data read-only access, end-user application development.
- Create transaction databases.

- Create databases for decision-support uses.
- Define data replication and synchronization process for decision-support data stores.
- Phase in application development (or rehosting) deployment plans.
- Establish processes for operating legacy systems in parallel with new distributed systems in an active data update mode until the source legacy systems are replaced.
- Phase in technology deployment plan.
- Define new data management processes for data and metadata.
- Phase in user training.

Some additional project-related steps may be:

- Gather and pin down business visions, objectives, and strategies.
- Develop linkage principles into technologies.
- Develop information technology architecture.
- Develop pilot projects to introduce technology.
- Coordinate business process reengineering with new technologies.
- Develop skills enhancement plans.
- Develop system design.
- Develop deployment plan.

Figure 9.1 shows how these various ideas fit in the overall scheme of transition. Each of the generic processes should be further decomposed to suit the requirements of a specific organization. A brief description of each of these process components follows.

From the business processes determine the data required and how it should be classified for management.   The business processes define the key macro-processes and the core competencies of a business. These are provided by the process owners. By using these processes, a high-level classification logic is arrived for both the data and metadata.

Create classes of data as released, shared, and private.   A data-driven view of transition will require an understanding of the scope of data and how it is integrated and managed (ownership, autonomy, etc.) across the enterprise. The classification logic of the previous process is used as input. An important concept is to classify the data in three classes as a minimum. The first, released data, consists of data that undergoes a process of formal release and subsequent changes are managed. The second, shared data, includes common data that is used as a resource and is not controlled by any specific application program.

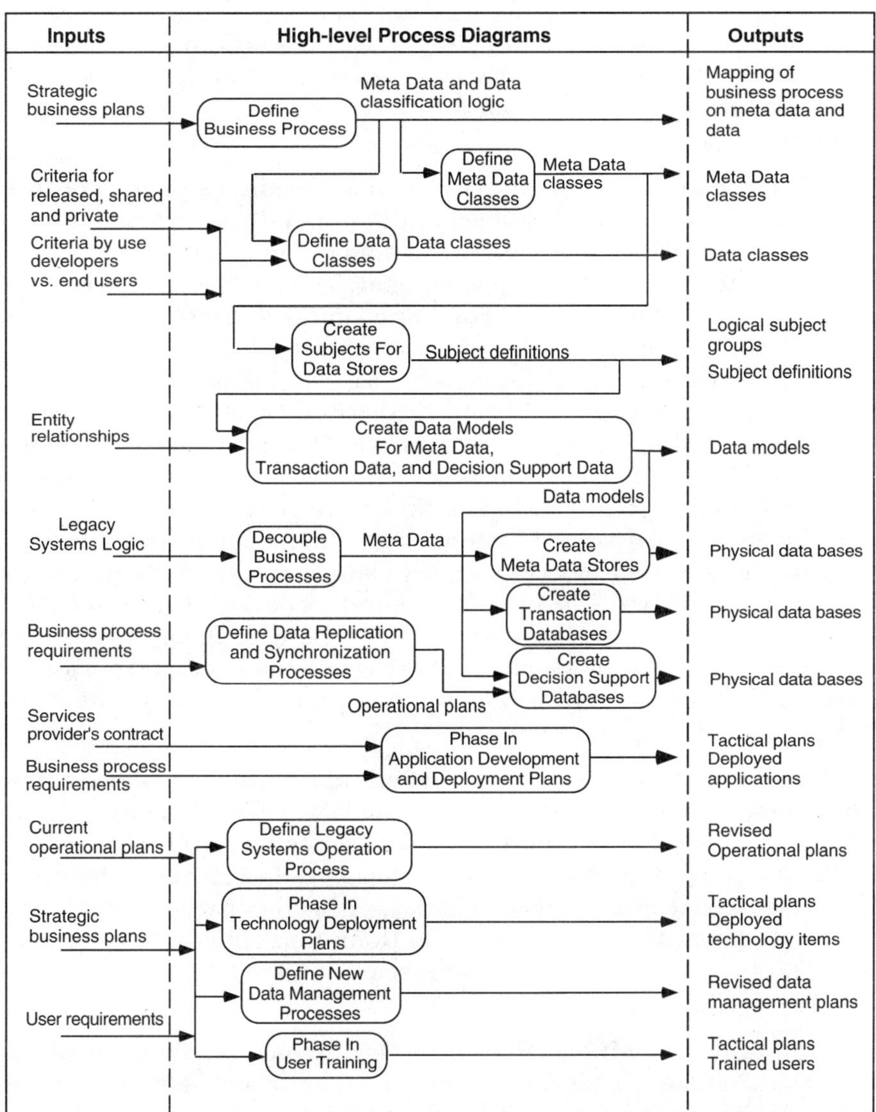

Figure 9.1   A high-level transition process diagram.

The third, private data, is fundamentally derived from shared data. Private data may include additional data that is created by end users. Such data can be of interest to a limited set of users. There can be many more classes depending on the business processes. The data classes also guide the physical delivery platform architecture and data management strategies.

Define classes of metadata based on business process rules. Metadata concepts were described in Chapter 4. It is important to recognize that there are many different kinds of metadata and each requires a different architectural treatment. The business processes will give us a clue to classify metadata. For example, the metadata used by application developers is different from that used by end users. It is conceivable that metadata classes will closely parallel data classes. The architecture for delivery platform will also be dictated by the metadata classification. Also, it will be clear as to what metadata should be made active during run-time environment.

Another useful concept is a run-time (active) logical data dictionary and directory. In a distributed computing environment, it is both impractical and unnecessary to locate all metadata centrally. The logical data dictionary and directory become the integrating part of all data. A logical data dictionary and directory provide a single data image to the user during run time. The metadata affords the various kinds of transparencies for data services. Figure 9.2 shows an example of how metadata can be classified based on user scenarios.

Create classes of metadata based on business process rules. The business process rules define the what, when, and where for data. All these physical data characteristics are described by virtue of the metadata attached to the data. Once again a classification should be performed based on these requirements. These requirements also drive the data management tactical plans. Definition of user views of data based on the business processes also require metadata containing the location, origin, and genealogy of data.

Decouple "Business Processes" information from applications and store these as metadata. The business process rules embedded in legacy systems define the data creation, read, update, and delete criteria. All these physical data instance activities are described by virtue of the metadata attached to the data. Once again, a classification should be performed based on these "CRUD" requirements. These requirements also drive the data management tactical plans. Managing this class of data as metadata formalizes the process—documentation in an accessible computerized format.

Metadata Components	Developer	End-User Developer	End User	Decision Support Analyst
Structure	yes	yes		no
Source	yes	yes	yes	yes
Transformation	yes	yes	no	no
Directory	yes	yes	✔	✔
Dictionary	yes	yes	✔	✔
Genealogy	yes	yes	✔	yes
Rules	yes	yes	✔	yes
Models	yes	yes	✔	no
Mapping Models	yes	no	no	yes
Ownership	yes	no	✔	no
Change Board	yes	no	✔	no
Platform Data	yes	yes	✔	no
Process Owner	yes	no	no	no
System Owner	yes	yes	no	no
Replication Rules	yes	no	no	no
Synchronization Rules	yes	no	no	yes
Storage Media	yes	yes	no	no

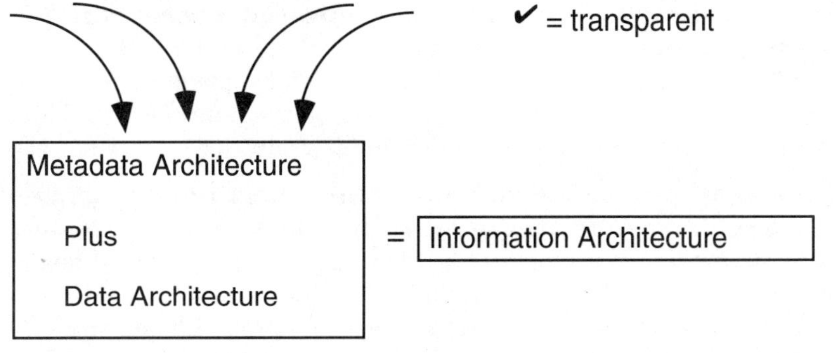

Figure 9.2   Metadata management concepts.

Create subjects for operational and decision-support data stores.   A classification of data by subjects will greatly minimize the data redundancy problem caused by the legacy systems. Subject definition will generate the logical subject classification for shared data. Subject orientation also affords data independence from applications.

Decouple "Business Processes" from applications and store these as metadata.   The legacy systems have some common business rules related to data updates encoded in them. Decoupling and storing of these rules is necessary in defining new operating procedures. The decoupling process will provide additional metadata.

Create metadata stores satisfying each business process class (e.g., application development, end-user data read-only access, end-user application development).   This process will create the physical data stores and delivery platform architecture driven by business process requirements.

Create transaction databases.   The preceding processes generate the information required to create the physical data stores. Normally, a variety of computer-assisted software engineering, CASE tools, are used for accomplishing the process step.

Create databases for decision-support uses.   The preceding processes relevant to decision support generate the information required to create the physical data stores or data warehouse.

Define data replication and synchronization process for decision-support data stores.   Decision-support data is derived or copied from transaction databases. Therefore, a process for replication frequency and synchronization for time-dependent, nonvolatile data needs to be defined. This process defines the details for implementation.

Phase in application development (or rehosting) deployment plans.   Once the data-related infrastructure tasks are accomplished, the entire application portfolio management process can begin. When we are linking the applications to the business processes in a continuous quality improvement situation, a one-to-one mapping of legacy applications to the new environment is not possible or required. In rare cases, some applications can be rehosted on the new delivery platform. An applications development plan and a deployment plan can be implemented, as we have established data as a "resource."

Establish processes for operating legacy systems in parallel with new distributed systems in an active data update mode until the source legacy systems are replaced.   It is very important to recognize that we are implementing an architecture in an ongoing production environment. Therefore, when we are rolling out new applications in a new data environment, we may have to operate some applications in parallel. This process will describe how we operate legacy systems and synchronize the data in a shared environment. Some strategies for data synchronization are described in Chapter 11.

Phase in technology deployment plan.   In most existing environments the implementation of distributed computing will require revamping of obsolete technologies and computing platforms. A technology deployment plan deals with network infrastructure, workstation modernization, and server deployment. These are the pacing items in an overall legacy system transition program.

Define new data management processes for data and metadata.   A key requirement is to understand that the old data management processes that managed the data via legacy systems will be obsolete in the new distributed environment. In this process step we define the procedures and processes used to manage the distributed data and metadata.

Phase in user training.   In the transition plan new technology, such as graphical user interfaces, platform access, security rules, has to be reintroduced to the users. The success of the plan is greatly enhanced by providing relevant training to the users as well as the developers of applications.

9.1   DOCUMENTING THE "AS IS" ENVIRONMENT

In most cases, the current environment will be as shown in Figure 9.3. It will be helpful for the transition planning process if we can document the "as is" environment from three viewpoints:

- Application
- Data
- Delivery platform

9.1.1   Application

Process-driven classification.   The legacy applications should be mapped against the new business processes. In most cases the mapping will show a confused picture of a single application going across multiple processes. This is normal because these applications were built along functional lines. However, if legacy applications cover the full

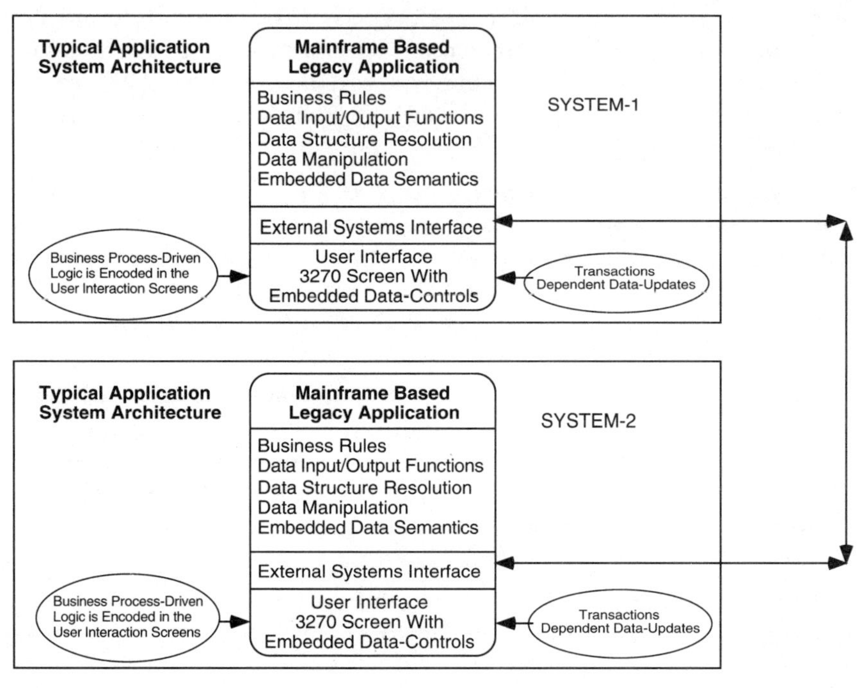

Figure 9.3   Current as is environment.

range of multiple processes, we may have to decompose the new applications into manageable chunks. Perhaps such a set of legacy applications can be phased out at a later time in the transition plan.

Business rules.   A mapping of what business rules are encoded in which application is useful in capturing the stored procedures for use in the transition process. These business rules can include data edit rules, and actions the application will launch based on the satisfaction of a process rule; for example, order inventory if the level reaches a certain point.

Simplification based on reorganization.   The legacy applications can be further classified to effect certain simplifications in the "to be" environment. A table containing a mapping of what process aggregations are encoded in a given application will let us determine a phase-out plan. This table is related to the process-driven classification as described earlier.

9.1.2   Data

A mapping of data elements (user object-view-driven) that each application uses is perhaps the most useful and tedious exercise. The information should include the structure, syntax, semantics (computational meaning, definition, contextual meaning, transformations made within the application, rules for altering its meaning, etc.). Semantics capture is the most complicated part of the exercise. As one goes deeper into understanding the data, certain aspects become apparent that should be included in the description footnotes of the data element.

It is permissible to ignore certain aspects of the data, especially those that are physical implementation-oriented. In the new environment we need not perform the heroics of the past years to save computing resources. We have a different set of challenges. The power and price of both storage and computing power is more favorable than 20 years ago when these legacy systems were built.

In some instances we may not have all the details. It is fine. We will guess certain details and verify as we go along from the actual performance. Transition process is not a one-shot deal with perfection guaranteed. It is wasteful to reengineer legacy application data models. These will take forever and the cost rarely justifies the expense. Classical data resource theoreticians will disagree, but practicality, experience, and common sense should guide our decisions.

9.1.3   Platform

The last set of details needed are the application platform details. A listing of processor, operating system, data management (file structure, database management system), communication protocols, programming language used, and so on for each legacy system should be captured.

In summary, the preceding information will aid us in completing the processes outlined in Figure 9.1.

9.2   TECHNOLOGY ASSESSMENT OF THE ENVIRONMENT

In most cases, the "as is" environment will be mainframe-centric. It is conceivable that most of the users with personal computers download data from legacy systems and manipulate these to suit individual requirements. In some cases, data can also be uploaded to the mainframes. In any event, the environment will be incapable of data integration or equipment interoperation. The data communications hardware will consist of gateways, bridges, routers, and data switches. A lack of a planned implementation of technology based on a meaningful architecture is the prime culprit for such a situation.

The following paragraphs contain some observations regarding information services for large organizations.

Desktop computing direction is proceeding into an object and reuse orientation. Data drives these applications. The current data delivery mechanisms—replication through extracts and refreshed copies—will not be feasible. We need to think how the mainframe-based data is best delivered to the users. The question is not when the mainframes will be unplugged. It is, rather, what we have to do so that the demand for mainframes goes down commensurate with the increased costs of end-user computing on desktop devices. When mainframe demand goes down, it will become easy to reduce the number of mainframes at the right time as dictated by business conditions—not when mandated by executives or as projected by technologists.

New applications will not look like the ones we have today. As a matter of fact we do not even know what these will be; for example, numbers, functionality groupings, and so on. If we trust the reuse concepts (the modules of prior years are called objects now), then applications will be assembled to order, not made to order. This means two issues. First, inter-process or communications between objects and second, provision of data access for data-processing. To solve inter-process communications, we have to think in terms of communications services. This service is message-based. The strategy is to keep only generic technologies with long shelf life implemented into applications and databases. Other essential components should be implemented in isolated layers akin to LRUs (logical replaceable units). These are units that will be change-managed, once again driven by business needs, not technology pushed. In Chapter 5 we discussed the architectural principles relevant to this discussion.

So, what are the essentials of data independence in the context of reuse principles? Is an organizational rethinking in order? What should be the focus of centralized "Information Services" ? Following are some thoughts:

- A data services-based architecture concept
- Model-driven application design (with a repository storing the models)
- An application assembly component supplier
- Making transparent all implements of technologies
- Users experience "Information Services"; they do not see these
- Users assemble, support, and administer application systems
- "Information Services" is an enabler and supplier of components and data resource

- Application-controlled data paradigm of the current environment should be abandoned.

Concepts of shared data are:

- Information that crosses ownership boundaries should be generated in an interchange standard.
- Information not shared should be left to local control
- In a continuous quality improvement environment "absolute" standardization of any data is counter-productive.

In a process-oriented thinking paradigm data is pulled, not pushed. This requires that we should provide an open and flexible data-access environment. The users decide what they need. The application programmer facilitates these transparently using the architecture principles described in Chapters 2–6.

9.3 THE "TO BE" ENVIRONMENT

The objective of the "to be" environment, from a data-driven viewpoint, is to increase independence between data and application components of computing systems. Increasing the data independence from applications will result in improvements along three dimensions:

- Support production processes cost effectively
- Have the flexibility for timely changes needed for process improvements
- Improve access to information

9.3.1 Criteria for Data Independence

The following computing architecture guidelines provide criteria that determine when data has been separated from applications.

Intuitive use.   Users and applications can use business *concepts* to access and use data without knowledge of database organization, format, or other esoteric computing system information. A simple functional interface to data is presented to the using application.

Change isolation.   Applications can migrate to new languages and computing paradigms without requiring any changes to the data storage layer and data storage can migrate to new products or new technologies without causing changes to application programs.

Portable data. Data is portable and can be moved or shared across multiple computing environments or locations without modifying application software.

Integration. Names, definitions, and interfaces are standardized and integrated across functional boundaries, so that the entire business process has concurrent and coordinated access to all data.

Single entry. The need to manually re-enter data is minimized.

Custom views of generic data. Applications can have custom views of data from multiple sources concurrently and in a locally meaningful form.

Universal access. Application and data implementation factors will not limit any user from getting to and using useful data as required by the business process.

Direct access. Information is available directly in a timely manner. Users will not have to go through legacy applications to access data.

Knowledge of the data. Users and applications have online access to information concerning format, definition, and location of available data. Contextual information is available regarding variables that can affect accuracy and validity.

Acceptable performance. Accessibility and usefulness of data is reliable and timely.

9.4   THE PREFERRED INFORMATION TECHNOLOGY ENVIRONMENT

The preferred information technology environment will have the following primary elements:

- Layered architecture using generic data definitions and intelligent, generic data services
- Incremental implementation approach using an iteration refinement process
- Engineering factors to guide the design and implementation process

The objective is to make data reusable and shared over many applications executing on different computing platforms. Data services will render the understanding of data to each of the application systems receiving it, while at the same time allow system efficiencies to be applied. The solution will provide generic data services that render data compatible with the intended usage including data types, formats, units of value, data item names, and the meaning of each value. Since the

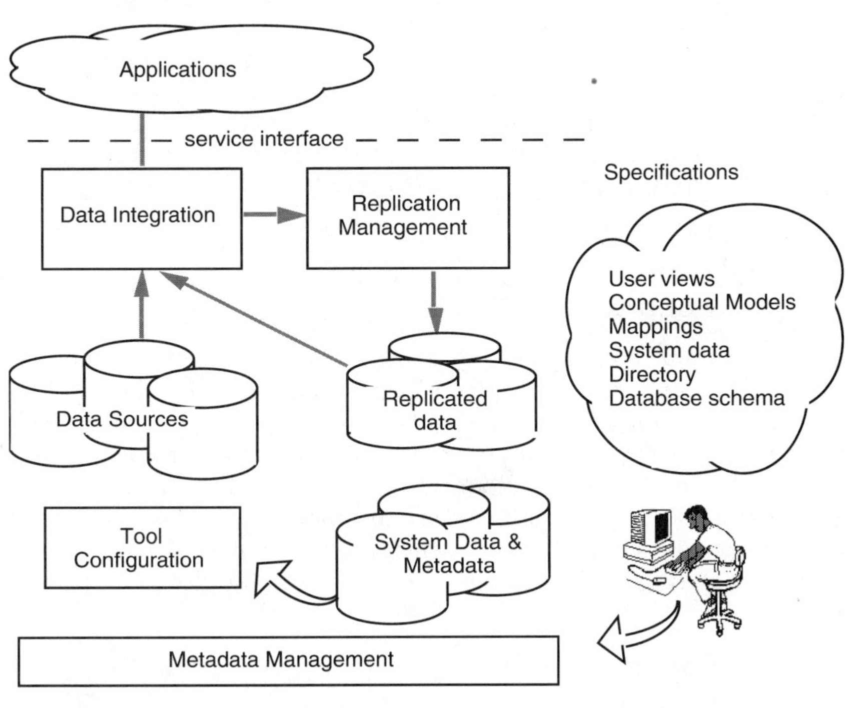

Figure 9.4   Data and application independence through data services concepts.

application's need to present data to a user in an understandable way is often incompatible with the need to store data in compact ways for the sake of efficiency, data services also provide low-level system services transparently to user operations.

An independence component, as shown in Figure 9.4, provides a number of data handling services through a "use neutral" model of the information. Separated from one another, applications can get their data in whatever form they need it, while data storage can use formats that best satisfy storage efficiency and fast access.

9.5   TECHNOLOGY READINESS OF THE PREFERRED ENVIRONMENT

The readiness from a technology viewpoint requires that a technology model of the "as is" environment be made and compared with the technology model of the "to be" environment. Typically, a technology model is based on the various standards, products, and business functions relevant to specific business operations. Based on the technologies selected detailed implementation plans are developed. If such plans already exist, key pacing items are identified for the dependencies of the transition program plan. Generally, network readiness is a key pacing item for distributed computing environments.

9.6   DATA DISTRIBUTION AND TRANSITION FOR LEGACY SYSTEMS

The transition of legacy systems is an important aspect of making a distributed computing platform perform. A fundamental theme of this book has been that the enterprises have a lot invested in their legacy systems. The legacy systems have data and process intelligence built into them by the lack of a deliberate architecture. The importance and the elements of the architecture were discussed in Chapters 1 through 6 of the book. Data distribution in the new environment is an essential part in completing the discussion of the transition process.

9.7   IMPLEMENTING THE DATA TRANSITION

There are three key parts to implementing the data transition. First is to understand the various considerations for defining and implementing a data-server environment. Second is to understand and specify the administration for these servers in the enterprise that will have shared data resident on them. Third is the data management methods that deal with data replication, synchronization, and storage issues.

9.7.1   Data-server Considerations

The data-server platform physically contains the data. The data-server environment will consist of the database management system and, additionally, several kinds of specialized software that provides the services described in Chapter 6. Figure 9.5 shows these service components. An important implementation consideration will be to map out the services with physical products. To a great extent, these products will be vendor-supplied or commercially available off-the-shelf software products. There is no unique way to fill out the building blocks. What is of importance is to adhere to good architecture principles of layering, using middleware, and open systems interoperability conditions.

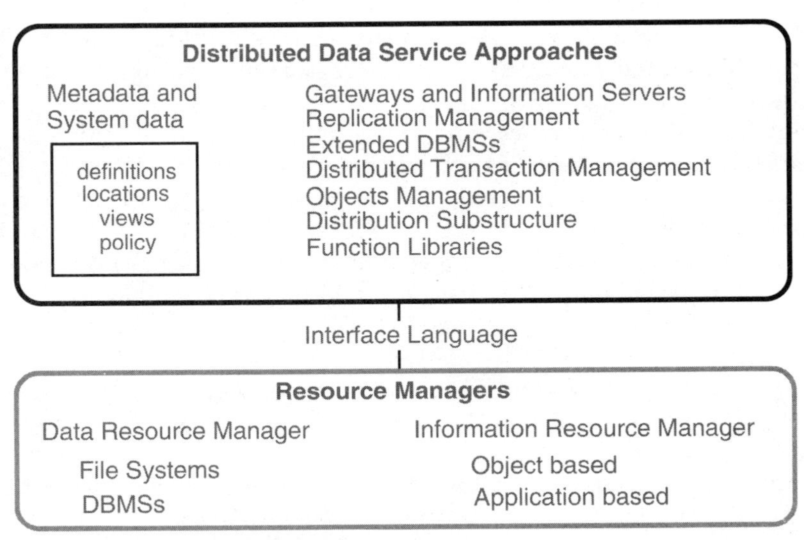

Figure 9.5   Distributed data service components.

9.7.2   Database Administration Considerations

The next set of considerations are administrative in nature. In the legacy environment for the mainframes we have very rigorous procedures for administering data. The nature of the problem here is slightly different in the sense that we have data distributed and, in many cases, replicated on selected servers. The new administration process should deal with replication and synchronization services for administering distributed data to the clients. Once again a detailed set of requirements are gathered and a review of available administration tools is performed to guide specify a set of products. A starting point can be the DRDA set of standards to establish the set of vendors who support these in order to start a formal evaluation process.

9.8   THE CRITICAL SUCCESS FACTORS

The most difficult part of transition is people and their habits. Expect to find very little support for ideas that will change information technology's role in the corporation drastically. That view is especially true of the conventional mainframe folks. These people are most isolated and feel extremely threatened by the new technology. Even the great mainframe company, IBM, became a victim of its prior success. IBM did not see the impact of distributed computing in a timely fashion to reengineer their business strategies. Today, IBM has to compete on an equal footing with distributed computing product vendors—a major cultural shift. The entrenched (old) legacy management is virtually abandoned by the trusted "big iron" salesperson. Therefore, the lead person for new projects may get worn down by a bureaucratic process that computing, finance, and procurement has created. The critical things are "patience" and a solid execution plan based on proven methods and mature technologies. The following are some more critical success factors.

- People: The users who will use the systems and whose business processes are the subject of the application systems must work as a team from day one.
- Technology: Introduce only tested mature technologies. This is especially true in network communications, data access, and Client/ Server application development tools. Technology must be focused, aimed, tailored, and applied.
- Project: Solve simple problems first. Projects should be simple, measurable, and delivered benefits should be apparent in a six-month period, not two years from project initiation.
- Management: Do not avoid cost/benefit analysis and justification. Provide the best data and facts that can be gathered.
- Quality: Use the principles of quality management for gaining customer satisfaction.
- Morale: The entire journey will be very difficult because of the entrenched old methods that run counter to distributed computing. Do everything possible to keep the morale of the development team high.

Transition Design Considerations

The legacy systems transition design is essentially a process reengineering task. The newly defined processes will suggest automation opportunities. Significant automation implies using current robust technologies to eliminate obsolescence in the "as is" situation. Information technology consists of computing platforms, computing applications, and data. The data can be both in electronic and paper media. The information systems should be specified in a computing environment supported by an architecture. Computing architecture specifies standards, rules, and interfaces necessary to enable systems to work cohesively in a dynamically changing environment. The business processes and information technology must be linked to achieve the mission to be a world-class supplier of information to customers.

Process reengineering is currently of great interest in the commercial sector. It will reconfigure the business processes. Business consultants and educators Michael Hammer[1] and Don Clausing[2] reaffirm that process redesign is the sole method to reshape and make U.S. businesses competitive in the world marketplace. This will require a transformation and customer orientation facilitated by appropriate information systems. The employees must be empowered to make decisions based on facts and data. Such facts and data are assembled as information made available by using data services and architecture principles. The newly defined and stabilized processes will guide them in using the information efficiently. Measurable positive effects will be diminished cycle times in completing tasks, reduced cost, and increased customer satisfaction. These should be measured by explicit contracted criteria.

To accomplish such a transformation we have to:

- Define all business processes
- Stabilize newly defined processes
- Implement "continuous quality improvement"
- Make data available transparently to the users
- Provide tools, techniques, and training
- Measure and document the changes
- Refine the processes and information systems to achieve the next level of improvement

By doing so, we are practicing a planning, implementing, checking, and acting cycle of activities.

Many companies have recognized the need to adhere to the principles of reengineering. The management structure is also changing from a hierarchy to a new corporate model, where the management of human resources is across, not up and down.[3] The seven key action elements of a horizontal corporation are:

1. **Organize around process, not a task.** Instead of creating a structure around functions or departments, the company is built around a few "core processes" with specific performance goals. An owner is assigned to each process.
2. **Flatten hierarchy.** Supervision is reduced. Fragmented tasks are combined, tasks that fail to add value are eliminated, and activities within each process are minimized. As few teams as necessary are used to perform an entire process.
3. **Use teams to manage everything.** Teams are the main building blocks of the organization. Supervision is limited by allowing the teams to self-manage themselves. The team is given a common purpose and is held accountable for measurable performance goals.
4. **Let customers drive performance.** Customer satisfaction, not stock appreciation or profitability, is the primary driver and measure of performance. The profits will come and stock will rise if the customers are satisfied.
5. **Reward team performance.** The appraisal and pay systems are changed to reward team results, not just individual performance. Staff is encouraged to develop multiple skills rather than specialized know-how. Rewards are correspondingly given those who develop multiple skills.
6. **Maximize supplier and customer contact.** Employees are brought into direct, regular contact with suppliers and customers.

Supplier or customers are added as full working members to in-house teams when they can be of service.

7. **Inform and train all employees.**   Sanitized information is not fed to the staff on a "need to know" basis. The staff is trusted with raw data and is trained in using it to perform individual analyses and make individual decisions.

The key action words to create a horizontal corporation[4] are:

- Identify
- Analyze
- Define
- Organize
- Eliminate
- Cut
- Appoint
- Create
- Set Specifics
- Empower
- Revamp

The companies AT&T, Eastman Chemical, General Electric, Lexmark International, Motorola, and Xerox[5] are implementing the horizontal corporation concepts. Other successful firms (e.g., Citibank's U.S. Card Products Group) are implementing the new competitive strategies of continuous improvement and mass customization. Continuous improvement means constant process improvement. Mass customization means a dynamic flow of goods and services via a stable set of processes.[6]

Response to a reengineered business climate requires that the information systems, computing delivery systems, and services be adaptive and flexible. The evolution of information systems has thus far supported the hierarchical functional management paradigm. Response to new challenges will require a strategic realignment of information systems with the business processes and strategies. Two major problems are: changes to current computing systems in a stable environment require long cycle times, and the operation and maintenance of current systems are extremely costly. Usually a third of the computing labor costs are directly related to data integration (or lack of) and access-related elements of the computing system. High costs and long flow times are attributed to a number of factors: system complexity, system design philosophy that depends on point-to-point data file exchange, business processes embedded in applications, data redundancy, functional duplication, impacts on related systems, and unresponsiveness to users. Simply rehosting old applications or having reverse engineered them is not the subject of this book.

The benefits of reuseability of computing codes, object-oriented applications and agents, and so on are unlikely to be achieved unless we understand that new tools and techniques are required. The transition design considerations consist of issues along three dimensions: business, technical, and logistic. These dimensions will help us visualize the process from a business perspective. A compelling reason for transition should not be based on technology push. Rather, it should be based on obtaining breakthrough improvements in cost savings and benefits. We should be able to perform functions with the new information systems that were not possible or within the realm of the vision at the historic point in time when automation was considered in the first place.

Figure 10.1 puts in context how functional organizations drove computing application delivery and design. These are the peripheral boundary conditions of our situation. We have monolithic applications hosted in a heterogeneous computing delivery systems environment. The challenge is to recast the functional teams as just described into cross-functional teams. These teams will be empowered to make decisions and are held accountable to deliver key capabilities in a process-oriented thinking environment.

The cross-functional teams will use a comprehensive description of the macro-processes of the enterprise. Almost invariably these macro-processes will be based on the core competencies of the business. The information services organization should have a mission supported by vision, goals, and objectives statements. A review of the services provided consistently and successfully by the information services organization will help define the core competencies. The core competencies help us define information systems strategies. The strategies are balanced with customer requirements to establish the driving parameters (e.g., design and build application systems, buy application systems, outsource data center operations, etc.). The macro-processes are defined based on these driving parameters.

The actual tactical plans are composed from these strategic elements, core competencies, driving parameters, and customer requirements. The tactical plans cast the processes into business streams in which these will be performed. A *business stream* is a formal definition of an implement or observed process phenomena (e.g., stable repetitive functions in a work-flow situation, customized processes based on customer preferences, etc.). Generally, simplification of the entire organization's processes is accomplished by defining multiple business streams. The process-oriented thinking forces us to examine how we are currently deploying the resources and what results are being produced. At the highest level we

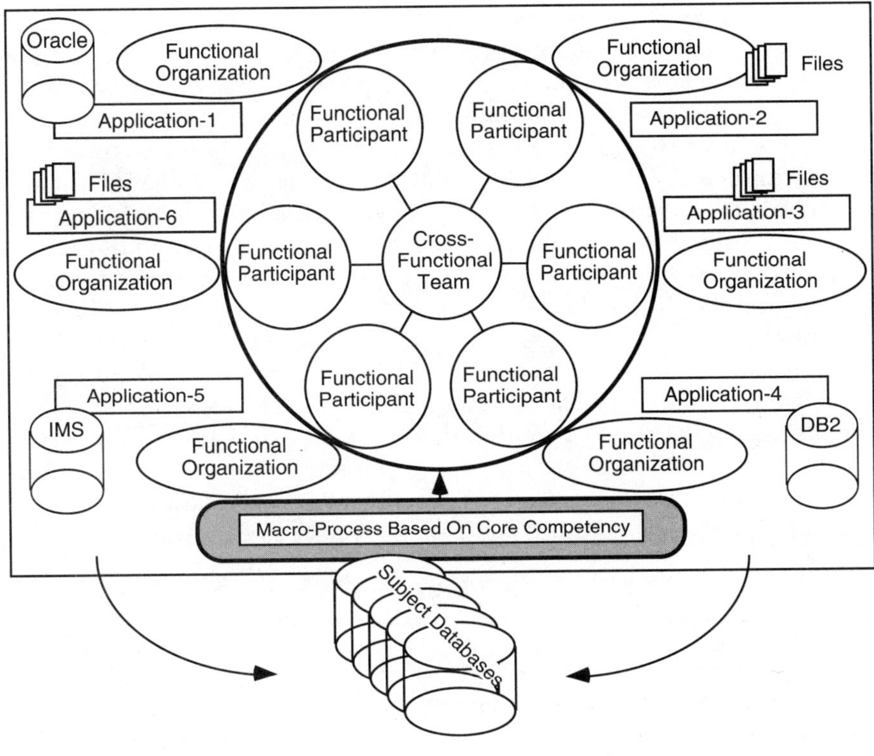

Figure 10.1   The business situation, the old and the new.

aggregate the basic "macro" or large processes that are logically different. For instance, in the case of information systems we can classify these into four macro-processes:

- **Define** the basic and constant work product that the organization produces.
- **Acquire** those components of the work product that are beneficial to buy rather than make in-house.
- **Produce** those components of the work product that are consistent with the core competencies of the organization.
- **Support** both external and internal customers by meeting quality, cost, schedule, and delivery commitments.

We will examine these four macro-processes in detail.

10.1   THE "DEFINE" PROCESS

The define process concerns defining the primary work content of the information services organization. The key drivers are process owners and system owners. In the case of the legacy transition context, a description of the "as is" application portfolio is used to target systems that are candidates for replacement. Figure 10.2 shows a high-level process diagram. The lowers levels of the process steps should outline the details of how the process will be developed for a specific situation.

A key deliverable of this process is a framework of how computing is applied to the business process. An example of a framework for marketing products in a telemarketing situation is shown in Table 10.1. The framework essentially describes the business process step, the functional activities to be performed in that step, and the application domain based on key characteristics. The scenario assumes that the telemarketing service is a small portion of a sophisticated selling style. The telemarketing representative is given key customer contact information on his computer screen to start a conversation (described in the functional activities column) with the prospect to find the geographic

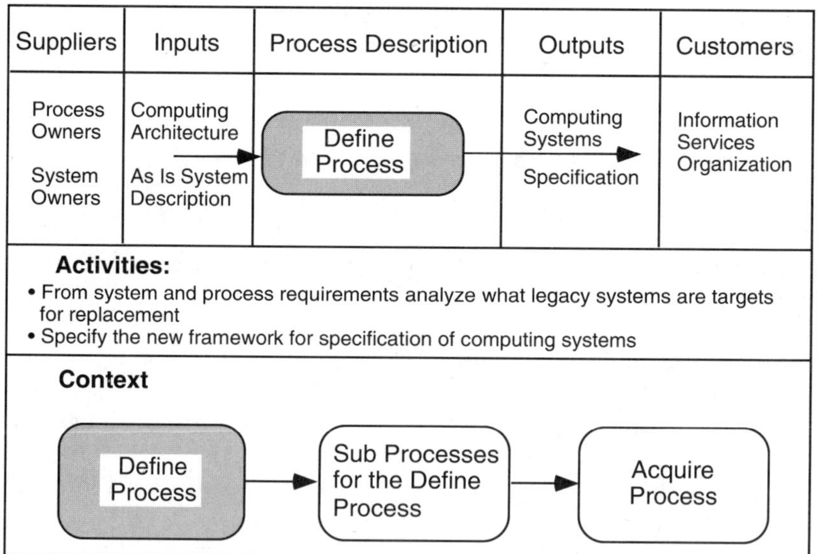

Figure 10.2   A high-level description of the "Define" process.

Table 10.1   An Application Framework For the "Define" Process

Process Step	Functional Activities	Application Domain
Initial Customer Contact	Computing Support: Geographic location Buying patterns and history Online credit information Freeflow text entry	Static data warehouse for read-only extract Simple minimum user-input user interface systems
Order Entry	Enter order locally Upload order to central	Simple transaction processing applications
Order Processing	Download order Process order, ship, and invoice customer	Backend complex transaction processing applications
Customer Service Feedback	Process returns Note objections for research Upload central with action information	Rapid transaction processing applications Simple minimum user-input user interface systems
Future Solicitation	Download customer activity data from marketing and other lead generation services Access previous history Gather data for order generation	Simple transaction processing applications Static data warehouse for read-only extracts.
External Relations	External Systems: Credit data Lead generation services Contract shippers Warehousing partners Buy/Sell customer lists	Complex transaction applications Online subscription services

location, buying patterns, and credit history. This will require extensive data mining from external databases. However, we do not provide all of the information. Only highly summarized, action-trigger information is furnished. The summarized data should be hosted locally. These characteristics are noted in the application domain column. The application domain provides explicit application architectural details that are captured in a computing systems specifications document. Many companies have such details in their tactical computing plans, division operating plans, and so on; regardless the define process should produce a deliverable describing how computing will be applied to solve the business process automation needs.

The first row describes the process step, functional activities, and the application domain for establishing customer contact. Now, in older legacy systems, rapid data entry based on telephone conversations in an online situation is very rare. In the legacy transition we can use sophisticated technologies, such as graphical user interfaces, voice annotations, and so on to satisfy the application domain requirements. In this very simple example we see the importance of business process redesign. In order to furnish the telemarketing representative with sophisticated customer contact technology, we have to understand the new process of customer contact and compare it with previous processes. The previous processes may be just taking notes long hand on forms that are keyed into computer databases as a follow-up activity. We can propose using stable new technology to accomplish the new process in a more automated fashion. We should review the suitability of the legacy systems in the new business process context and identify opportunities for buying or building new applications. The next process step in Table 10.1 describes the framework in more detail which is self-explanatory. A business case analysis may be required to pursue any of the opportunities suggested by the application framework. The acquire process is designed to answer these requirements.

10.2   THE "ACQUIRE" PROCESS

The acquire process builds upon the define process. Once the application framework for a set of business processes is specified, we have to decide what applications to build in-house, what applications to retire, and finally what application to buy. Figure 10.3 shows the process. If the approach is to acquire applications, a thorough application architecture assessment of the acquired product must be documented. The architecture is the driving force to attain a managed environment to cope with business process redesign and new technology implementation requirements.

10.3   THE "PRODUCE" PROCESS

The produce process acts upon the decisions made during the acquire process. The produce activity is concerned both with assimilation of acquired applications and legacy systems, and new development efforts for production of information systems. Figure 10.4 shows the process.

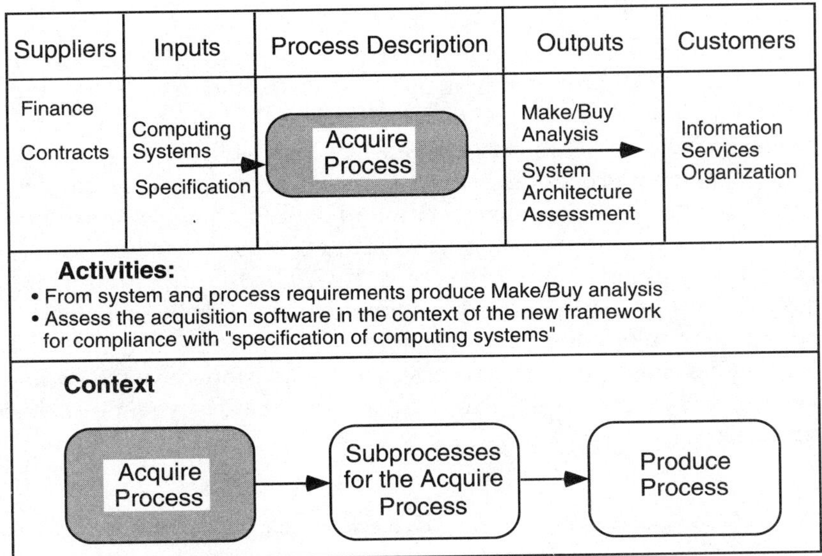

Suppliers	Inputs	Process Description	Outputs	Customers
Finance Contracts	Computing Systems Specification	Acquire Process	Make/Buy Analysis System Architecture Assessment	Information Services Organization

Activities:
- From system and process requirements produce Make/Buy analysis
- Assess the acquisition software in the context of the new framework for compliance with "specification of computing systems"

Context

Figure 10.3   A high-level description of the "Acquire" process.

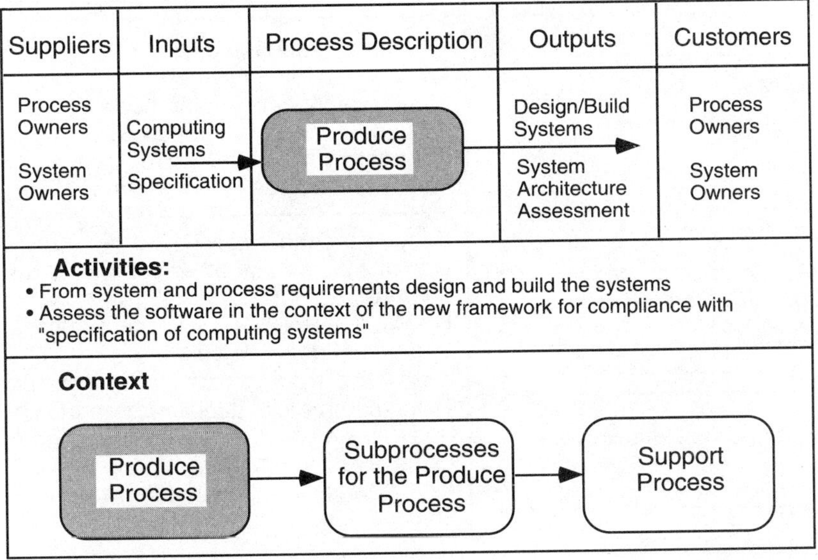

Suppliers	Inputs	Process Description	Outputs	Customers
Process Owners System Owners	Computing Systems Specification	Produce Process	Design/Build Systems System Architecture Assessment	Process Owners System Owners

Activities:
- From system and process requirements design and build the systems
- Assess the software in the context of the new framework for compliance with "specification of computing systems"

Context

Figure 10.4   A high-level description of the "Produce" process.

The key driver is core competencies of the information services organization. It will not be uncommon to find that critical skills for implementing distributed computing may be lacking. We may have to address those concerns in the support macro-process as well.

The high-level process shown will have to be decomposed into various lower levels. The lower levels can and should adopt or adapt many of the existing development processes. In Chapter 7 we discussed a rapid application development process. It will be highly appropriate to include the rapid application development techniques in lieu of outdated mainframe application development paradigms.

In the produce process, training of application developers is an important consideration. Figure 10.5 shows generically some training requirements.

Capabilities	Generic Description
Building Client/Server Applications	Services hosting strategies Interprocess communications Remote procedure calls Networking methods
Building Distributed Data Management Applications	Relational database design Transaction processing Database connection and access using middleware database servers Connecting client and server based database management systems
Building Graphical User Interfaces	Windows technologies Use of widgets and other common user interface objects Low-level objects, e.g., scroll bars, buttons and Visual Basic objects, etc.
Building Data Access Applications	Using commercial decision support applications and building navigation aides using layered middleware products Using data mediation middleware Using database schema mapping tools

Figure 10.5   A high-level description of the training requirements.

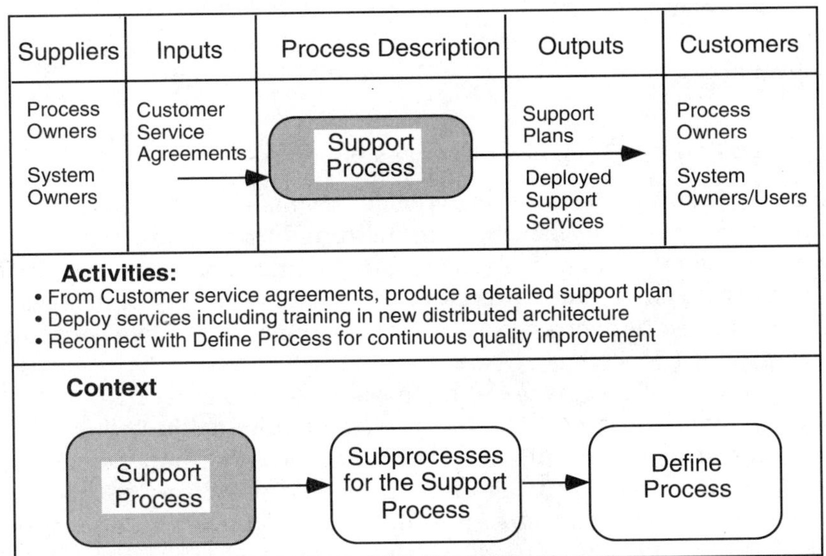

Figure 10.6   A high-level description of the "Support" process.

10.4   THE "SUPPORT" PROCESS

The last macro-process is the support process. Figure 10.6 shows a high-level description. The support plan is essentially produced from the service agreements. Customer training may be required for some of the new systems that may be different from the old user interface techniques.

10.5   BUSINESS PROCESS REDESIGN

Business process redesign is regarded as the single driving force to examine the legacy systems from a transition perspective. As explained earlier, the transition process is not a platform rehashing or technology implementation task. The key processes and activities relevant to information systems alignment with newly defined processes are as follows.

- Define all business processes
- Stabilize newly defined processes
- Implement "continuous quality improvement"
- Make data available transparently to the users

- Provide tools, techniques, and training
- Measure and document the changes
- Refine the processes and information systems to achieve the next level of improvement

10.5.1 Define All Business Processes

Figure 10.7 shows a description of the define business process. The core competencies play a decisive role in defining business processes. Core competencies fully support the mainline business strategy and direction of the company. Macro-processes are defined at a very high level. In many instances these processes are typically performed in various functional organizations.

The newly defined processes are assigned to key executives who are already playing an important role in a closely aligned functional area. The macro processes should map well with the core competencies, unless the company is venturing in a completely new direction. The success of the reengineering effort lies in choosing a few focused processes for deployment. The major consideration is cost versus benefits ratio. In

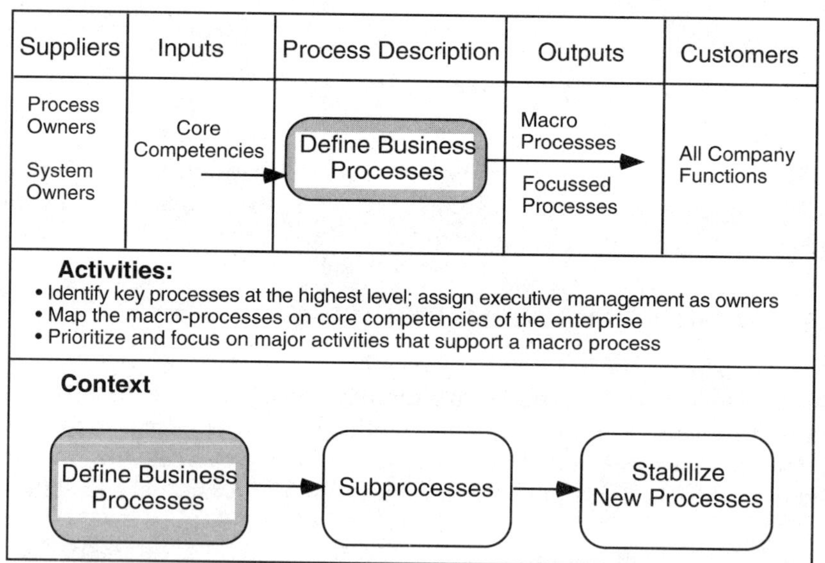

Figure 10.7   A high-level description of the define business process.

an evolving business it may not be unusual to find that the basic processes got complicated by the old legacy system's way of doing things. The old systems had very little human engineering built into them. People and processes were forced to follow arcane computerization. When we rethink the total picture and analyze the cost of implementation with the benefits, the focus areas emerge naturally. The experience obtained from implementing focused processes may even alter the originally postulated business processes. Such an occurrence is not rare.

10.5.2 Stabilize Newly Defined Processes

The newly defined processes are implemented on a prioritized schedule. Meaningful metrics are defined for measurement. For instance, if the quality is to be improved, the new macro-processes will have defects to parts (or product) ratio as a measure. If the cost to manufacture is the key indicator, then the cost is a metric. Stabilization is accomplished by reducing variations in the processes used to perform an activity. Reliability in the processes is determined when a set of consistent desirable results are produced. Figure 10.8 shows a high-level depiction of the

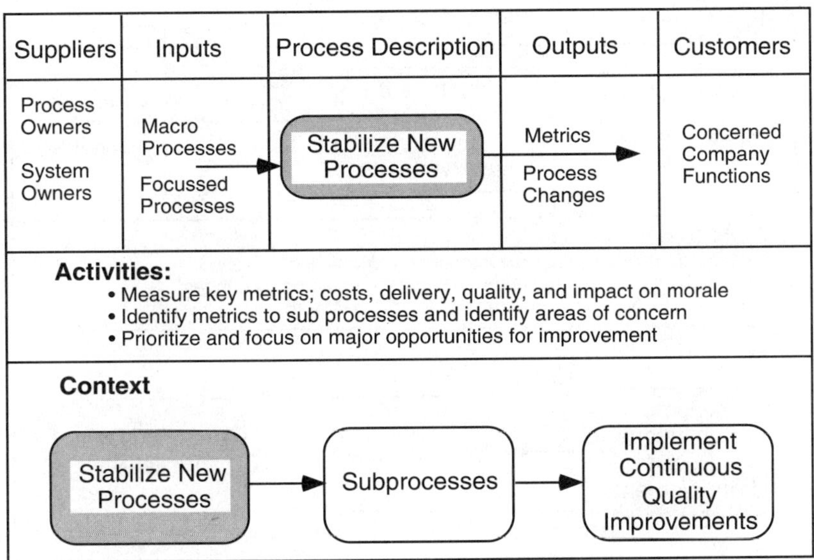

Figure 10.8   A high-level description of the stabilize new processes.

stabilization process. The metrics collected during this process feed into the continuous quality improvement step. We tactically assumed that business process redesign and continuous quality improvement require activities to be performed integrally.

10.5.3 Implement Continuous Quality Improvement

The process is shown in Figure 10.9. The activities are very similar to the process stabilization process. The definition and collection of relevant metrics is the cornerstone of these activities.

10.5.4 Enhance Data Availability

The next process step is to make the right data available to the users at the right time in right quantities. This particular concept was discussed in some detail in the architecture principles section in Chapter 6. Data warehouse concept to provide integrated data from legacy systems is a key deliverable of this process as shown in Figure 10.10.

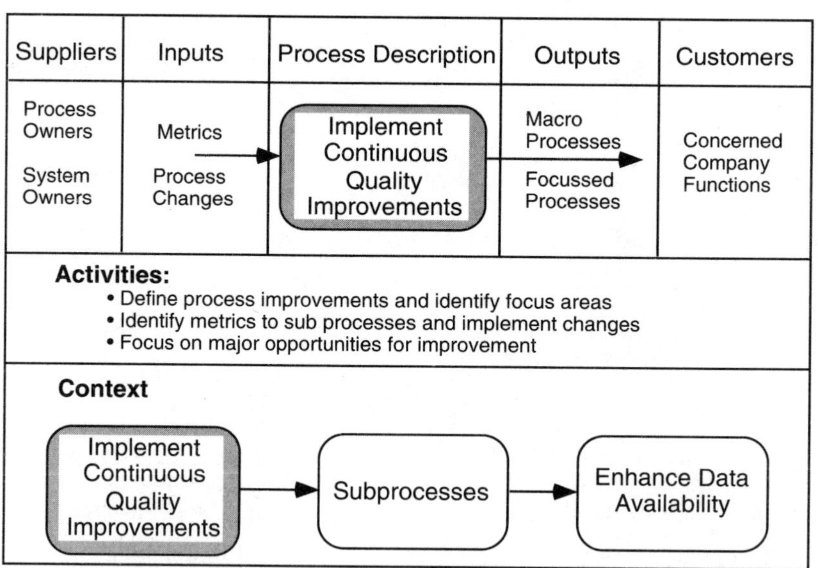

Figure 10.9   A high-level description of the "CQI" process.

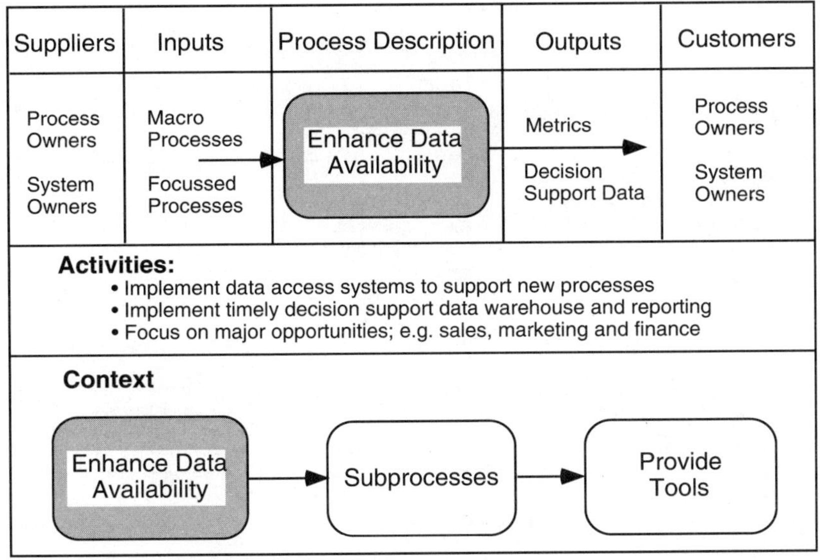

Figure 10.10   A high-level description for enhancing data process.

10.5.5 Provide Tools, Techniques, and Training

The new processes cannot be deployed without provision of tools and new business techniques (see Figure 10.11). Training to use these is a key requirement. Most reengineering efforts have failed because this particular aspect of the transition process was not emphasized.

10.5.6 Measure and Document the Changes

The next process is to measure and document the changes from the continuous quality improvements efforts. The importance of meaningful information systems that include automatic and transparent storing of the enterprise data can perhaps be appreciated. Employee surveys are a valuable tool in this regard. Figure 10.12 shows the process.

10.5.7 Refine Processes

The last step is to refine the macro-processes based on a large sample of real experience data and customer satisfaction criteria. The focus of the

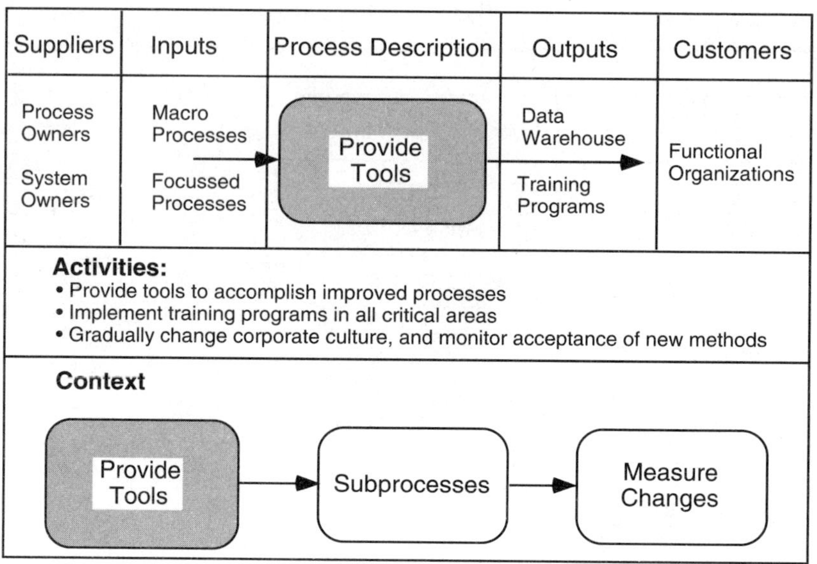

Figure 10.11   A high-level description of the provide tools process.

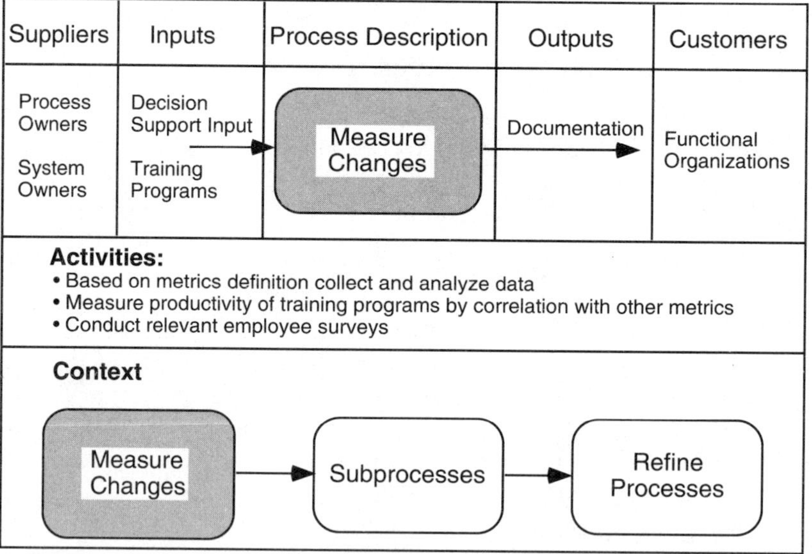

Figure 10.12   A high-level description of the measure changes process.

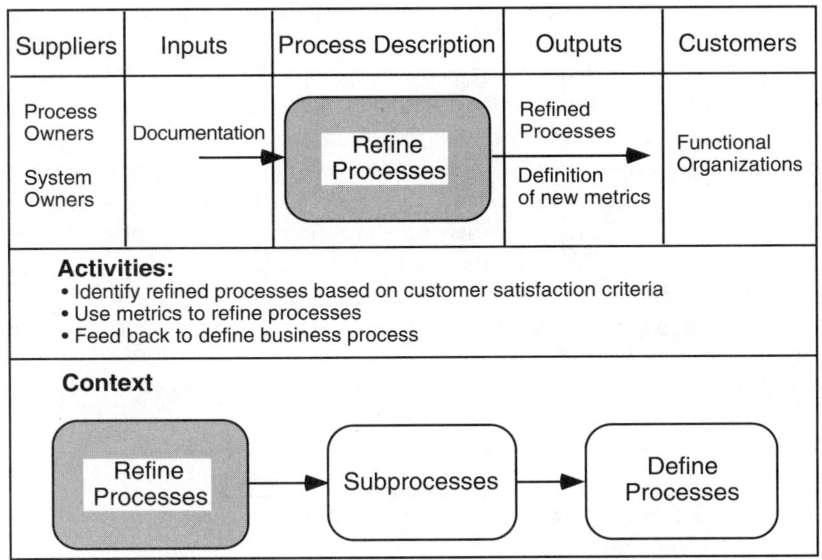

Figure 10.13   A high-level description of the refine process.

business is to delight the customer in all aspects of cost, quality, schedule, and morale of the operating divisions. Figure 10.13 displays the process.

10.6   INFORMATION DESIGN CONSIDERATIONS

The transition design consideration requires an understanding of how information is obtained, analyzed, and used in an organization. The message of the previous chapters may lead one to conclude that all the information in an enterprise can be computerized, modeled, analyzed, and presented in any way the customer desires. In reality, quite the contrary is true. People obtain information based on the culture of the workplace. Notwithstanding the importance of computers and databases, people will continue to obtain information in myriad ways. We can broadly classify information sources in two categories. The first is human-centered and the second is computer-centered. Figure 10.14 shows a model of information acquisition. Human-centered information can be seen as based on experience, investigation, and analysis. Most decisions are based solely on such sources. However, with databases becoming more available, we partially depend on computerized information for facts, trends, and other quantitative data.

Computer-centered information is generally collected from three different sources: central corporate sources, particular department sources, and external subscribed sources. The data models supporting corporate sources should be governed by the common rules of data resource management, so that applications can run against these sources to provide consistent information. At the local level, a high degree of autonomy and flexibility is required. Some level of data redundancy is also desirable at the local level. At each level a separate focus is necessary, as shown in Figure 10.14. The ideas captured in the model closely parallel the observations made by Thomas Davenport in an article published in the *Harvard Business Review*.[7]

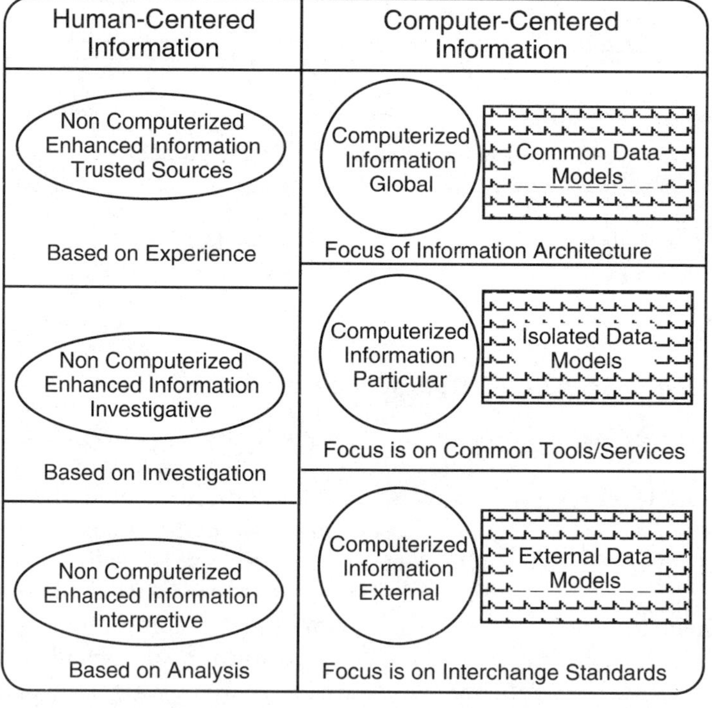

Figure 10.14   A model for "Information" acquisition.

10.7   THE BUSINESS REQUIREMENTS

As observed in the beginning of this chapter, businesses are organizing horizontally and reducing vertical hierarchies. Functional organizations are recast into cross-functional teams to perform the activities that are key to the strategic business plans. Cross-functional teams are empowered to support a specific macro process. If the macro-process involves computing technology in any significant way, then the situation of resolving the demands between legacy systems and requirements arises. There can be various business problems that become drivers for designing a transition. Figure 10.15 organizes the problem, solution demands, and finally a solution is suggested for recasting regenerated legacy data into information. The technology is pulled by the processes. The legacy systems transition process consists of synthesizing all the design considerations discussed in this chapter to assure that practical implementation barriers are removed and processes are in place before we proceed with individual projects.

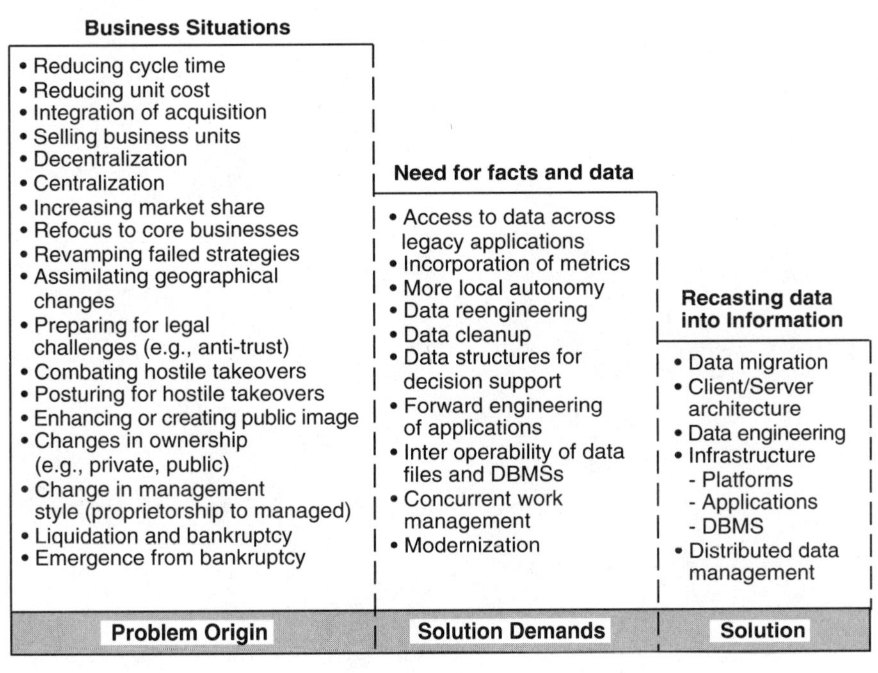

Figure 10.15   Transition design is business-driven.

CHAPTER NOTES

1. Hammer, Michael. "Reengineering Work: Don't Automate, Obliterate." *Harvard Business Review* (July–August 1990).
2. Clausing, Don. *Total Quality Development.* New York: The ASME Press, 1994.
3. "The Horizontal Corporation." *Business Week* (December 20, 1993).
4. Frank Ostroff, Consultant, McKinsey & Co.
5, Data: *Business Week*, McKinsey & Co.
6. Boynton, A.C., B. Victor, and B.J. Pine II. "New Competitive Strategies: Challenges to Organizations and Information Technology." *IBM Systems Journal,* vol. 32, no. 1 (1993).
7. Davenport, Thomas H. "Saving IT's Soul: Human-Centered Information Management." *Harvard Business Review* (March–April 1994).

11

Transition Overview

A brief overview of the transition process will be presented in this chapter. The two essential considerations for understanding the transition requirements, as described in Chapter 2, are the need for an architecture and the requirement to increase the level of data abstraction. Together, these considerations, when linked with the business processes, will produce design specifications for the new applications. The new applications will not have the deficiencies of the legacy systems. A basic assumption is that the transition requirements are not driven by a need to rehost applications on UNIX delivery platforms. The problem addressed here deals with an enterprise-level requirement to implement distributed computing using a variety of server platforms that are scalable and facilitate forward engineered[1] or purchased applications. These applications generally will use new reusable code components and objects. The business processes, information services strategies, core competencies, and information architecture are the primary drivers for the transition design.

A high-level diagram of the transition process is shown in Figure 11.1. There are three distinct sets of activities with these processes. Details are presented in the following sections.

11.1 OVERVIEW OF THE ROAD MAP

The overview road map will be explained in a series of executable steps that are derived from Figure 11.1.

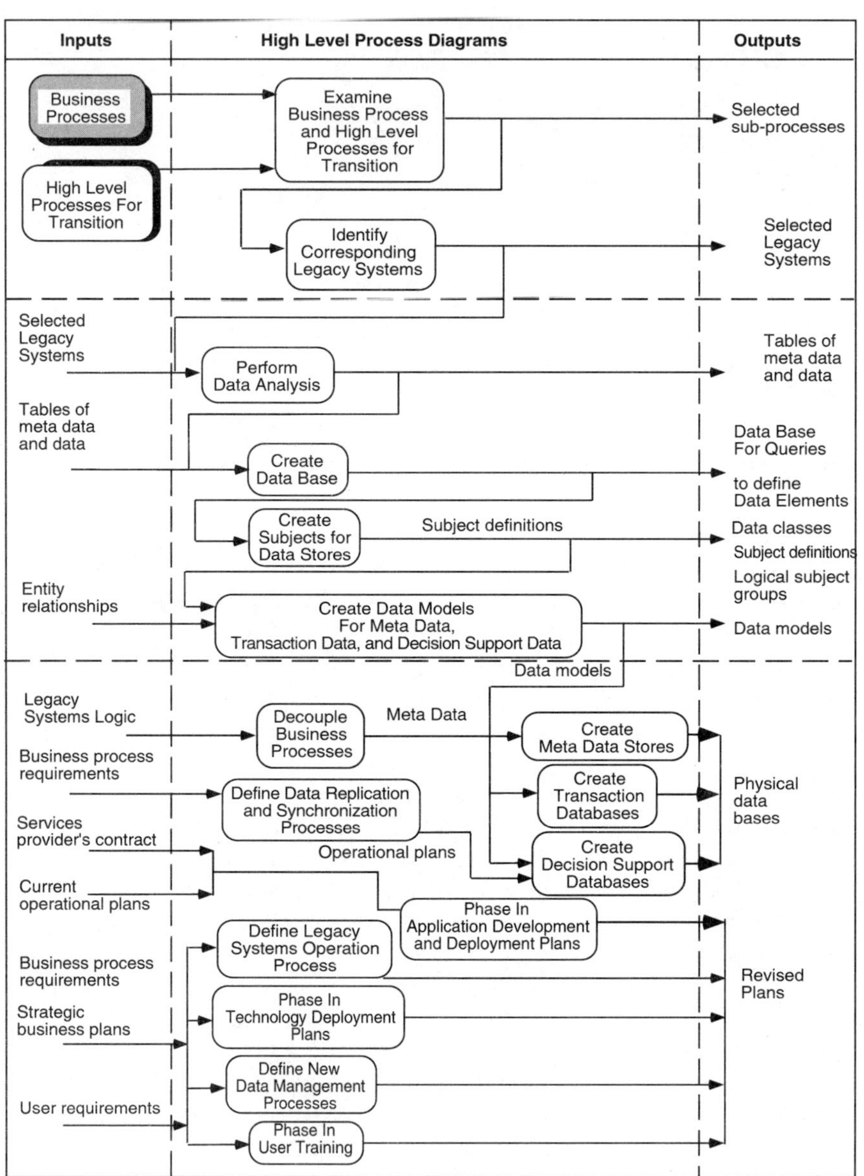

Figure 11.1   Transition process diagram.

Step 1   Examination of Macro-Processes

Objectives:

1. To link information systems with business processes as defined in the new reengineered environment.
2. To determine which legacy systems have data and embedded process logic of value that have to be extracted and retained for use in the transition environment.

Approach:

1. Examine all the redefined macro-processes of the enterprise.
2. Create a process to legacy application mapping.
3. Separate legacy applications within the context into transactional and decision support.

Step 2   Select and Prioritize All Processes

Objectives:

1. To define a subset of the problem that has most immediate benefit.
2. To define a repeatable and a reliable process for follow-on projects.

Approach:

1. Consider cost and benefit analysis recommendations.
2. Apply total quality control principles. Perform only those tasks where a benefit can be measured and attributed directly to a process improvement.
3. Select processes that are supported enthusiastically by users.

The process diagram for Steps 1 and 2 is shown in Figure 11.2.

Step 3   Perform Data Analysis for Selected Legacy Systems

Objectives:

1. To separate useful information from legacy data in the context of new processes.
2. To establish a repeatable process for legacy data analysis that is extensible to other selected business processes.

Approach:

1. Gather information in a structured form.
2. Collect the metadata applicable to legacy systems.

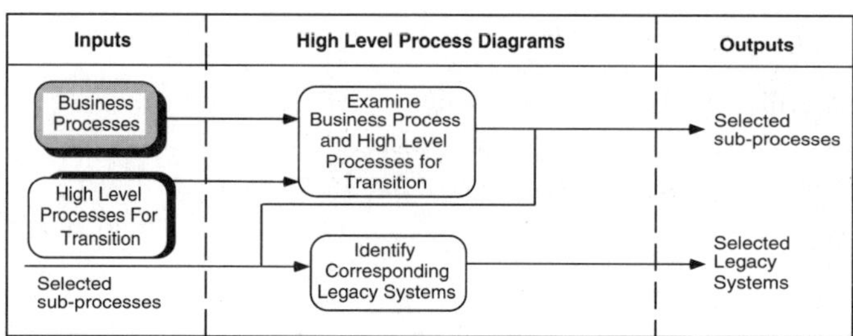

The Selection Of A Subset Of Legacy Systems

Figure 11.2   Process diagram for Steps 1 and 2.

3. Separate metadata within the context into transactional and decision support.

The gathering of information can be accomplished in tables (Tables 11.1 through 11.4) described as follows. There can be some guidelines to assist the analysts. Some examples are as follows.

1. Consider the user-interaction screens as the predominant source for capturing data information as opposed to chasing individual data elements in an application.
2. A data element belongs to the creating application.
3. Data alias is also identified by its standard name.
4. Virtual data elements created by concatenation are identified as user view elements. There can be many more depending upon the situation and how complex the legacy implementations are. In general, IMS implementations are the most challenging.

Step 4   Analyze data for creating an extensible metadatabase

Objectives:

1. To convert the tables into a relational database for analysis.
2. To determine which legacy systems have data and embedded process logic of value that have to be extracted and retained for use in the transition environment.

Approach:

1. Normalize the data in Tables 11.1 through 11.4.

Table 11.1   Data Element

1. Data Element Name	Lexical name in dictionary
2. Data Type(Format)	Character, number, string, etc.
3. Create	Created in which application
4. Read	Read from which application
5. Update	Updated by which application
6. Delete	Deleted by which application
7. Creation Rule	Rule for creation, e.g., for reporting
8. Read Rule	Rule for read, e.g., data manipulation
9. Update Rule	Rule for update
10. Delete Rule	Rule for delete
11. Alias Name	If alias, name of original name
12. Concatenated from	Screen View, from data elements
13. Parsed From	If data element parsed from what element

Table 11.2   Semantic Information

1. Data Element	Lexical name in dictionary
2. Semantic Information	e.g., functional dependency
3. Application	Semantic information in what application

Table 11.3   Data Coding Information

1. Data Element	Lexical name in dictionary
2. Application	Name of application
3. Code Value	Meaning of code, e.g., 1= Male

Table 11.4   Metadata Mapping

1. New Data Element Definition	Lexical name in new dictionary
2. Data Type(Format)	Character, number, string, etc.
3. Created in legacy application	Name of application where created
4. Update rules, application name	Rules for update in applications
5. Delete rules, application name	Rules for delete in applications
6. Data instance in application desired	Name of application for instance
7. Subject classification	Subject database name

2. Create a relational metadatabase for legacy data.
3. Generate meaningful queried information from the metadatabase.

Step 5   For the macro-process under consideration, determine what data is required

Objectives:

1. To establish data element definitions based on real-world objects.
2. To obtain a cohesive set of data from legacy systems.

Approach:

1. Analyze the legacy systems data definition metadatabase.
2. Determine required data for newly defined processes.
3. Perform coherency analysis on legacy and new data to determine common data and metadata to be retained from legacy systems.

Step 6   Rename the data elements for the new reengineered macro-process

Objectives:

1. To arrive at consistent and standard data element names.
2. To standardize user view-based data element names as real-world objects.

Approach:

1. Compare the various definitions of the legacy data with new data requirements for macro-processes.
2. Determine required data by decomposing the process to atomic levels. Assign most meaningful names to data elements as understood and agreed to by the process owners and users.
3. Standardize the process by which data-naming activities will be conducted repeatedly in the future. The process should also have a name-change (add, delete, and modify) management defined as well.

Step 7   For the new data elements, create corresponding metadata

Objectives:

1. To collect the data for creating metadata.
2. To gather information for creating the metamodel (data model).

Approach:

1. For common data elements existing in legacy systems, collect the metadata from the database created in Step 4.
2. For new data, create Table 4 as described in Step 3.
3. Combine the data and check for coherence and consistency.

Step 8   Create subject definitions for decision support and transactional databases

Objectives:

1. To establish a standard subject orientation.

2. To establish separate subjects for decision support and transactional users.

Approach:

1. Define subject areas based on real-world data objects and new processes.
2. Define subjects as unique and nonredundant.
3. Create separate subjects for decision support and transactional uses.

Step 9   Create data models for metadata, transactional, and decision-support databases

Objectives:

1. To establish data models.
2. To create manageable flexible classification.

Approach:

1. Use CASE tools to create data models.
2. Check all data models and verify that these are consistent with metadata.

The process diagram for Steps 3 through 9 are shown in Figure 11.3.

Step 10   Decouple business processes from legacy systems and store these as metadata.

Objectives:

1. To capture data management information from legacy systems.
2. To enhance metadata for follow-on legacy systems transition.

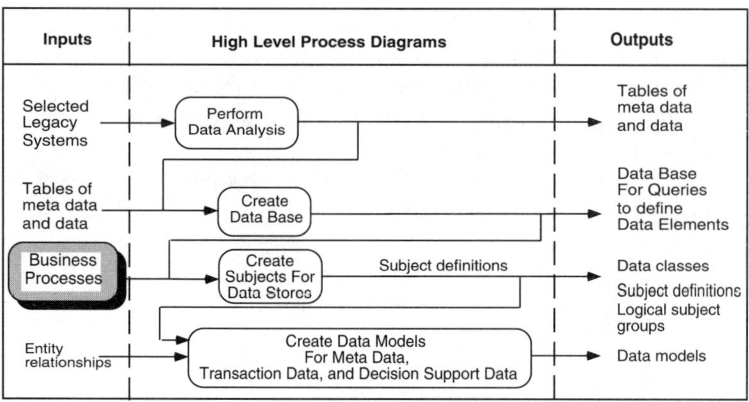

Figure 11.3   Process diagram for Steps 3 through 11.

Approach:

1. Capture data in tables as described in Step 3.
2. Resolve conflicting rules for update and delete.
3. Store these as metadata in appropriate tables.

Step 11   Consider all the metadata and create a relational database system.

Objectives:

1. To establish a manageable and usable metadatabase.
2. To establish a bridge between legacy and new systems.

Approach:

1. Combine decoupled business rules with new metadata.
2. Check the data for consistency and coherency.
3. Normalize and create a relational database for the metadata.

Step 12   Create transaction databases

Objectives:

1. To establish separate transaction databases for access through data services layers by new applications.
2. To establish the data as a resource separate from applications.

Approach:

1. Define an application architecture for the applicable macro-process.
2. Validate the subject classifications of the transaction database.
3. Employ the data models created in Step 11 and create the database.

Step 13 Create decision-support databases or data warehouse

Objectives:

1. To establish separate decision-support databases for access through data services layers by decision-support applications.
2. To establish separate data for query purposes as a resource.

Approach:

1. Define decision-support application architecture for the applicable macro-process.
2. Validate the subject classifications of the decision-support database.
3. Employ the data models created in Step 11 and create the database.

A summary of the how to establish the decision-support and transactional databases is shown in Figure 11.4 for a representative heterogeneous legacy systems environment.

Step 14 Extend data in data warehouse by logical (integrated schema) methods

Objectives:

1. To provide facts and data to support decision investigation.
2. To accommodate for unforeseen circumstances of data requirements.

Approach:

1. Provide required data without physically extending warehouse data.
2. Use data mediation techniques described in Chapters 4 and 5.
3. Gather user statistics for defining data warehouse extension strategies.

Step 15 Define and implement the data replication and synchronization models for the decision-support data warehouse

Objectives:

1. To define data replication strategies.
2. To define data synchronization strategies.

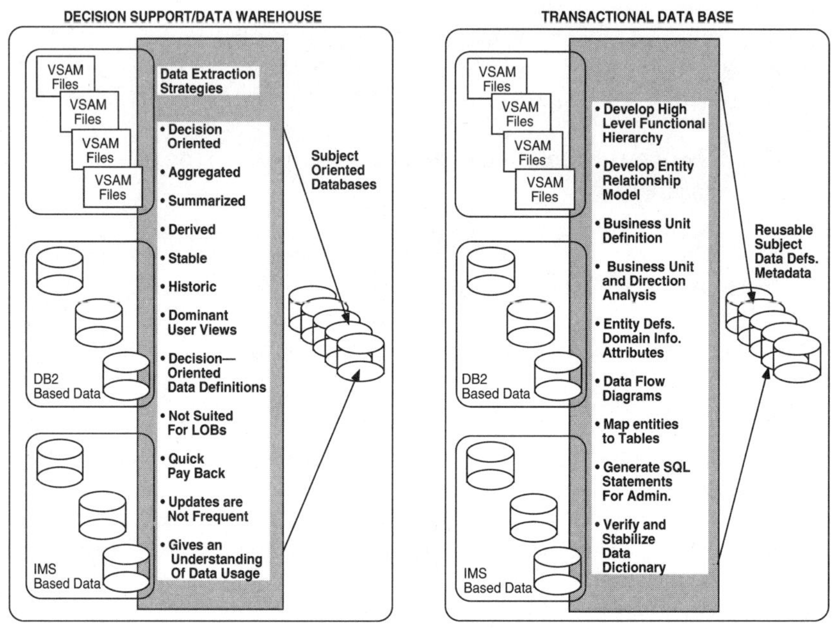

Figure 11.4   Summary of database creation process.

Approach:

1. Define criteria for replicating data.
2. Define time characteristics of data.
3. Define data refreshing strategies that will result in synchronized data.

Data replication needs can be classified into types based on some common criteria. Table 11.5 describes four types based on some commonly known criteria. The actual typing of data replication will be dictated by the process needs and data management policies used by an enterprise. Table 11.6 shows the time-related characteristics. Table 11.7 shows the data synchronization characteristics. Some advanced strategies are also described in Chapter 11.

Step 16   Define application development and deployment plan

Objectives:

1. To assure that current activities are congruent with overall vision.
2. To assure that new applications are deployed at the appropriate time.

Table 11.5   Criteria for Data Replication

Replication Characteristics	Replication Reasons	Replication Approach
Making a copy of transactional data available at users' proximity. **Type 1**	Data management policies limitations; network architecture limitations; End-user empowerment	A personal data replica is made during non-primetime. Data replication is done by using service layer, e.g., SQL server as opposed to writing a hard-coded extract routine.
To create a derived database based on transactional data. The derived data is personal, not shared data. **Type 2**	Data management policies limitations; Network architecture limitations; End-user empowerment; Process improvement investigation; Special volatile data requirements.	Data replication is done by using service layer, e.g., SQL server as opposed to writing a hard-coded extract routine. The metadata is used to isolate derived data from being affected by upstream changes. A Mediation services layer is highly recommended for flexibility and reuseability.
For creating a shared decision-support database, complete with its own metadata. Creation of a data warehouse. **Type 3**	To facilitate the separation of transactional and decision support users. To create summarized historical non-volatile time-variant data.	Data replication is done by using service layer, e.g., SQL server as opposed to writing a hard-coded extract routine. The metadata is used to isolate summarized-derived-data from being affected by upstream changes. A Mediation services layer is highly recommended for flexibility and reuseability. Meta mapping models and replication data mappings should be stored as metadata for data warehouse management.
To facilitate data backup and archiving. **Type 4**	For routine and normal data management functions.	Use standard defined operating procedures.

Table 11.6   Time Characteristics of Data

Data Element Properties	Natural Properties	Process Related
Stable data descriptor	Chronology related	A condition is imposed
Variable data descriptor	None	Online data collection
Historical data descriptor	Aggregation rules	When available in time
Research data descriptor	Theory in study	When available in time

Table 11.7   Data Synchronization Characteristics

Natural Properties	Data Center Constraints	Regulatory Event Driven
Protocol related	Pull On Data Center	As applicable
Process triggered	Online/Batch contracts	As encoded in process
Cost based considerations	Least cost approach	None
Transition conditions	As specified	None

Approach:

1. Consider macro-processes to prioritize activities.
2. Identify applications that will require make or buy analysis.
3. Make or buy applications as determined.

Step 17   Define legacy systems interoperation with new applications

Objectives:

1. To operate applications in the transition environment.
2. To assure the integrity of data.

Approach:

1. Integrate legacy data update rules with new processes.
2. Monitor data integrity and revise operating procedures.
3. Keep users involved to validate computerized procedures.

Chapter 5 describes advanced techniques for co-processing legacy systems with new applications in a mixed legacy and distributed environment.

Step 18   Define technology deployment plans

Objectives:

1. To retire obsolete technologies.
2. To introduce mature new technologies.

Approach:

1. Define an equipment upgrade plan.
2. Identify training requirements for new equipment operation.
3. Identify systems training plans for new applications and user interfaces.

Step 19   Define new data management policies

Objectives:

1. To establish revised data management policies.
2. To implement data resource management policies.

Approach:

1. Regard data as a resource as opposed to being managed by applications.
2. Use distributed data management principles. Recentralization of server-based data can also be a viable strategy, since, in most cases, robust vendor products may not be available at times.
3. Establish set of policies for decision support and transactional data.

Step 20   Define user training requirements and procedures

Objectives:

1. To introduce new systems at the right time.
2. To make training an ongoing activity through the transition process.

Approach:

1. Establish new procedures and use computerized methods to train users.
2. Include user help documentation into the application.
3. User hypertext methods for contextual help.

The entire series of Steps 1 through 20 should be repeated for the prioritized macro-processes. Figure 11.5 shows the process flows.

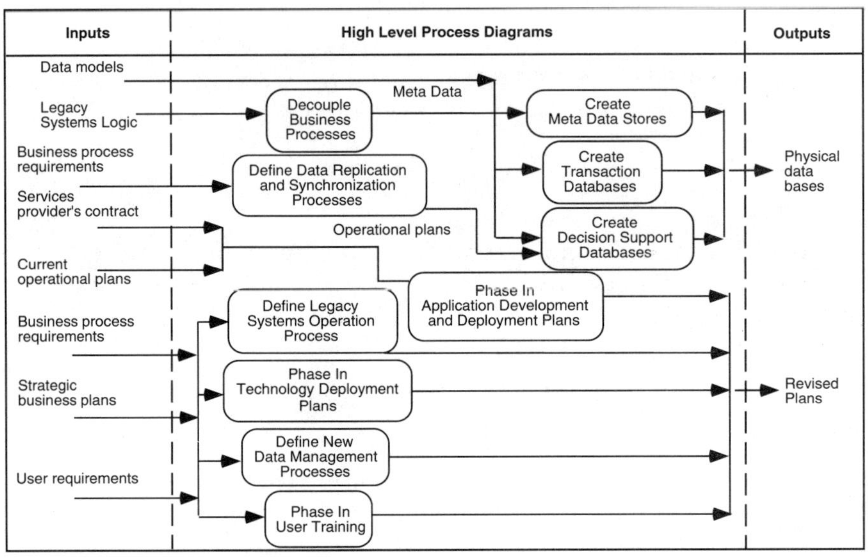

Figure 11.5   Process diagram for Steps 11 through 20.

11.2   HOW TO HARVEST SHORT-TERM BENEFITS

The legacy systems transition process will be able to yield immediate short-term benefits. In the longer term, when we have succeeded in establishing the environment for retiring more legacy systems, the benefits accrued will be permanent in nature. Key benefits are derived from the following categories.

- Using the data warehouse for decision support
- Reducing data variation and replication costs
- Capturing lost opportunities
- Phasing out mainframe processing

11.2.1 Using the Data Warehouse for Decision Support

The data warehouse data will be used to generate *required* reports to replace existing "legacy reports." Practically, it will be difficult to determine who was using or paying for the legacy systems based reports in most cases. Chances are that the legacy reports (printed on mainframe print resource centers, established by central MIS organization) are used by end-user computing analysts to manually rekey the data from paper reports into PC-based spreadsheet to produce meaningful reports for the decision makers. Once the data warehouse is established as the authoritative source for data resource, it will be unnecessary for users to manually rekey data to obtain reports. By understanding the push and pull of the operating environment, we get an appreciation of the massive number of legacy systems generated reports and the ineffectiveness. The ineffective reports should be eliminated first.

The key issue is that the legacy systems propagate a lot of data. However, the noise level in the data is very high. By utilizing the data warehouse, we can eliminate such noise and increase the quality of information. The data warehouse also provides a capability for ad hoc queries that were once impossible in the legacy environment. The data in the warehouse is integrated schema-wise across legacy applications. The painful process of obtaining same information and resolving manually from desperate systems is unnecessary. Further, the ad hoc query capability will provide facts and data to improve current processes and data quality. In short, meaningful implementation of data warehouses across the enterprise provides savings for supporting information systems improvement incrementally. The incremental improvement is the life blood to sustain the transition process. Without this arrangement, the transition process will not produce favorable return on investment.

11.2.2 Reducing Data Variation and Replication Costs

The data warehouse (if so defined) accomplishes integrated global data schema mapping across legacy applications. The warehouse data should also be resolved from structure, syntax, and semantic viewpoints. The data synchronization process assures data integrity, if followed flawlessly. Such a rigid cleanup is a resolve in building the data warehouse. Once these conditions are meticulously followed, we reduce data variation, such as multiple definitions for the same data element, aliases for convenience to work around "change boards," and such related occurrences. The data replication costs are eliminated because a credible source of data is now available in the data warehouse. The established extract-related processing that was the backbone in providing data to end users can be gradually phased out.

11.2.3 Capturing Lost Opportunities

The distributed Client/Server architecture, if properly applied to data replication and synchronization design, will give one access to data in a form not possible before. Trend analysis and sifting through validated data will provide new insights into competition and the business intelligence. Lost opportunities that were a result of overloaded systems can be recaptured. This is especially true during peak business season for merchandising and mail order houses. These firms are at times forced to outsource work because the mainframe-based legacy systems are running to capacity. Additionally, adding more processing power incrementally is not a viable option in that architecture.

11.2.4 Phasing Out Mainframe Processing

As the data warehouse-based processing takes hold and legacy systems are turned off for reporting purposes, the mainframe processing should reduce. A strategy for consolidating processing and reducing direct access storage should be implemented to harvest additional benefits.

All the previously discussed benefits should be monitored and documented. A persistent problem is that management usually gets little visibility of benefits actually accrued. Monitoring capability can be built by design into the decision-support application to eliminate guesswork.

Figure 11.6 shows a relationship between the processes and the transition steps essential to effect a planned transition of legacy systems to a distributed environment.

11.3   HOW TO FINE-TUNING METHODS

The transition processes described in this chapter may not apply or work well for all possible situations and environments. Following are some observations worth pondering that are based on experiences in real-world transition programs.

11.3.1 Evaluating Monitored Data

Project programmer analysts.   Attempts to change the mind-set of "IMS-thinking" is challenging. The analysts' system-by-system application development paradigm, where requirements are known a priori, could not be easily changed to a broad "data"-oriented thinking paradigm, where the requirements evolve as we progress with the end users of data. A description of issues related to the paradigm is given in Chapter 3.

Project data modelers. The data-modeling efforts progress slower than planned . . . again the primary reason is that the requirements are not known a priori. Data independence requires increasing the levels of data abstraction. The data modelers are tuned towards optimizing implementations with respect to a database management system. It is a physical data view with the least abstraction. Such conflicts take longer than anticipated to resolve.

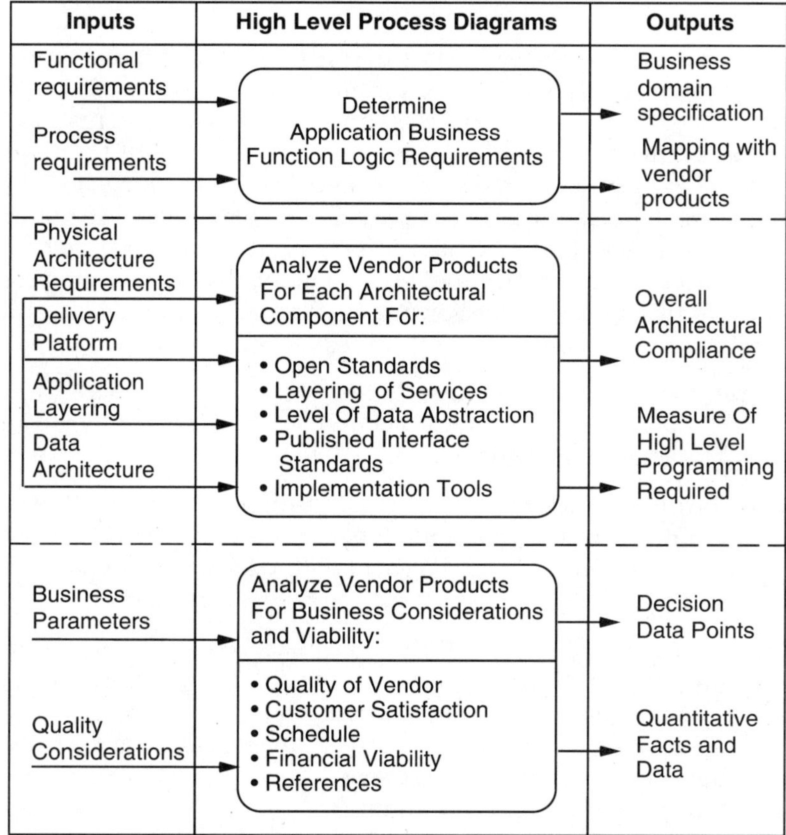

Figure 11.6   Transition processes and benefit opportunities.

Data abstraction skills are neither practiced, nor do these generally exist in the current data practitioner's repertoire. Absolute physical data models as applied in the construction of a database is the only skill available in most modeling staff. Anything outside of that comfort zone has to be acquired.

Metadata generation and linking it to data instances is talked about, but has never been practiced before. This leads to modeling paralysis.

Project advanced thinkers.   Most of the advanced methods are well-debated theoretical approaches for increasing the levels of data abstraction, as proposed here. The degree of success will enhance as actual implementations mature it in a production environment. We have to collect metrics and fine-tune the theories based on facts and data.

Deploying distributed computing in a mainframe environment.   System administration and commissioning the equipment are an adventure. Security, keyboard mappings, and software installation become a learning experience. Once again, not having all the requirements for things known, unknown, anticipated, and unanticipated in a crisis situation forces the services providers in a defensive situation. It usually takes longer and costs more than originally planned for. There is a perception in the distributed environment that no simple process exists to do things that were routine in the mainframe environment. Everything seems to be mired with untested processes.

Legacy system knowledge base.   Finding people who understand all data in legacy systems is a challenge. At best, one has to guess one's way through many instances.

Cost/benefit analysis.   Cost/benefit analysis of any situation is suspect. Fundamentally, the kind of data needed for proving a return on investment scenario cannot be gathered by legacy systems.

Data warehouse concepts.   A complete consensus of what the data warehouse is takes some time to be absorbed in the minds of the designers and users. Data warehouse proved to be an essential step in understanding legacy systems transition.

The need for separating production database transactions from decision-support processing is gaining acceptance. It is a key requirement of the processes proposed in this chapter.

General observations.   There is no need to force a distributed architecture along with data warehouse building in one single step. The problem of understanding data and separating it for decision support is, in itself, a big challenge. A phasing is suggested.

Information services group really owns the data . . . the systems that generate and control it are very fragile and brittle. The only way to get at data is to make your own copy and change the ownership. Ninety percent of end-user computing is copying and rekeying data. Information services group is an unsuspecting conduit to keep this process perpetual. The need for data is mostly decision-support at various levels. Transactional access is not part of the end-user equation.

11.3.2 Recommended Techniques

The previous observations have led to some proposed actions in a large project environment, as follows.

Step 1   Build data warehouses in at least two separate but related areas. This will ascertain the following:

1. Data abstraction can be practiced and modeled successfully.
2. Server-based data can co-exist with mainframe-based production data, and data refreshes (synchronization) can be reliably performed.
3. Reports generated from data warehouses are acceptable and older reports can, in fact, be turned off.
4. Assess how the new information distribution method is benefiting the process owners.
5. Team concept to rapidly generate application does work in our transitional culture.
6. Separation of production transactions from decision-support transactions are indeed beneficial from a data currency and availability view.
7. Verify that new data management principles can be applied well.
8. Subject and facet models can be implemented.
9. The data knowledge gathering process can be formalized.

Step 2   Simulate updates to legacy systems based on warehouse data by using middleware products. The simulation will ascertain the following:

1. Hard-coded interfaces can be substituted by loosely coupled middleware components running on different processors in an architected environment.

2. Systems with different characteristics can co-exist successfully in a data-driven environment.

Step 3   Build metadata for reengineered processes based on existing resolved data definitions common to warehouse data and new definitions. Define stored procedures from stable processes of legacy systems. This will accomplish the following:

1. New processes will have a baseline for data definitions in constructing new systems.
2. Stored procedures are available for stable transition from legacy systems with least disruption.

The growth of technology constantly challenges us. It is especially true with the rapid introduction of Client/Server computing technology products by several vendors. The one aspect of legacy systems transition that transcends these considerations is that the data-related problems are fundamental. These were created by a different computation paradigm. It will take a reasonable amount of time to resolve all data problems. Once we have made a substantial effort in that direction, maturation of technologies will happen. Therefore, the recommendation is not to get too wrapped up with technologies. All implementations should be project-pulled instead of being technology-driven.

11.4   APPLICATIONS ACQUISITION OPTIONS

A kcy activity in the transition journey is approaching the problem from a data architecture view. This is because the monolithic legacy mainframe applications had two vital elements—data and process-based data edit rules embedded in them. We have discussed in detail how data independence can be accomplished, in conjunction with establishing a distributed computing architecture infrastructure as described in Chapters 2 through 6. Having crossed the data-bridge, we have to determine how applications will be available to the users. In this regard, there is a relationship between make or buy approaches, technical, and product standards. We have to understand these considerations in the context of the business processes and the pull relationship with computing as a whole. The following sections describe these considerations.

11.4.1 Make versus Buy Decisions

The focus is on applications that are critical to business operations. Such applications are also called line of business applications. These applications are tactical in nature. However, some applications can be strategic. Regardless, we have to specify a process for a make or buy decision. Figure 11.7 describes these considerations. The outputs from the processes shown in Figure 11.7 are analyzed to determine whether the application should be made or bought. Figure 11.8 shows how to synthesize the process.

CHAPTER NOTES

1.   Forward Engineered Applications: These are a new class of application systems that are produced by using modern code generation toolkits and object-oriented methods. These have no resemblance with the COBOL legacy application programs. The forward engineering requires using the reengineered business processes in application system design that the process owners define as "Continuous Quality Improvement" steps.

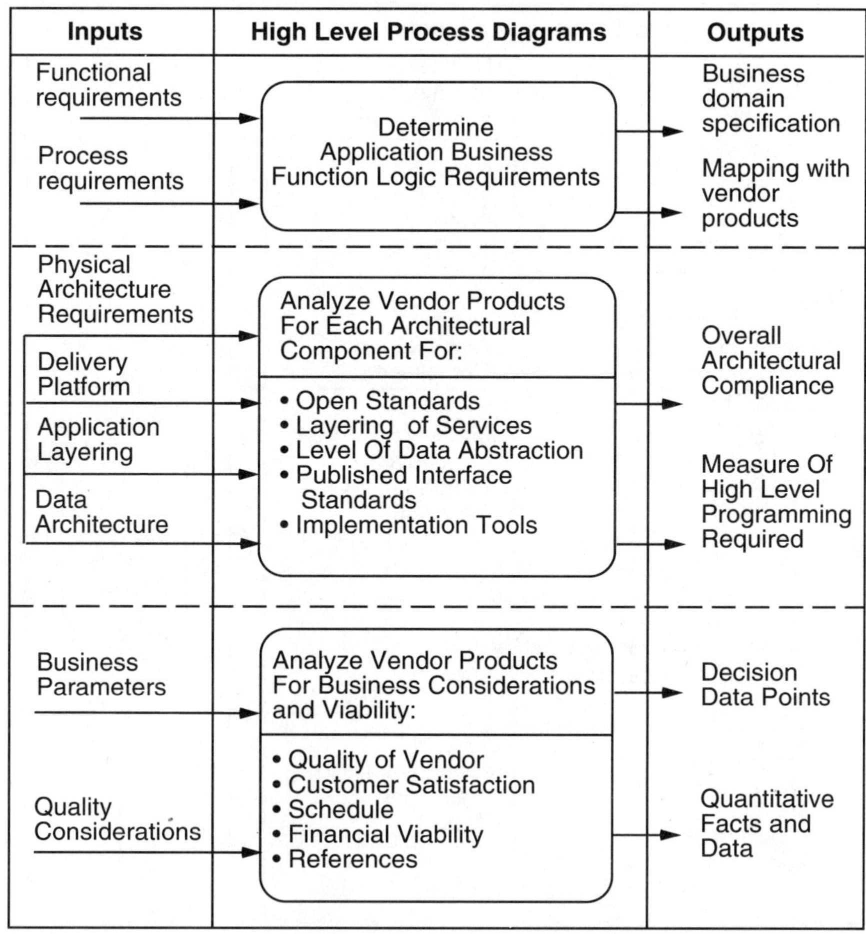

Figure 11.7   Make or buy process diagram.

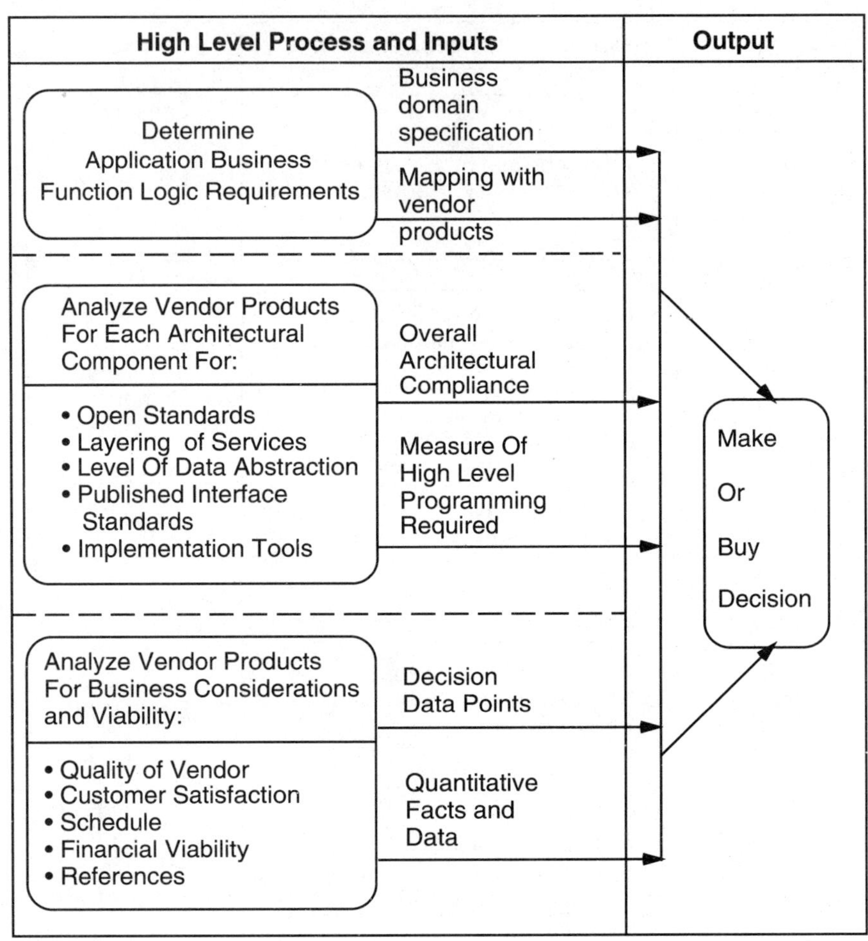

Figure 11.8   Make or buy decision process.

12

Road Map of Transition Process of Legacy Systems

The legacy systems transition to a distributed environment requires a careful and planned approach. The most important aspects are data, metadata, and business processes. As explained in Chapters 4 through 7, the legacy systems web bundles all of these in a very complex monolith. The complexity requires us to resolve the systems one step at a time. The transition is a process for accomplishing gains in increments. The "big bang"[1] approach of system conversion in one step is rarely successful. A chosen subset of business processes and corresponding legacy systems should be considered for the transition process to yield incremental benefits. Such an incremental approach should be used to develop a plan for execution. Some key components for developing the transition process follow.

12.1 A ROAD MAP

Figure 12.1 shows how these various incremental processes fit in the overall scheme of transition. Each of the generic processes should be further decomposed to suit the requirements of a specific organization.

In this section a road map is presented in detail. The road map is kept general to accommodate situations from across various segments of industry. Some generic issues are detailed below. The purpose of the road map is to set the stage for getting started. Once these steps are completed we are able to follow all the processes described in Figure 12.1.

The starting point is the legacy systems operational environment.

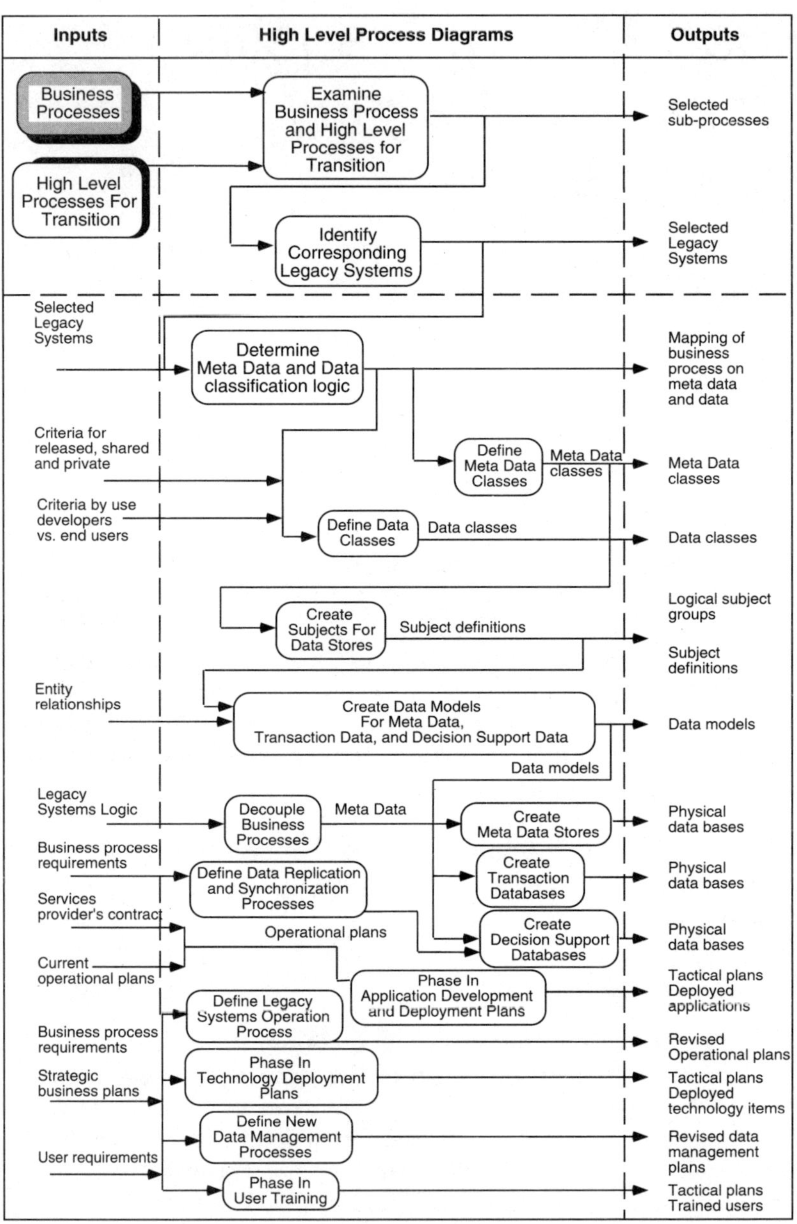

Figure 12.1   The legacy transition process.

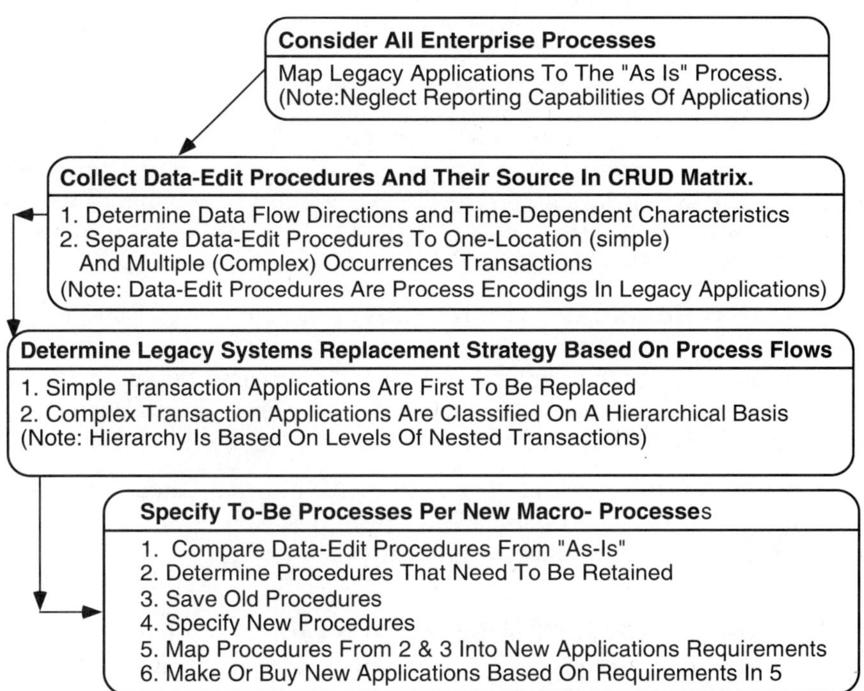

Figure 12.2   High-level road map of the transition process.

An assumption is that the transition will happen in an ongoing production environment. Figure 12.2 describes the various steps. Explanations of several new terms in the figure follows.

Enterprise processes.   These are processes that describe the key competencies of a business at high level, common across all interacting divisions. Generally these will be cross-functional in nature for a vertically managed company. In vertical management, hierarchies are described in layers of management responsible for functions, such as engineering, manufacturing, sales, finance, and so forth.

Data edit procedures.   Data edit procedures specify what data instance will be created, read, updated, or deleted by what application. Further, in cases where more than one application is involved, the rules specify and launch transaction monitoring functions. In monolithic legacy applications the data edit procedures are embedded in the application code. The consistency of data edit rules is managed through application interface control definition documents manually. Capturing these rules in computer-sensible format as metadata affords the capability to manage these by automated procedures.

CRUD matrix.   A matrix shows applications' control of Create, Read, Update, Delete activities as executed by the encoded program logic for a particular data element. The complexity or nonsparseness of a CRUD matrix shows the levels of nested transactions occurring in a group of legacy applications.

Data flow direction.   This is a vector describing the CRUD activities between and among applications. In the case of read-only applications, we can classify the applications as upstream (created), midstream (read and update), and downstream (read-only) purely from a data viewpoint. These vectors help in devising an application transition strategy.

Time-dependent characteristics.   All data instances have certain time-dependent characteristics. These describe temporal nature, persistence, and the sensitivity (volatility) to change with respect to time.

Process encoding.   The embedded programming logic (instruction set) describes the process; for example, the simplest is a binary action (release order yes/no) in an application.

Hierarchy or nested transactions.   This is a set of transactions that the data edit procedures launch in a set of related applications sequentially and automatically. This indication was described in Chapter 7 as an accepted past-programming practice.

Macro-processes.   These describe of the major activities of a company such as design product, build product, sell product, and support product. A detailed discussion of macro-processes was given in Chapter 8.

Figure 12.3 shows how end users, process, and system owners are part of the transition process. It is important that the end users, the process, and the system owners are involved in defining the various data resolution rules embedded in legacy systems. When we are able to separate the data edit rules, surface semantics, and deep semantics from the legacy applications, then we are enabled to create the environment for a data services-based architecture. In such an environment, data is physically and logically separate, and communication with the application is established through service layers. These new data management concepts were described in Chapter 5. The data resolution and rationalization rules along with data edit business rules are also the

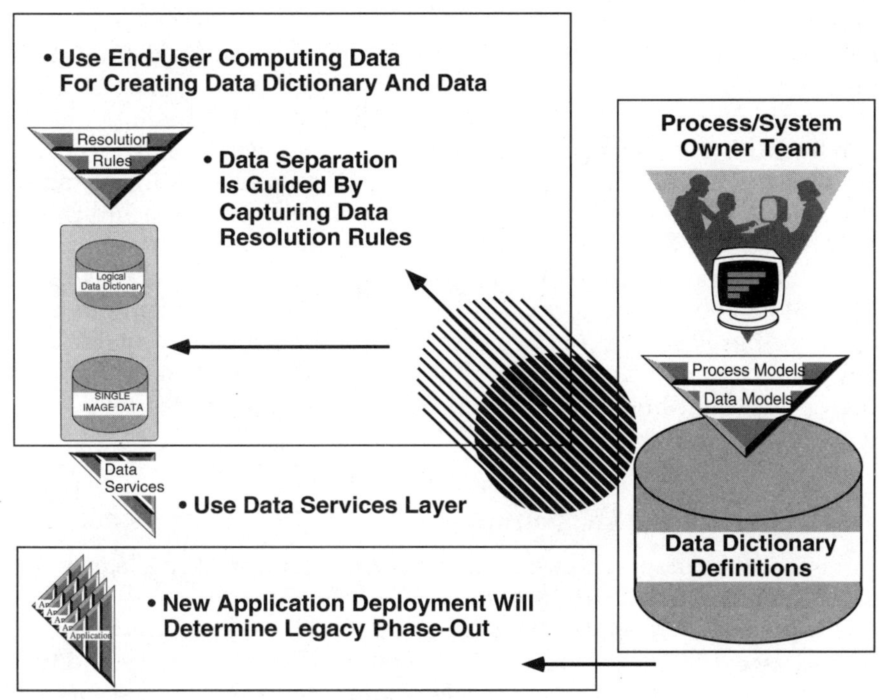

Figure 12.3   End-user participation in the legacy transition process.

metadata. Where and how metadata is stored and managed is part of the data architecture. The right-hand side of Figure 12.3 shows the process of collecting the information, such as process and data models, data resolution rules, and data dictionary and semantics. The left-hand side of the same figure shows how these are captured as the data definitions and metadata. The lower part of the figure shows the data access through data services layers. In essence, the figure is a high-level description of the tactical portion of the entire transition process.

12.1.1 Classification of Existing Legacy Systems

A meaningful transition process can be understood by taking an inventory of the current legacy systems. One quick way is to classify these into strategic, tactical, and decision-support applications. The characteristics for these were described in Chapter 7. It must be noted that in many cases when these legacy applications evolved, there may not have been such classifications present. We have to introduce one more dimension in our classification process; that is, to determine the owner of the system, and how the application replicates and transmits data to and from other legacy applications. The model shown in Figure 12.2 can be used to answer such questions. This will help us in understanding the degree of data-edit complexities built into the system interfaces. Another way of looking at this is to understand the data management culture that gets embedded into the application logic. While we will not decouple all such dependencies, we at least understand the data management-based issues and are able to define a solvable problem. The key result obtained at this stage is a good documented understanding of the application, business process, and data dependencies within the legacy systems web.

12.1.2 Functional Decomposition of Key Legacy Systems

Functional decomposition into distinct code chunks of the legacy systems includes understanding the legacy web. In some cases, it is possible to trace what applications feed data to what applications. But, in many cases, the data is physically copied into the application and fictitious data elements are added to effect data integration (preservation of contextual information). From a simple data flow view, one can identify upstream, midstream, and downstream applications. The classification need not be perfect. As a matter of fact, it may be very difficult to find the design documentation that supports the current processing environment. The analyst will be in a constant discovery mode. Figure 12.4 is representative of a typical situation.

The following description of the current application environment is adapted from situations in many large companies that are predominantly mainframe-oriented.

- Users generally have requests for changes to legacy applications for enhancing capabilities or for providing data for decision support.
- In cases where data structures need not be altered, the changes are accomplished rapidly.
- In other instances, the work backlog grows to an unmanageable size.
- The user copes with the situation by writing simple extract programs and then develops an application to provide data analysis capabilities based on the extracted data.

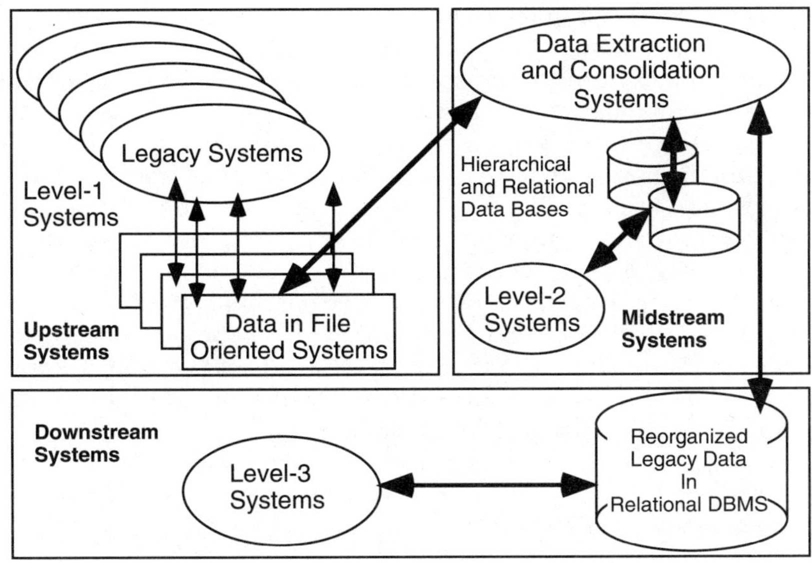

Figure 12.4   Current application environment.

- At times the PC-based programs also send transactions back to the mainframe using screen-pumping techniques.
- When data is in no direct usable form in databases or flat files, the user writes screen-scraping programs that execute on a PC. Screen scraping, though very useful, may cause the greatest impediment in transitioning from mainframes.
- The use of screen-scraping[2] in combination with screen-pumping[3] for data uploads to the mainframe is the ultimate bridge for gaining access to data and services that the MIS community was not able to provide rapidly. While this is beneficial to the end-user organization, it is not a robust architecture-based solution. Creative marketing types go as far as calling this design technique first generation Client/Server systems.
- A legacy transition strategy should be able to supplant the above mode of computation with proper data and application services in a distributed environment.

With the legacy application situation being so complex initially, it may appear challenging to effect a meaningful transition process. The starting point should be to classify common shared systems using the levels shown in Figure 12.4. Normally, the classification into these levels may closely follow the chronology of the application development process itself. In other words, the oldest of applications will fall into level 1 and the newest in level 3. Regardless, the most common starting point will be at the level 2. Once we restore or reclaim all the data in these level 2 and 3 systems and replace the application capabilities based on newly defined processes, we never have to go back to level 1 systems. The applications in level 1 will be operated simultaneously till we synchronize all data and gain sufficient production robustness in the new environment. At that time we can sunset the level 1 applications. The assumption behind this kind of phasing is that the oldest systems have the most obsolete technologies and business rules encoded in them. As such, there is no redeeming value in reverse engineering those sets of applications. Related ideas were supported by arguments given in Chapter 7.

12.1.3 Creating the Data versus Application Matrix

The transition process requires an understanding of how data is managed in the current suite of legacy applications. A data versus application matrix describes how data is managed in the current environment. An example is shown in Table 12.1.

The CRUD matrix provides insights for specifying the data replication and synchronization rules when we transform source data obtained from legacy systems and reformat or map it to target data stores. The transition process requires that the data be reclaimed from legacy systems. The reclaimed data will be stored by subjects for the purposes of transaction and decision-support processing. The CRUD matrix data should also be part of the metadata for a period of time until the comple-

Table 12.1   A Generic CRUD Matrix

Application	Data Element-1	Data Element-2	Data Element-3	Data Element-4
Application-1	C= Create	R	U,D	D
Application-2	R= Read	U,D,C	C	C
Application-3	U= Update	R	R	U
Application-4	D= Delete	R	R	R

tion of the transition process. Storing such information in metadata (in a computer) further enhances the quality of data, because errors in recording can be readily corrected by launching a database transaction, as opposed to paper documentation.

12.1.4 Establishing the Data Warehouse

The legacy systems have evolved over a period of time. A general observation is that the user community satisfies its informational needs by writing extract programs that populate individual databases or application file systems. These individual systems (Level 3 in Figure 12.4) are unable to provide an integrated view of the data. The subject of data integration across applications for the purpose of storing these in a database (data warehouse) for "Read"-only access is discussed in detail by W.H. Inmon (*Building the Data Warehouse.* QED Publishing, 1990).

In a legacy systems environment all the data is controlled and managed by applications and change control boards for configuration control. Further, the same source data in operational systems is physically used for decision support and report generation. Operational requirements dictate that we separate these two different classes of users for efficiency and ad hoc query capability. Inclusion of a data warehouse creation step greatly simplifies the legacy transition process. The data warehouse is a transition element, not a transitory solution. The data warehouse is required in the distributed environment. As a matter of fact, it was a mainframe solution but never caught on because of the application backlog situation. Distributed computing, PCs, and advanced 4GL tools rejuvenated the dormant concept in the current situation. There are many advantages to do so. The principle drivers to create data warehouses are as follows.

Driver 1.   Decision-support users are interested in summary data. Derivation of summary data at various levels of aggregation requires computation and mapping of production (transaction) data. Some data may be mapped with no transformation; however, most data will require a detailed mapping model. In Chapter 6, various mapping and models were discussed. The definitions of these models and mappings have to be completed in order to establish a data warehouse. The concepts to build a data warehouse are much more sophisticated and evolved from those discussed by Inmon. The new concepts are model-configured data-refreshing capabilities, and specification-driven extendibility of the data as we proceed to new releases of the warehouse and decision-support application.

Driver 2.   Decision support requires ad hoc query capability.
It is almost impossible to normalize and optimize a transaction database for ad hoc queries. Read-only data structuring is very different and relatively simple from read/write transaction databases. Rich data indexing strategies are the key to access optimization. Large indexes in multidimensional databases eliminate complex joins and intermediate joins of relational tables. These details were discussed in Chapter 10. A data warehouse need not be burdened with transaction-optimization features. It is permissible to have long response times in some situations. However, once the query is understood in terms of repeated use, the data warehouse data can be restructured.

Driver 3.   Data integration is a prerequisite for cross-functional data access. The nature of decision-support queries requires data from various legacy sources. Once we begin to resolve and rationalize data for structure, syntax, and semantics across applications (data integration), we have a wealth of metadata-related knowledge. This knowledge is the key in making the transition process successful. The data warehouse will enhance the integrity of the data, because most data-value (instance) problems arises from asynchronous data. By design, we have a synchronization model defined that will enforce data coherency and consistency in the warehouse. Therefore, creation of a data warehouse is an essential step in the transition process.

There are several other characteristics and advantages for data warehouses as described by Inmon. For our purposes, we recognize the importance of creating data warehouses. The legacy transition plan, therefore, includes a warehouse creation step. Figure 12.5 shows the schematic diagram of how a data warehouse is constructed. The logical and physical architectural elements used to create a data warehouse are discussed in Chapters 5 and 6.

12.1.5 The Operational Data Store

The data warehouse consists of time-variant, nonvolatile, subject-oriented data. The data instances do not change. Historic snapshots of data are stored in time increments dictated by the synchronization and data replication models. The data is used for read-only purposes. Any data derived by the users is not stored in the data warehouse. Users do not update or delete data in the data warehouse. The use is generally limited to support queries, both standard and ad hoc. This requirement is usually satisfied by providing access to the metadata for end-user private application creation at level 3, as discussed in Chapter 9.

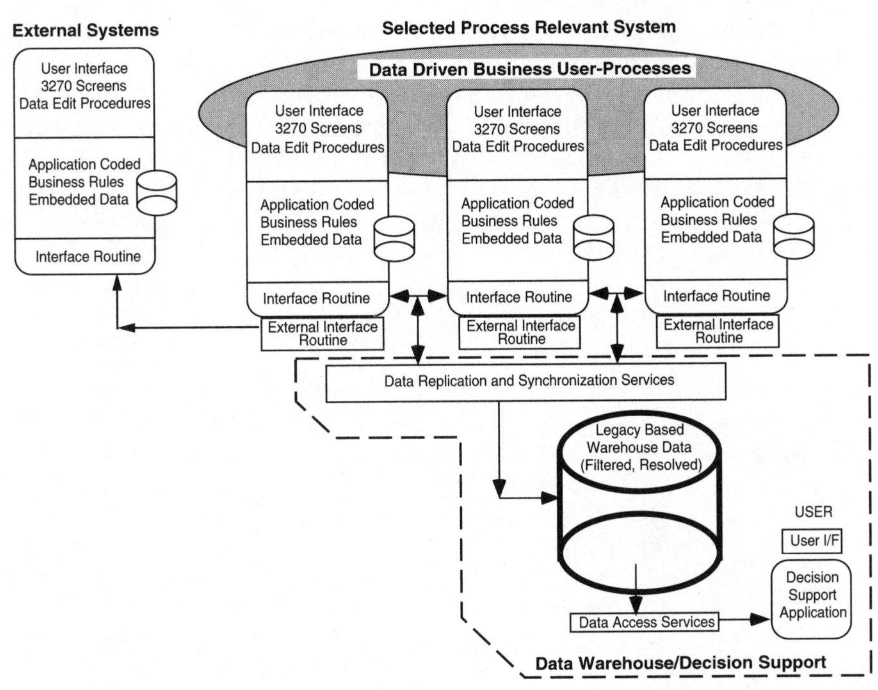

Figure 12.5   Building the data warehouse.

Given this scenario, it is conceivable that a class of integrated data will be required that needs to be updated, deleted, and created in concert with the source data derived from legacy systems. Inmon defines such a data store as an operational data store. The application using the data in an operational data store is not any different from a production application. The only conceivable difference from a legacy system is that it supports the new processes and does not contain the baggage of a monolithic legacy system. In that context, operational data stores are yet another bridge to arrive at an architected environment.

An important distinction between an operational data store and a data warehouse is that part of the metadata is in common with the data warehouse's metadata. Additionally, certain data edit rules, described in previous sections, are included as stored procedures. The data instances are not obtained from the legacy applications, but are created from the forward engineered new applications.[4]

The operational data store should have one more important feature. When we examine the stored procedures, we will find that certain updates to legacy systems which are still part of the overall applications require updates. These updates are caused by dependence of external systems on the phased-out systems (replaced by the forward engineered applications) for transactional integrity. One way to handle these in the interim is by a message-based external interface, as shown in Figure 12.6. There can be other strategies, too. The important point to understand is that the operation of legacy systems in parallel with new systems, operational data stores, and data warehouse is a challenging problem. Chapter 6 discussed some of these challenges and ways to face them.

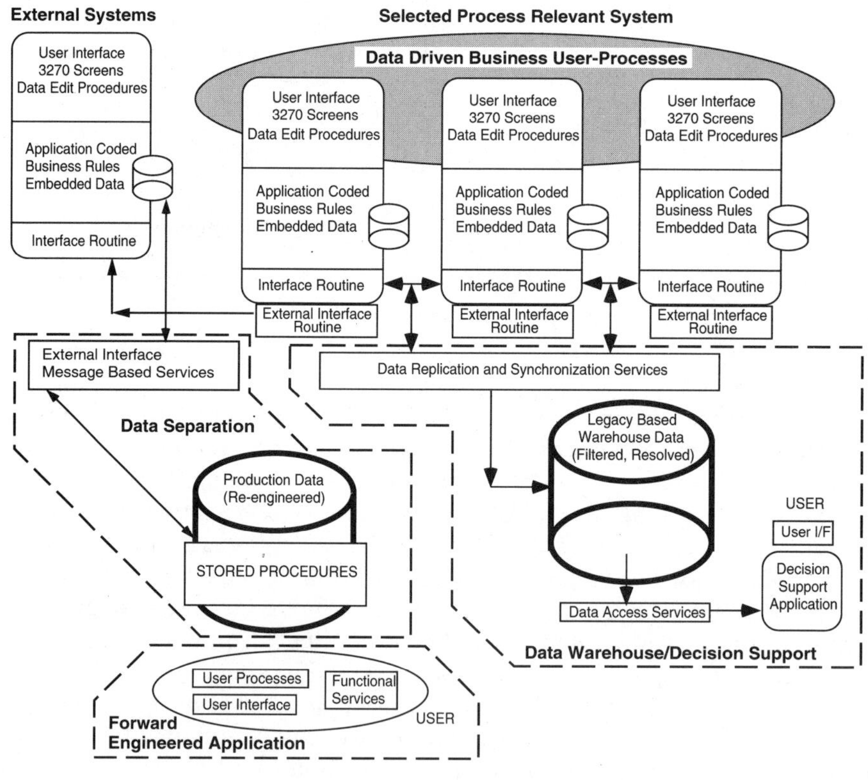

Figure 12.6   Legacy systems interface with data stores and data warehouse.

12.1.6 Monitoring Data Usage

The data usage patterns of the data need to be monitored. As a requirement of architecture design we should allow for collecting statistics on what data is used, where, and by whom. An analysis of such data will allow us to optimize the use of storage devices by frequency of use. The legacy system architecture is too complicated to make such analysis possible. The guess work in designing a large-scale, data-serving environment is mitigated with the availability of metrics. Various database products are poor in this regard and we may end up designing our own middleware servers to facilitate meaningful architecture transitions. Environment management tools are inadequate in the current vendor product set. All proponents of quality improvement insist on metrics for continuous improvement.

12.1.7 Enriching the Operations Data

The operation of the systems, as summarized in Figure 12.7, provides us with some important insights. These ideas were discussed in detail in Chapter 6 and are not repeated here. The data warehouse portion of Figure 12.7 shows the manner in which the data mappings have to be altered or extended. The operational data store along with the stored procedures, in the same figure, show the enhancements required to the rule set.

An important aspect of the client and server model of the distributed architecture is a loosely coupled system of processors along with layers of software filling the requirements of an end-to-end transaction. Figure 12.7 shows an example of how operational data stores can interact with external legacy systems in the interim transition environment.

In Figure 12.7 several middleware components are brought into interaction. In such an environment, it will be possible to examine the rule set and what additional rules have to be established to satisfy the user. The user will inevitably be in a discovery mode. The data delivered in this environment was seldom available in a timely fashion . The old legacy systems deluged the user with a whole lot of data. All of it was not required. So, in this changed environment the user will become an integral part of defining the succinct data needed to complete a process step. The user participation in this area will enrich the operations data. Thus we will be positioned to arrive at an optimum data management operation situation—the dream of any information services organization.

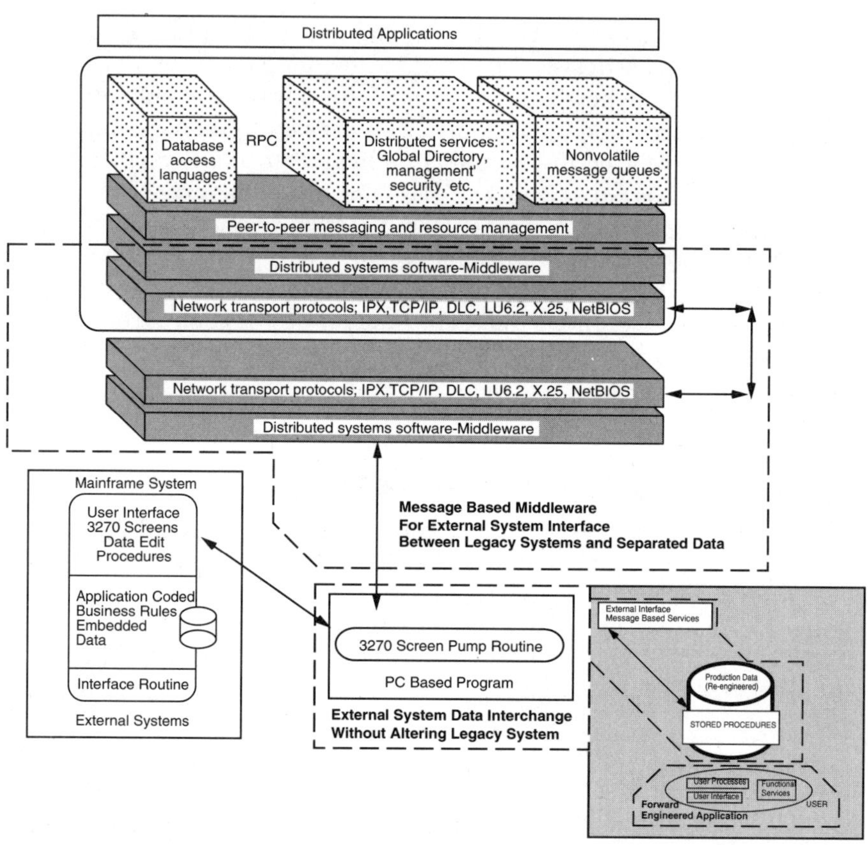

Figure 12.7   Architectural components of an interim transition environment.

12.1.8 Creating the Extensible Enterprise Metadata

The previous discussion should bring the attention back to metadata. Any time we deal with data and the associated rules of usage, we are implying and implicating metadata. The treatment of metadata is not any different from data as a common resource. Just some of the concepts of use are different. The extendibility of metadata is implemented by the various contents of the cloud model shown in Figure 6.2 and discussed in Chapter 6. These are the specifications for everything connected with data.

12.1.9 Creating Business Rules for the New Applications

The legacy systems transition process road map is designed to provide incremental benefits while we are establishing a proper architecture environment as described in Chapters 2 through 7. Chapters 8 and 9 discussed creating rules, linkages, and computing processes to satisfy the needs of the newly reengineered processes. Instead of encoding these into applications, we now want to add these to the metadata. This type of metadata should be used by the developers of new applications. Metadata is the principle resident of the repository. The repository of the past designs started too ambitiously. It went as far as to profess that reusable code in a stable environment can be stored for assembly to order for a customer request. While the concept is theoretically acceptable, the practicality is highly questionable. The insights given by Thomas Davenport[5] are compelling and supportive of this view by virtue of the examples he quotes in the paper. The idea that all data, regardless of its origin, scope, and usage, can be defined by one single standard definition is staggeringly difficult in a large company. The key culprit is time and lack of consensus. The concept was based on the assumption that computing platforms will be a precious resource. It has become a commodity. A commodity design approach is highly desirable. That means data replication is acceptable. Distribution means autonomy and less conformity. Conformity is accomplished by data abstraction techniques; it is logically coerced not physically mandated. These are powerful new ideas for our road map.

Data filtering (metadata-based management techniques as opposed to voluminous canned paper reports), when linked with processes, will give the order and cohesion. This is the new paradigm. Gigabytes made to look like just "bytes" is the architecture. It is flexible and transparent. The user experiences it and does not know or care how complex it is. The computers adapt to the user, not the other way around. This is not so because we are smarter than our predecessors (who in some cases manage us): We have the right technology and the commitment to be business-driven; the price is right; the risks make it fun; and we have the urgency to solve the problem the right way, right away.

12.1.10 Business Rules Based on Total Quality Improvement

Total quality improvements will require implementation of metrics. We have to measure the benefits afforded by virtue of the new applications, data warehouse, and operational data stores. We may discover that some assumptions may be invalid. The modified business rules supporting processes should accordingly have to be changed. The concepts of business streams are new to application delivery. We used to go back to the drawing board each time a functionality had to be added. Now, we think in terms of objects, reuseability, and separate databases and data-server environments. These are driven by micro-process improvements suggested by quality improvements. The key requirements and improvements are generated by the people who use the data, not middle layers of computing professionals who made computing seem like some sophisticated, scarce technology of a privileged few. The PCs and graphical user interfaces shield the users from arcane computer language. Really not much has changed. The complexity is still there; if anything, it has increased substantially. However, the user is hidden from the complexity behind object and data abstractions. Now the business rules get communicated and implemented in very rapid situations. Developments are tuned to yield benefits and capabilities. The legacy transition process has to happen with the push to reengineer businesses. Business rules are based on facts and data, and human intelligence to interpret the data. Figure 10.14 discussed such a human-based information technology model for decision-making. The model is an important road map milestone.

12.1.11   The Conceptual Application Architecture and Principles

The conceptual architecture, while difficult to understand, is a critical milestone on the transition road map. The new systems should be specified using the models described in Chapters 5 and 6. An important tabulation of the dimensions of user satisfaction is shown in Table 12.1 and was discussed in Chapter 2.

Table 12.2   Dimensions of user satisfaction

Information satisfaction	System satisfaction	Support group satisfaction
Availability	Ease of use	Technical competence
Accuracy	Ease of learning	Attitudes
Timeliness	Flexibility	Responsiveness
Precision	User control	Services
Reliability	Response time	Development schedule
Currency	Error control facilities	Charge back methods
Completeness		
Output format		

The architectural principles are repeated here to put the road map in context. Most architectural principles derive from three principles concerning abstraction, integration, and balance. These principles forge a strong link between business purposes and selected standard computing approaches.

Abstraction.   This principle provides critical *independence* between the specification of a system and its implementation. Independence allows improvements to occur with minimal impact. The principle of abstraction guides the design towards a system that appears simple and intuitive to the user. Esoteric operations of the information technology are made relatively *transparent*. The operations of the system closely match the operations of the user and the business process. Abstraction is achieved by designing system functionality in layers of increasing system organization.

Integration.   The principle of integration guides the design to provide opportunities for cooperation—cooperation among machines, individuals, and groups within the same or different contexts and stages of a process. Cooperation among machines requires that they *interoperate*. The integration principle guides the design towards an implementation of the metaphors of communication, sharing, and coordination.

Balance.   The principle of balance guides the design towards optimization. This principle requires that objectives must be concrete and explicit in order to know when they have been met. A good design adjusts key system variables within the limits of constraints to meet the objectives. The principle guides the design to attain desirable system properties by using the right structural elements and parameter settings that affect those properties.

12.1.12   Specifying the Layered Architecture

The layered architecture described in Chapter 5 should be mapped with a corresponding product set of vendors. It is possible that in certain areas new developments have to be launched to fill the blanks not satisfied by vendor products. Figure 12.8 shows an enriched model of the layered architecture. The key element of this milestone of the road map is the addition of work-flow management and coupling with process management services and intelligent agents to retrieve data. Work-flow managers are emerging and require key elements as directory and dictionary services.

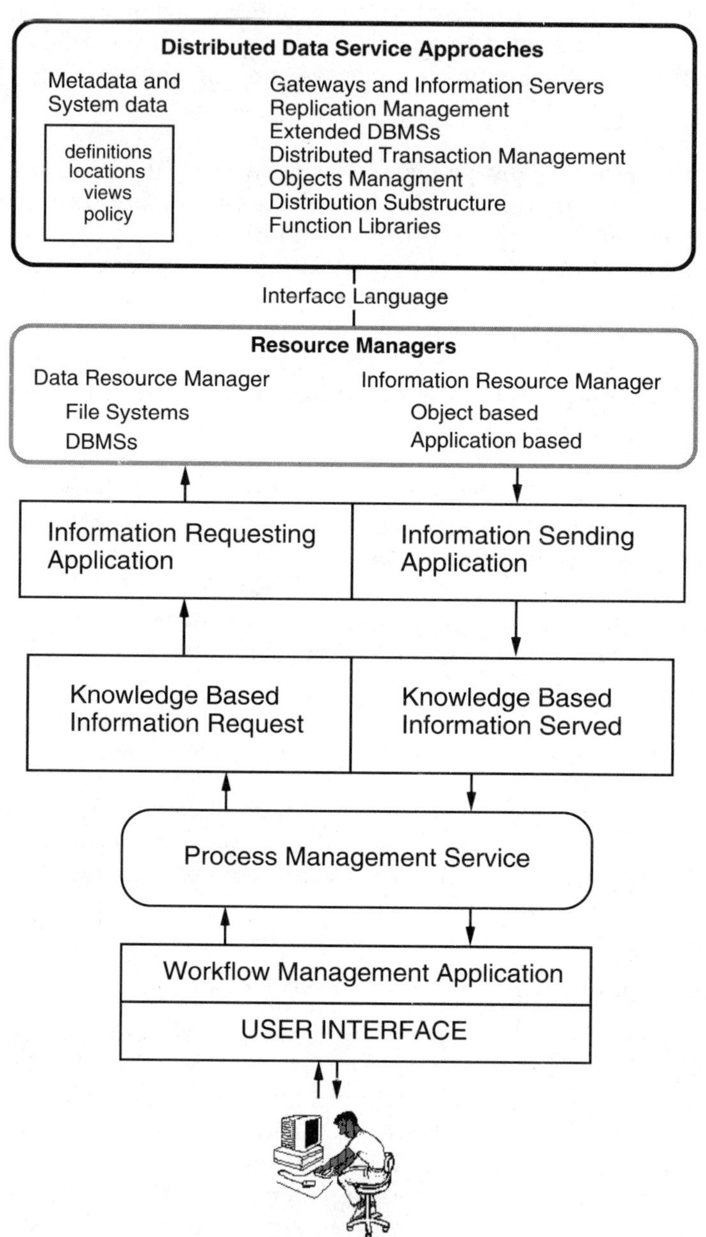

Figure 12.8   An extended services-based architecture model.

12.1.13   The Final Steps of the Transition Process

The final steps of the transition architecture are to deploy technology based on considerations of readiness. The technology option can be better understood in the context of a framework. Figure 12.9 is an example of a framework.

Figure 12.9 consists of eight distinct architectural elements; related concepts were discussed in Chapter 10. We extend the discussion

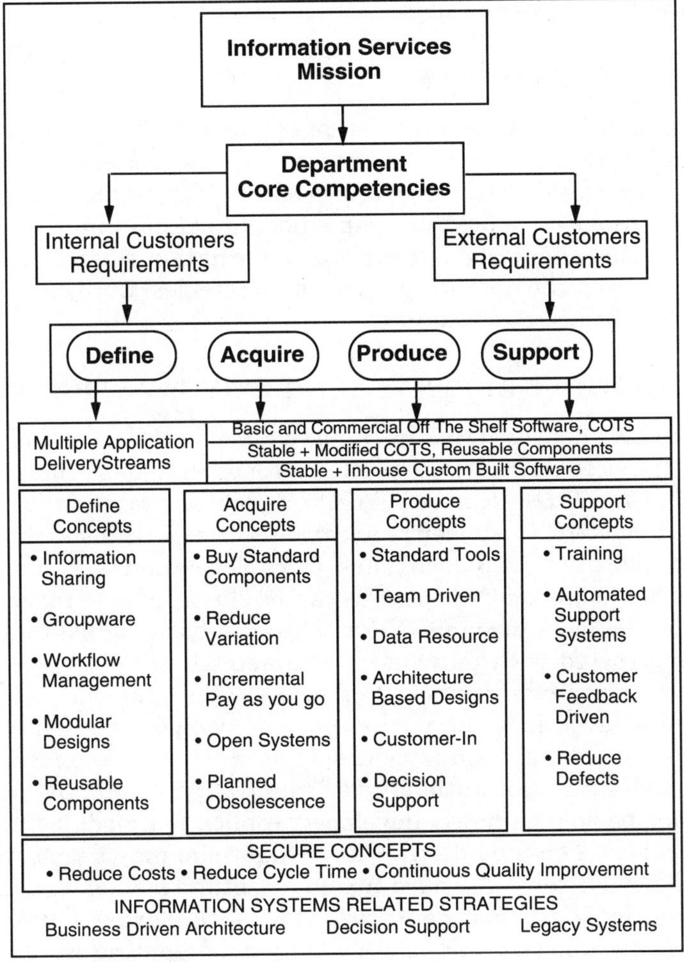

Figure 12.9   The components framework of the transition road map.

to show some physical components to improve the legacy transition program. These are as follows:

1. A mission statement
2. The core competencies of the information services (IS) group
3. Key requirements of the internal and external customers
4. The fundamental macro-processes of the IS group
5. Definition of the business streams for the macro-processes
6. Essential concepts for each macro-process
7. Secure concepts
8. Information systems-related strategies

12.2   THE STRATEGIES

A tactical plan to reshape information services starts with a statement of strategies. In an ongoing concern, the strategies are derived from both top down and bottom up approaches. Universally, incremental implementations have provided rapid benefits at minimum risk; therefore, strategies should be supportive. Information services strategies are derived from the operating divisions strategies. Core competencies must be recognized at this stage.

12.3   MULTIPLE APPLICATION DELIVERY STREAMS

The application delivery streams can be defined in the context of computing systems based on the business stream concepts by Don Clausing in his book *Total Quality Development*. We can classify and standardize between changing and stable customer requirements or expectations, thus reducing the complexity of introducing new technologies and concepts.

Generally, information systems can be classified into three distinct application delivery streams. First these are basic and stable components constructed with purchased, commercial off-the-shelf software. The second stream is composed of stable, plus previously developed components saved in a library as reusable components (an emerging concept in the software industry widely used by the National Aeronautics and Space Administration organization, NASA). Finally, the third stream has basic plus newly developed application modules to protect strategic ideas. The modules in the third stream may be one of a kind and may not be reused. There are many other models expressed as taxonomies by NIST (National Institute of Standards). Other models are commonly known as DCE (Distributed Computing Environment) by Open Systems or its latest manifestation, the object-oriented model of OMG (Object Management Group) called CORBA (common object request broker architecture), and so on. There is no shortage of models, only shortage of robust vendor products. At times, it is not clear whether the standards are created for the benefit of vendors or the general good of the consumers; regardless, having a framework including the one described in the current book helps us to focus on specifying a road map for the legacy systems transition.

The first stream consists of the basic infrastructure elements of the information delivery systems. Examples are communication networks, computing platforms including operating systems, standard ubiquitous utilities, and so on, that have a fairly long shelf life. The second business stream deals with the applications that utilize the elements of the first business stream. However, in this stream we include applications that are supporting stable business processes. Generally, the bread-and-butter applications are included, such as payroll, human resources, and so forth. The third consists of new and evolving demands from the users that require certain custom programming or adaptations. Examples are inclusion of new productivity tools such as word processing, spreadsheets and such adapted with proprietary company models for analysis of information. Integration from a data-sharing standpoint is an important business requirement. Both the second and third business streams are predominantly customer-driven. The first is usually industry-driven, based on a wide customer base.

12.4   KEY CONCEPTS

Key concepts are defined for each of the four macro-processes to further define the strategies of information systems. These concepts are further detailed here over the high-level processes described in Chapter 10 as applicable to information systems.

12.4.1 The "Define" Macro-Process

Key concepts for the "define process" are as follows.

Information sharing.   The architecture should facilitate sharing of information. Information is the commodity that passes from worker to worker and is enhanced at each step. This key concept means we have to be concerned with database management systems, decision-support systems, layered and open architectures, and flexible delivery systems.

Groupware.   Groupware is the term loosely used to describe a group of technologies that mediate interpersonal collaboration through the computer.[6] Current groupware product categories are:

- Electronic mail and messaging (e.g., cc:Mail from Lotus)
- Shared-screen products (e.g., Aspects from Group Technologies)

- Shared-memory products (e.g., Lotus notes, Word Perfect Office)
- Calendaring and scheduling (Meeting Maker from On Technologies)
- Group decision-support systems (e.g., GroupSystems V from Ventana)
- Group editing (e.g., Face-to-Face from Crosswise)
- Workflow (e.g., ATI from Action Technologies)
- Document image management (e.g., Filenet from Filenet)
- Workgroup utilities (e.g., Workgroup for Windows from Microsoft)
- Groupware development tools (e.g., Notes from Lotus)

Groupware or workgroup products let workgroups or individuals transfer and share information with one another. The key ingredient is information. It is easy to see how this concept meshes with the information-sharing concept.

Work-flow management.   Work-flow management as a key concept helps to tie together diverse applications, people, and processes. In a work-flow application, the process knowledge that applies to the information is also managed, transferred, and routed. The key ingredient is the process.[7]

Modular designs.   The information systems of today should eventually be built using object-oriented technologies. That way the applications are modular and can "plug and play" to provide rapid capability to the users. Modular designs are produced only if we specify an architecture at the highest level of abstraction. The inter-communication is facilitated by specified interface definitions and procedure calls. By using open systems standards we can establish an environment where diverse vendors' products can work as a cohesive unit.

Reusable components.   Software reuse is a major opportunity of the 1990s. Reuse is facilitated by a repository containing the applications' business rules, the data definitions, data meanings, and processing rules.

It is now possible to see how these key concepts play an important role in understanding the "define" process. There can be many more key concepts. However, the idea is to drive the strategy down to meaningful levels to move the organization to a distributed computing environment.

12.4.2 The "Acquire" Macro-Process

Based on the define process, there will be certain components that can be acquired from vendors. The key concepts follow and are self-explanatory. The key consideration is, once again, to specify an architecture that enables the purchased components to work as a unit.

- Buy standard components
- Reduce variation in both hardware and software acquisitions
- Implement capabilities incrementally
- Use and specify open systems standards
- Manage acquisitions by policy to allow for planned obsolescence

12.4.3 The "Produce" Macro-Process

This macro-process supports the application production process. In those cases when it is beneficial to design and construct the application system in-house, the following key concepts apply.

Standard tools. This concept enables the groupware and work-flow concepts explained earlier to perform in an application generation environment. The hand-crafted code of the past is rapidly changing. Programmers use graphical user interface building tools, application generators, and such. The concept is to standardize on tools that will adhere to the architecture principles.

Team-driven. The new paradigm is to include the customer or the users of the application involved through all the process from beginning to end. The old concepts of gathering requirements and then building the application in isolation have contributed largely to the legacy systems mess.[8] In a team concept, we define a design/build team that includes representation from all groups that design, build, and use the final product. In concert with the concepts explained earlier, we can see how responsive software can be built by using these processes.

Data resource. This concept formally defines the processes required to make the data available as a separate resource from the application.

Architecture-based designs. The purpose of architecture is to create a designed system that satisfies a client's purpose. Clients of a computing system design range along a continuum from operational users to business stakeholders. Clients come from different functional areas of an enterprise, function at various levels of the organization, or have various relationships to the enterprise. The architect, by virtue of the designs, should establish the criteria that the client, that is, the users in the broadest sense, should be satisfied with the implemented system. Architected designs are based on principles. The following characteristics of AT&T's GISA development projects would be good candidates for principles to ensure linkage between information technology and business objectives:[9]

- Standard data designations and format
- Standard interfaces to common external systems
- Minimal size of local development groups
- Avoidance of redundant software development/searches
- Multiuse licenses for the same software
- An experienced team to coordinate global implementations
- Coordinated customization and upgrade maintenance
- User group to share ideas and experiences
- Backup among multiple users in same area
- Improved communications between locations

Customer-in.   The fundamental thesis of world-class information services organizations is to delight the customer with products and services that are used, influenced, and built in a cooperative environment with the customer-in concept. This concept is in direct contrast with the product-out philosophy that says, "give me requirements, all the requirements then I will build the application and deliver it to you."

Decision support.   The concept of decision support is to create a separate database from the operational database so that we can perform all activities that need data to make a decision or understand a problem. It will be impossible to collect metrics for continuous quality improvement without a decision-support system.

12.4.4 The "Support" Macro-Process

The final process is to support the applications serving the user community. The key concepts are:

Training: Training is an essential part of system deployment. The training should be designed and conducted with the customer-in concept.

Automated Support Systems: With the advent of technologies such as CD ROM, Hypertext, and multimedia, it is possible to put a lot of help at the users' finger tips. The automated support systems concept deals with such technology implementation.

Customer Feedback-Driven: The support delivery should be, once again, customer-driven. An automated feedback system can be built into the application user interface as a background application. E-Mail and messaging systems can be put in place to act rapidly on feedback received from the users. It is important to include such strategies right up front to make a transition to the information age.

Reduce Defects: This concept is complementary to the customer feedback concept and must be a secure concept of the information services organization. Defects are based on lines of code metrics.

12.5 SECURE CONCEPTS

The information services organization should also specify certain secure and abiding concepts. The most common in the industry—at least those adopted by the Fortune 100 companies—are as follows:

- Reduce costs to produce products and services to offer lowest priced products to the customer
- Reduce cycle time to produce product to meet with market elasticity
- Total quality improvement for process improvements based on empowered employees

12.6 INFORMATION SYSTEMS RELATED STRATEGIES

Information systems related strategies defines certain broad requirements. For instance, these can be:

Business-driven Architecture: The architecture should be driven by the realities of the business. The details were discussed in Chapter 8. If the architecture is business-driven, then we will see technology being pulled not pushed on the user. Every major decision will be driven by a cost/benefit analysis and return on investment criteria.

Decision Support: Increasingly, we are seeing that most of the information systems budget is consumed in providing data for decision support. A recognition of this aspect of service should be acknowledged in the management strategy as opposed to being an afterthought.

Legacy Systems Transition: Legacy systems transition is an important strategy. In addition to implementing newly defined business processes, the strategies include cooperative processing of the legacy systems in addition to the new distributed applications. It will be impossible to shut down the shop when we are modernizing the infrastructure and the application portfolio. This strategy and the supporting tactics were the principal contents of the current book.

Figure 12.10 shows the groupware environment adapted from the same paper cited in Chapter Note 6.

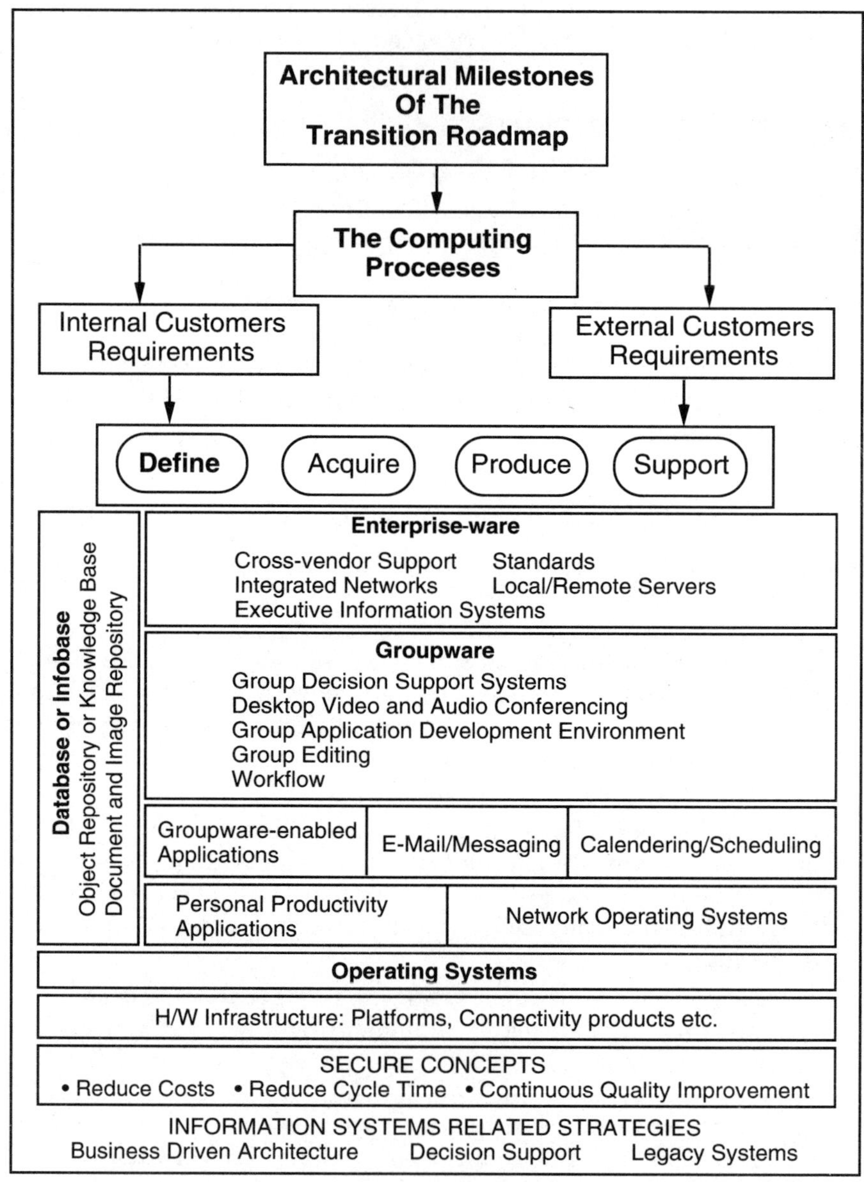

Figure 12.10   An extended model of architectural components of the milestones of the transition road map.

12.7 CONCLUSION

The emphasis of the book was, in first, presenting the architectural principles and second, in applying these to the problem at hand. Transition of legacy systems is not a platform conversion task. Also, it is not taking old COBOL programs and rewriting these in C language and changing the mainframe operating systems to a server-based operating system. It is much more than that. We are actually reengineering our business processes and then determining what aspects of the business requires automation. The automation is supported by information needs which, in turn, demand data. The need for the right information and data was driven by an architecture that demands a high level of data abstraction and independence with the computing application. We have recognized that perfection cannot be reached overnight. We have to perform each activity on the basis of sound business practices and business linkage. That invariably means an incremental approach, guided by a vision of information technology. Ad hoc implementations that solve a specific business priority should be outside of the vision.

The transition will be successful if no compromises are made to deviate from a process-oriented thinking. It is the combination of process-oriented thinking and business process reengineering that will provide the critical success factors in transitioning legacy systems to a distributed architecture.

CHAPTER NOTES

1. Brodie, Michael L., and Michael Stonebraker. *DARWIN: On the Incremental Migration of Legacy Information Systems.* TR-0222-10-92-165.
2. Screen scraping: In the PC environment a specialized set of products are available that essentially emulate a 3270 character mode session for legacy application. The screen-scraping products allow one to capture the actual data entered on the screen and later use it to define a legitimate data element.
3. Screen pumping: Screen pumping allows a PC program to emulate 3270 sessions for a legacy system and allows mass updates of data rapidly. The practice of screen pumping can be used with caution in a production environment. Several commercial products are available as bridge products in the PC local area network for screen pumping and communication with mainframes.
4. Forward engineered applications were described in Chapter 7 as rapid application development techniques.
5. Davenport, Thomas. "Saving IT's Soul: Human-Centered Information Management." *Harvard Business Review* (March–April 1994).

6. "Collaborative Strategies." A White Paper by David Colemen in *Computerworld*, vol.28, no.7 (February 7, 1994).

7. An example of such software is XSoft's InConcert product.

8. Inmon, W.H. *Information Architecture*, QED Publishing.

9. "AT&T Adapts a Global Manufacturing Architecture." *Manufacturing Systems* (January 1994).

Index